FAILED

FAILED

GOVERNMENT POLICIES
IN THE EAST AND THE WEST

BONG K. LEE, PH.D.
AUTHOR OF *THE UNFINISHED WAR: KOREA*
IN ASSOCIATION WITH
BONG-SUH LEE, PH.D.

iUniverse, Inc.
New York Lincoln Shanghai

Failed
Government Policies in the East and the West

iUniverse books may be ordered through booksellers or by contacting:

iUniverse
2021 Pine Lake Road, Suite 100
Lincoln, NE 68512
www.iuniverse.com
1-800-Authors (1-800-288-4677)

Because of the dynamic nature of the Internet, any Web addresses or links contained in this book may have changed since publication and may no longer be valid.

The views expressed in this work are solely those of the author and do not necessarily reflect the views of the publisher, and the publisher hereby disclaims any responsibility for them.

ISBN: 978-0-595-43364-3 (pbk)
ISBN: 978-0-595-87689-1 (ebk)

Printed in the United States of America

Contents

Acknowledgments

I am particularly grateful to Dr. Bong-Suh Lee, no relation to the author, for his collaboration in writing this book. After receiving his PhD in economics from Harvard University, he worked for the Federal Reserve Bank of Philadelphia and the World Bank in the U.S. After his return to South Korea, he held cabinet level positions in the Office of the President, the Ministry of Energy and Resources, and the Ministry of Trade and Industry. He served five years as Vice President (West) of the Asian Development Bank (ADB) in charge of the operations of 13 developing member countries of South and Southeast Asia. Currently, he teaches part time at the Kyung Hee University, mainly on the subject of the global economy.

We are grateful to many people who have made valuable comments on the manuscript. Tan Sri Radin Soenarno (historian and development economist) commented on the chapter on Malaysia. His last position in the Government of Malaysia was as the Director General of the Economic Planning Unit (EPU) in the Prime Minister's Department. Since his retirement from government service, he has served as the chairman of several banks and corporations. Mr. Yong Cheng and Mr. Willy Lim, Singaporeans with extensive international experience in finance and consultancy, commented on the chapter on Singapore. Mr. Farrokh Kapadia has kindly provided comments on the chapter on India. He was a former Indian Administrative Service (IAS) officer in diplomatic service before joining the Asian Development Bank (ADB).

Mr. Jan Johnson, a Canadian transportation economist with an MA from Stanford University, has commented on the chapter on China. He has consulted for the World Bank and other international agencies. Recently, he spent some time in China on a consulting assignment. Mr. Ping-Yung Chiu, a Taiwanese financial analyst with extensive international work experience, commented on China and Taiwan. Dr. Yoshihara Iwasaki, who has a PhD in economics from Stamford University, has commented on the chapter on Japan. His last job at ADB was as the Director General of South Asian Country Operations. Mr. Min Rip has reviewed the chapters on Japan and South Korea. He was a former executive of the Bank of Korea and the Director of the Treasury Department, ADB. Mr. Woo-Chul Chung, who has an MBA from the University of Indiana, has also commented on Japan. He is the Director General of the ADB Office in Japan. Mr. Ernest Perez, who has a BA in political science, the University of California Berkeley) and Mr. Lester Bataclan (MA in Business Economics, the University of the Philippines) have commented on the chapter on the Philippines.

American physician and professor Joanne Allport, M.D. has commented on the chapter on health. Mr. Peter Paolino, who taught in the California school system and served as a school counselor, has commented on U.S. public education. Mr. Lawland Long (MA, the Kennedy School of Government, the Harvard University), the CEO of several non-profit organizations commented on U.S. domestic policy issues. Mr. Philip Petersen (Australian) read a previous draft of the book from cover to cover and commented on the various aspects of the book. Mrs. Anita Garcia, who speaks French, German and English fluently, has commented on and edited the text.

Introduction

How does a nation increase the wealth and social wellbeing of its people? That is the central question of this book. It starts with facts such as the economic growth rates of different countries. We then search for the explanations. The proof of the pudding is in the eating. The right or wrong policies will show up over a long period of time if everything else is more or less the same. For example, communism is wrong not only because its theory is flawed but also because it has failed in every communist country. Today, a key policy question is the relative success and failure of Anglo-American capitalism, the welfare socialism of euro-economies and the state-controlled capitalism of Asia.

The book makes some generalization on the East and the West, but a number of different countries have been examined individually before any generalization is made. Asian countries are far from homogeneous. Japan and Singapore are both in Asia but their economic policies have been very disparate. There are, however, some common factors that distinguish the East from the West such as the limitation placed on individual freedom and government-business relationship. International comparison and perspectives are important for other reasons also. The world has shrunk due to better communication (Internet and satellites), the mobility of technology and the dismantling of trade barriers. As a result, what happens in China and India directly impacts the jobs, wages and home ownership costs of the U.S. or EU. Globalization is the most significant phenomenon that is changing the world today.

The book also discusses social order, crime, drug abuse, healthcare, education, income distribution, races, wars and other moral and social issues because they are very important to the wealth of a nation and living well. To those who have not read Adam Smith's *The Wealth of Nations*, capitalism may be nothing more than a "dog-eat-dog" ideology but his philosophy is as much about morality as economic efficiency. This is why the book discusses them.

Historical facts and cross-country data are more important to this book than everyday news and events. For such data, we rely a great deal on the socio-economic records of the World Bank, UN agencies, national censuses and authenticated secondary sources. We also rely on our personal experience of, and insight gained from, studying and working in several different countries and international organizations. Such observations and insights have been always backed up by empirical evidence. We have also benefited a great deal from peer reviews. Many of the reviewers, like the authors, have a multi-cultural background and spent a number of years in different countries working on international development and socio-economic research.

Part One
The West

o o o o o o o o o o o o o o o o o o o o o o o o o o o o o o o o o

The West in this book is more than geography or racial heritage. It is scattered around the globe today and is racially mixed. Is the West in decline like the final phase of the Roman Empire? The answer depends on what and where.

Chapter 1

Transition of the United States

Questions

How have U.S. social and economic policies changed by the Great Depression, the stagflation and Reagan's supply-side policies? What caused the stagflation and recovery from it? Who is right: Adam Smith, John Maynard Keynes, Milton Friedman or supply-side economists? Does tax cut stimulate the economy and raise tax revenues? Answers to these questions divide the liberals and conservatives in the U.S. Verdicts are available below.

Learning from Experience

The Great Depression was a turning point for the U.S. as well as for other industrialized countries. It appeared that Adam Smith's "invisible hand" was broken for good. It did appear that a big government and deficit spending, advocated by English economist Lord John Maynard Keynes, was the answer. When Franklin D. Roosevelt came into office in 1933, he started alphabet soup agencies and programs called New Deal, which were Keynesian in nature. The era of a big government and deficit spending began. Both the New Deal and Keynesian theory reigned supreme until the 1950s. Milton Friedman, the Nobel laureate and the most influential economist during the past half century, emerged with an alternative view: "the Depression was the consequence of an incredible sequence of blunders in monetary policy." Money was excessively abundant and the interest rate was too low for a period leading to the Crash. As the Depression started, the Federal Reserve system cut the money supply by one-third from 1930 to 1931. According to monetary economists, this was precisely the opposite of what should have been done. The capitalism of Adam Smith was still a viable system, but it overlooked the importance of money in the modern economy.

Roosevelt was not a big spender in the beginning. In fact, during the election campaign, Roosevelt attacked Hoover for incurring deficits, which was caused by shrinking revenues. He promised that he would balance the budget if elected. He did not keep his promise although his deficits were small by the present standard. It may surprise some people that during the first year of the Roosevelt Administration in 1933, government expenditures were below the level of 1931 under the Hoover Administration. Unless otherwise mentioned in this book, government expenditures include state and local expenditures, social security and interest expenditures as well. Even without huge deficit spending, the economy was already on a modest recovery path in 1933. Roosevelt's spending programs, however, increased gradually and this did stimulate the economy starved with demand deficit. The U.S. economy limped on until massive spending started during World War II. Government expenditures increased by 66% in 1941, 135% in 1942 and 49% in 1943. With such high government expenditures, the demand-starved U.S. economy boomed. After the war, the myth was created that the remedy for a sagging economy is a war and immense government spending.

Therefore, even after World War II, the government expenditures (including Social Security and interest payment) of the U.S. government expanded continuously at all levels. Government expenditures as percent of GDP were merely 9% in 1930 but went up to 15% in 1940. The percentage shot up to 23% in 1960 and then to 28% in 1970. Strangely, however, bigger government spendings did not expand the economy in the 1970s. Instead, inflation and unemployment rates rose simultaneously. This phenomenon was given a name: stagflation. It began to show up all over the Western economies. It was not exported from the U.S. like the Great Depression. The UK experienced it even before the U.S. Some economists tried to explain it by pointing to a series of supply shocks such as crop failures and two huge oil price increases, the surge of baby-boomers and women entering the labor market. But all these explanations were variously inadequate to explain what was happening.

Stagflation

Why? The economy was no longer demand starved but supply starved. Monetarists had a simple explanation. Milton Friedman "came on [TV] camera with the Treasury's printing presses in the background spewing out sheets of $20 bills. "'This is how you stop inflation,' he said while pressing a large red button that stopped the printing presses."[1] Keynesian spending, known as "priming the pump," was doing more harm than good in the 1970s. More demand was creating inflation rather than more supply. The constraints were in supply, not in the demand. Along with it the Keynesian theory and its companion theory, the Phil-

---

1.   See Kit Sims Taylor, Human Society and the Global Economy; 1998

lips curve, were discredited. The Phillips curve essentially states that when inflation is high, unemployment will be low.

This was no longer true. The monetarists had predicted all along that inflation
can occur with high unemployment if the government increases the money supply in a period of rising prices. Their prediction turned out correct. During the
Carter Administration (1977–1981), inflation, unemployment and interest rates
were all in double digits. The "misery index" (the sum of inflation and unemployment rates)[2] shot up sharply during his administration. In 1980, Carter's
final year as the president, the Misery Index rose to 20.8 from 13.6 in 1977. The
economists and common people began to believe that inflation was the greatest
evil and it must be tamed at any cost. Increasingly, Milton Friedman's view that
the primary objective of monetary authorities is to contain inflation became the
dominant public policy.

The "bad" cop who carried out this policy was Paul Volcker (the chairman of
the Federal Reserve Board), first appointed by Jimmy Carter in 1979 and reap-
pointed by Reagan later. He raised interest rates so high that the economy went
into a recession. In 1980, the inflation rate went up to 13.5%., the unemployment rate reached 7.3%, and the prime rate was as high as 21.5%. Volcker continued with high interest rate policy into the early years of the Reagan
administration. It killed inflation but brought the economy to a recession as well.
It was, however, a worthy sacrifice. The Misery Index was 18.0 in 1980 (the first
year of Reagan presidency) but it dropped to 10.7 with the inflation of 3.6 in
1985—the first year of his second term. See Table 1 for the index during Carter
and Reagan presidencies. After taming inflation in the 1980s, the monetary
authorities in the West have not allowed inflation to go out of control. There is
now a near consensus among economists that inflation is a bigger problem than
low growth, and that inflation should be checked by raising interest rates to whatever level necessary to maintain its level to 2% more or less per year.

---

2.   It was originally created by Chicago School economist Robert Barro, now a Harvard
      economics professor.

Table 1

Misery Index
Carter and Reagan Years [*]

	Inflation rate (%)[1]	Unemployment rate (%)[2]	Misery index[3]	Prime rate %[4]
Carter				
1977	6.5	7.1	13.6	6.5–7.5
1980	13.5	7.3	20.8	11.0–21.5
Reagan				
1981	10.3	7.7	18.0	15.7–20.7
1985	3.6	7.1	10.7	9.5–10.7
1988	4.1	5.5	9.6	8.5–10.5

[*]   Notes:
(1) Federal Reserve Bank of Minneapolis, Consumer Price Index; 6/9/04.
(2) The Department of Labor
(3) The U.S. Misery Index—1948 to 2003; Misery Index = Unemployment rate + Inflation rate.
(4) HSH Associates; The original source was *The Wall Street Journal*, 6/9/04

The U.S. has enjoyed low inflation and high growth rates since 1985. Between 1992 and 2003, the inflation rate dropped even further. This was due to a combination of tight monetary policy, the supply-side economic policies of Ronald Reagan (explained later in this chapter), and cheap goods and services imported from Asia. The cheap imports from these Asian countries have kept inflation low although the Fed Funds rates were pushed down gradually to 1%. This brought about an unprecedented period of sustained growth.

There has been a trace of inflation in 2004–2005 and the Fed Fund rate has gradually been raised to 5.25 %. This has not brought down the inflation rate by much, which may be because the world has entered yet another economic paradigm. It is a global economy that matters. The inflation rate in the U.S. is as much a function of what goes on outside of the U.S. as inside. In the past, raising or lowering short term interest rates affected long terms interest rates immediately, but this is no longer the case. This has been a conundrum for the Fed. It is all because of the global nature of the present economy.

The U.S. is still the biggest consumer market in the world. Therefore, a recession in the U.S. would slow the world economy. However, the U.S. is now a smaller part of the global economy than before. Since so many of the long-term debts are being bought by foreigners, the Fed rate does not influence the long bond rate as much as global liquidity. American wages are also regulated by global wages. When American wages relative to productivity are too high, American industries outsource or even move production facilities to cheap-labor countries. Under such conditions, the labor does not have the kind of bargaining power that it used to.

Supply-Side Economics

The Keynesian policy does not work in an environment where the constraints are in factors affecting supply and global competitiveness. Not surprisingly, supply-side economics became popular in the 1970s. The concept originated from Say's Law, which is named after French economist Jean-Baptiste Say (1767–1832). It states: "There can be no demand without supply." There was no demand for a computer before it was invented. Supply-siders, therefore, believe that prosperity can be created by stimulating production, improving technology and providing incentives to invest. This is abundantly clear in developing economies where no amount of printing money or stimulating consumption would do any good to the economy unless the bottlenecks to production are eliminated. The bottlenecks may be the lack of entrepreneurs, skilled labor, technology, machinery, infrastructure or all of the above.

The supply-side economics in the U.S. was articulated by Jude Wanniski in the 1970s in *The Way the World Works*. In the book, he details the failure of high tax-rates and U.S. monetary policy under Keynesian economics in the 1970s. A tax is also a supply-side issue because if taxes are too high, no investor would want to invest and no worker would want to work. Arthur Betz Laffer Sr., Reagan's chief economic adviser, pointed out that a decrease in tax rates could result in an increase in tax revenues. Reagan's supply-side economic policies are based on such belief. He cut taxes, eliminated regulatory bottlenecks and fired illegal strikers (air traffic controllers).

Tax Cut

"Government's view of the economy could be summed up in a few short phrases: If it moves, tax it. If it keeps moving, regulate it. And if it stops moving, subsidize it."

Ronald Reagan (President of the United States, 1981–1989)

During his presidential campaign of 1980, Reagan proposed a 30% across-the-board marginal income tax rates cut. He did not get that much of a cut but he managed to get 25% cut in the Kemp-Roth sponsored Economic Recovery

Tax Act (ERTA) of 1981. It was implemented over a three year period.[3] The tax cuts were on individual and corporate incomes, interests and dividends, and capital gains. Tax brackets were indexed to prevent tax hikes through what is known as "bracket creep," which previously pushed up one's tax rate to a higher bracket for no other reason than inflation. The fact that Reagan got so many cuts is a uniquely American phenomenon. A ballot initiative known as Proposition 13 of 1978 in California passed with a whopping 70% support. It placed a cap on property tax rates in the state and reduced them by an average of 57%. Politicians all over the country took note. It paved the way for the Reagan tax cuts.

According to the Treasury Department Office of Tax Analysis, ERTA slashed what would have been federal taxes by $38 billion the first year, $91 billion the second year, and $139 billion the third year. These cuts amounted to 8.5% in 1981, 19% in 1982 and 26% in 1983 of what might have been taxes. Yet, Reagan's so-called massive tax cuts caused just a modest one-year drop in the federal tax revenue. The corporate tax collection did not even drop for a single year. Whether a tax cut decreases tax collection depends on the time frame. In a short term, it can reduce tax collection. In the long run, tax cuts boot the economy and increase tax collection. Federal budget deficits increased during the Reagan Administration because of rampant spending increases, both for national defense and social programs, rather than a drop in tax revenues.

The whole point of tax cut is that it stimulates economic growth, lowers tax burden and eventually increases tax revenues. In fact, tax cuts have never reduced the collection of current tax revenues except in the first year after the Reagan tax cut. The tax collection of the federal government increased from $290.6 billion in 1981 to $402.9 billion in 1988 in spite of tax cuts. The increased fiscal deficits during his two-term presidency were entirely due to spending increases. Reagan supply-side policies, not confined to tax cut alone, reversed the downward trend of the U.S. economy and brought in an unprecedented era of prosperity to the U.S. economy. The U.S. economy created more jobs, and the people earned more money and paid more taxes for years to come. In 1976, Carter's first year, the economy grew by 4.6% but during his final year in the White House, the economy contracted (-0.2% in inflation-adjusted 2000 dollar). Reagan inherited a weak economy but left behind a strong economy. His tax cuts are working even today because the impact of low tax rates continues indefinitely until erased by subsequent tax increases. But the big government liberals will not admit it. To do so would undermine the very foundation of their belief system.

---

3.   A 5% cut in 1981, 10% cut in 1982, and 10% again in 1983.

It needs to be mentioned that although a tax cut of 25% sounds impressive, Reagan also took action, in subsequent years, to increase tax revenues. Such measures include the Tax Equity and Fiscal Responsibility Act (TEFRA) of 1982, which eliminated various tax loopholes, and instituted tougher enforcement; the Highway Revenue Act of 1982, which increased the gasoline tax temporarily from 4 cents to 9 cents through September 30, 1988; and the Deficit Reduction Act of 1984. The net percentage of his tax cuts was, therefore, appreciably smaller than 25%. In 1983, Reagan also accelerated the implementation of previously passed payroll tax rate hikes to save the Social Security system from going bankrupt. It involved the timing of implementation rather than creating new payroll tax rates. This followed the recommendation of the Greenspan Commission on Social Security Reform. It added more employees to the system, raised the full benefit retirement age, and made some Social Security benefits taxable incomes.

Economic recovery after tax cuts happened every time. It also worked when John F. Kennedy and George W. Bush cut taxes. In each case, federal budget deficits were significant concerns but it did not matter so much at the end. Using the Bureaus of Economic Analysis data, a CATO Institute study indicates that the real economic growth averaged 3.6% during the Reagan years versus 2.8% during the Ford-Carter year.[4] The same study concludes, "Real median family income grew by $4,000 during the Reagan period after experiencing no growth in the pre-Reagan years; it experienced a loss of almost $1,500 in the post-Reagan years." The study was conducted in 1996.

Politicians tend to take credit or blame for the economic performance under their watch. This is not right. For example, the economic boom during the Bill Clinton Administration owes much to the supply-side reforms that Reagan had instituted earlier, the tech boom which he had nothing to do with, the welfare reforms that Republican Congress forced on Clinton, monetary policies engineered by Greenspan and the global economy which he did not create. Clinton deserves credit for cooperating with Republican Congress although he vetoed the welfare reform bill until he no longer had the vote to sustain his veto. A president, however, can and should take credit or responsibility for his budget (tax cuts or increases) and other economic policies that he has initiated.

Tax cuts have a short term and long term impacts on the economy in a different manner. In the short run, it acts like pump priming to the private sector by providing more money to the hands of individuals. It was pointed out by an

---

4.   William A. Niskanen and Stephen Moore, "Policy Analysis: Supply Tax Cuts and the Truth About the Reagan Economic Record"; October 22, 1996.

economist in 1961that "when the private economy is floundering, it was the task of government to increase the total amount of purchasing power at the disposal of the people. It has taken us a long time to learn this lesson, and there are still many politicians who either do not believe it or have been unable to convince their constituencies of its potency."[5] On a short term, therefore, tax cuts during a recession stimulate the demand. The difference between this and a typical Keynesian demand stimulation is that tax cuts put money in the hands of individuals and corporations rather than the government. Is it always best to cut taxes and give the money back to individuals and corporations which paid them? There are many situations in developing countries where taxes are better collected and increased to build roads, generate and distribute electricity and telecommunications, and supply water. However, this is hardly the case in advanced countries. The private sector takes care of most public utilities. Even fiscal conservatives do not object to building and maintaining roads, water supply systems or waste collection and disposal. By and large, advanced economies are taxed too heavily and spend too much on social programs, which have more negative than positive impacts on the economy, and create problems such as unemployment. This becomes clearer when economic growth, taxes, social security and unemployment rates of the euro-economies are compared with the U.S.

On a long term basis, tax cuts provide supply-side incentives to producers and workers alike. When taxes are high, individuals and businessmen do not want to work hard and invest in productive ventures. Therefore, the economy does not expand. If tax cuts reduce the tax rate to zero, however, the economy may boom but tax revenues would be zero. It is also easy to understand that if a tax rate is 100%, no one would want to work or invest; therefore, there would be no tax revenue. This argues that there exists an optimum tax rate at which tax collection is highest. This is the view of Arthur Laffer. His hypothetical curve is shown in Figure 1.

---

5.   Seymore E Harris, "Fiscal Policy" in Seymore E Harris, ed., *American Economic History* (1961) p. 131.

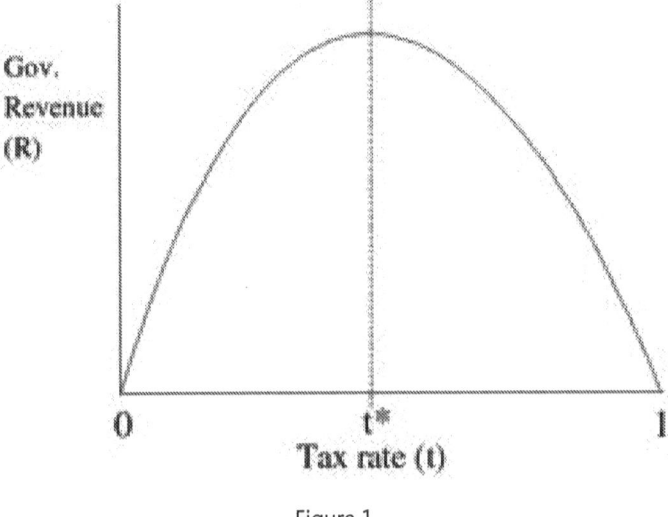

Figure 1

Edmund Morris, Reagan's official biographer but no admirer of Reagan, wrote: "[Reagan] committed the American economy to eight years of self-compounding deficits, and a trillion-dollar shortfall, greater than the entire debt of the past two centuries. Yet—such is the mad logic of economics—he also initiated the greatest sustained peacetime boom since the founding of the Republic"[6] The advocates of tax cuts would point out that ERTA created 6.3 million new jobs between 1982 and 1984 although one can argue correctly that all that job increase was not due to the tax cuts alone.

Did President Reagan plan for the huge fiscal deficits when he made tax cuts? Not according to a Republican Party website, which says: "[Democrats] succeeded in keeping the deficits growing, all the while blaming the White House, as they porked up every bill he wanted to pass with millions and millions of unneeded spending. Once he [Reagan] even threw the budget down in disgust and said, 'You expect me to sign this crap?' Ultimately, he had no choice. He wanted to rebuild the military and in Washington you play the 'Potomac Two-Step'. He got his military spending and they got to rob the American taxpayer with wild abandon." This was a partisan statement, of course, but it sounds familiar. Even today the Democrats blame the George W. Bush administration for the huge fiscal deficits. Yet, the Democrats are never satisfied with the level of Bush's spending on education, health and social entitlement programs.

---

6.   Edmund Morris, *Dutch: A Memoir of Ronald Reagan* (1999), p. 447.

Much has been said about Reagan's immense defense spending causing soaring deficits. This is true but Federal government expenditures under the Reagan Administration, which grew at the rate of 12.2% per year, were one full percentage point lower than under the Carter Administration, which was 13.2%. Strangely, there seem to be no opinions about excessive spending under the Carter Administration. Reagan was somewhat effective in holding down spending increases in social programs. Another entirely different controversy was: did Reagan's tax-cuts benefit the rich at the expense of the poor and middle class as some have accused? A short answer is "no". Since this is a point of a significant contention, it is worth discussing later in this chapter. A proper way to look at the size and the impact of tax cuts is to look at tax burdens, not tax rates. Most increases in tax burden took place between 1930 and 1980, from 11% of GDP to 29% of GDP. During Reagan's presidency, it remained flat at 29% in spite of all the excitement about tax cuts not withstanding. It is surprising that during the Bush (I) Administration, the tax burden went down slightly in spite of Desert Storm and the much touted Bush (I) tax increases, which deprived him the second term. The Clinton Administrations raised the tax burden from 29% to 32% at the end of his term in spite of the fact that the Cold War ended and there was no war during his presidency. His tax increases came toward the end of his second term. This has contributed to the slow down of the economy as well as the tech bubble burst.

Deregulation and the Labor Market Reform

Another side of the supply-side policy is labor market reform and deregulation. Over time, every government tends to pile up too many regulations in the name of progress such as public safety, protecting the environment and promoting the general welfare. The U.S. began to undo them even under Democratic President Jimmy Carter. He started the deregulation of the trucking industry and the airline industry. Carter also deregulated the railroads and telephone industries. However, when push came to shove, the Democrats have been more inclined to impose restrictions on the economy than the Republicans. For example, Carter regulated the price of gasoline, which caused long lines in front of gas stations. Carter promised to decontrol it gradually while pushing for a "Windfall Profits Tax" at the same time. In 1980, Carter's Democratic challenger Ted Kennedy advocated outright nationalization of the oil industry.

On the other side, Republican Ronald Reagan was calling for complete decontrol. When elected, Reagan lifted controls over gasoline price almost immediately. Reagan was consistent in applying the principles of the free market. Reagan let many of the Savings & Loan (S&L) institutions go bankrupt. It was costly to rescue innocent depositors, about 600 billion dollars or about $1,500 from every person in the U.S. but it removed the cancer from spreading. After the 1990 bubble burst, Japan suffered 10 years of economic stagnation by not letting insolvent banks go bankrupt. Lately, the U.S. has been adding more cumbersome regulations. The Sarbanes-Oxley Act of 2002 is an example. The environmental impact review and environmental activism are another example. The Sarbanes-Oxley Act adds so much cost to public companies that they are turning into private equity companies in a record number. At this rate, the New York City might lose its status as the financial capital of the world. All that the government has to do is enforce the existing laws rather than creating more laws. This is also the case with immigration laws.

Reagan was also strongly against the illegal strikes of the labor union. He fired all air traffic controllers who implemented illegal strikes. This sent a strong message to the labor. In the final analysis, being a supply-sider is being pro-business, whether small or large, and supporting a free labor market. A free labor market is good for the business, and what is good for the business is good for the economy and the labor. Only a strong economy and free job market—as against labor union monopoly—will increase the bargaining power of the labor.

Chapter 2

Two Economies of Western Europe

Questions?

The euro-economies have been falling behind the U.S. and the UK economies for decades. Why? The answer to this question is critical since the ultimate goal of American liberals is to move U.S. closer to the welfare socialism of the euro-economies.

Lesson from the United Kingdom (UK) Economy

The Great Depression spread from the U.S. to the Great Britain because the U.S. restricted imports from the UK to protect the dwindling number of jobs for American workers. The British exports to the U.S. plunged by 50% between 1929 and the end of 1930. This in turn caused the British unemployment rate to soar to 20% of the insured workforce. The flight of gold started in earnest. The government tried to stop it by introducing extremely high interest rates, but this only depressed the economy further. In late 1931, the government abandoned the gold standard. Immediately the exchange rate of the pound fell by 25%, from $4.86 to a pound to $3.40. This stimulated exports and led to a gradual economic recovery. Another positive step that the government took was to lower the interest rates from 6% to 2%. In some hard hit areas, the government enacted a number of specific programs to create or protect existing jobs such as road building, providing loans to shipyards, and imposing tariffs on steel imports. The British government also had modest unemployment and health insurance systems although they ran out of money rather quickly.

What pulled Great Britain completely out of the Depression was war preparation to counter the military buildup of Nazi Germany. The war that followed further wiped off any trace of the Depression. Following the end of World War II, the majority of the British people refused to return to the austere old days. In the 1945 general election, socialist Clement Attlee of the Labour Party defeated Winston Churchill, to the surprise of the world.

The Marshall Plan or the European Recovery Program (ERP) that followed the war was critical to Western Europe when its homes and infrastructure were devastated. The UK received the largest chunk of the aid, $3.297 billion out of $13 billion when the value of money was not the same as today. The International Bank for Reconstruction and Development (IBRD) was created to help rebuild Europe and the International Monetary Fund (IMF) to stabilize the exchange rates after World War II. But most European countries decided to seek aid under the Marshall Plan rather than IBRD loans because the Marshall Plan aid was in grant. The Marshall Plan also transferred American managerial and industrial technology to Western Europe.

Attlee's Labour government, in the meanwhile, was turning the UK to a cradle-to-grave welfare state. National Health Service was established in 1948, with free medical treatment for all. A national system of benefits was also introduced to provide social security to all so that the population would be protected from the "cradle to the grave". The fact that unemployment disappeared during the war and the Keynesian theory appeared to be working gave confidence to the policy makers and the public alike that with a high level of government spending full employment could be maintained during peacetime as well. These policies became known as the "post-war consensus," and were accepted by all major political parties.[1] The Attlee government also created a boom in the Council House program, in a form of public housing. For many working class people at that time, the council houses "provided the first experience of private garden space (usually at front and rear) and the first private and indoor toilets and bathrooms. The Attlee government, then, went on to nationalize the Bank of England, the fuel and power industries (coal, electricity, gas, and atomic energy), transportation, and most of the iron and steel industry. British socialism started with a big bang.

Like Americans, the British in the 1970s found out later that a big public spending did not create continued prosperity. Keynesian economics began to fail earlier in the UK than the U.S. Rationing had to be maintained and economic recovery was slower than in other Western European countries. In 1949, the British pound was devalued from US$4.03 to US$2.80. This brought the defeat of the Labour government in the 1951 general election, although it regained power since then. The promise of "cradle to grave" was too tempting for the British. In

---

1. Few would disagree with this statement but one may see a statement to effect in J. Bradford DeLong,
    University of California at Berkeley and NBER;Slouching Towards Utopia?: The Economic History of the Twentieth Century; 1`/24/1997; available on the Web.

1976, the pound had to be devalued again to $1.57. In 1974, the inflation rate jumped to 15% and 27% in 1975. The excesses of socialism taking toll from everyone.

This set the stage for Margaret Thatcher's Conservative Party to gain power in May 1979 and introduce supply-side reforms. This was two years before Ronald Reagan was sworn into office. The inflation rate began to recede starting in 1981 and declined to 3% in 1986. Thatcher did not and could not cut taxes but curtailed spiraling tax increases. She also curbed strong unions, which were creating huge inflation rather than productivity gains. The UK as well as other industrialized countries has long ignored supply-side problems since they believed that producers would respond if there was demand. Thatcher also restricted the growth of the money supply and went on to privatize public enterprises, deregulate cumbersome rules and regulations, downsize industrial policy, reform industrial relations and restrain the growth of government expenditures. She also encouraged direct foreign investment. Many of these policies would have been inconceivable to the "Old" Labour governments of Attlee, Callaghan and Wilson.[2] Inflation during her tenure remained at 5%-6% range. Her supply-side reforms did not bring instant prosperity to the UK but the economy gradually bounced back and grew not only faster than its Western European neighbors but also faster than the U.S.

Margaret Thatcher's policy clearly reversed the UK's slide toward a banana republic. She subdued Britain's trade-unions. The privatization of government enterprises such as the British Airways and the British Steel made them the leaders in their respective industries rather than bankrupting. The per capita GNI of the UK stood at 64% of that of the U.S. in 1980 but it rose to 75% of the U.S. by 2003 even as France, Germany, Sweden and even Finland slipped further behind the U.S. in terms of per capita income. Refer to Table 2. Unemployment rates in the UK were higher than in the U.S., although lower than those of other Western European countries. Notwithstanding the bitter medicines she prescribed to the labor, Thatcher was elected to three consecutive terms. She resigned in 1990. By that time, she turned the country around and earned the nickname "The Iron Lady." The success of Thatcher's economic policy was so convincing that it even changed the Labour Party. Tony Blair and Labor defeated Thatcher's successor John Major by a landslide in 1997, but they did so by moving the party's economic policy to the Thatcher's position rather than to the old Labour position of income redistribution and strong labor unions.

---

2.   ibid

Table 2

Unemployment Rates and Per Capita Gross National Income[1]

in Selected European Countries and the U.S.

in current US$ *

	1980	*1990*	*2000*	*2003/05*
France				
GNI per capita	$12,760	$19,620	$23,990	$24,770
% of the U.S.	98%	84%	70%	66%
Growth rate in %		4%	2%	1%
Unemployment rate in %	6%	9%	10%	10%
Germany				
GNI per capita	$12,340	$20,160	$25,150	$25,250
% of the U.S.	$95	$86	$73	$67
Growth rate in %		$5	$2	$0
Unemployment rate in %			$8	$12
Sweden				
GNI per capita	$16,490	$26,390	$28,680	$28,840
% of the U.S.	127%	113%	83%	77%
Growth rate in %		5%	1%	0%
Unemployment rate in %	2%	2%	6%	6%
United Kingdom				
GNI per capita	$8,380	$16,190	$25,220	$28,350
% of the U.S.	64%	69%	73%	75%
Growth rate in %		7%	5%	4%
Unemployment rate in %	7%	7%	6%	n.a.
United States				
GNI per capita	13020	23440	34360	37610
Growth rate in %		6.06	3.90	3.06
Unemployment rate in %	7	6	4	.5.2

* Source: World Development Indicators (WBDI) database except "% of the U.S." and growth rates calculated by the author, and the unemployment rate for 2003/05, which are as reported by *The Economist*, June 4th-10th, 2005; 96.

Note: Gross National Income (GNI, formerly GNP) per capita is converted to U.S. dollars by using official exchange rates except in certain circumstances. To smooth fluctuations in prices and exchange rates, the World Bank uses the Atlas Method of conversion. It averages the exchange rate for a given year and the two preceding years.

In summary, there was no free lunch after all. The British had to swallow the bitter medicines that Thatcher prescribed. This is just another confirmation that the supply side policy works.

Lessons from the Welfare Socialism of the Euro-economies

Germany

The Great Depression had a devastating impact on the German economy. Germany was suffering from the burden of war reparations after WWI, hyperinflation in 1923 and then a high unemployment rate. This brought the Nazi party to prominence. In 1928, the party captured 2.8% of the vote for the German legislature (*Reichstag*). At that time, some 1.25 million workers were unemployed. Hitler was considered a fool in 1928 to predict a coming economic disaster but in 1930 he was considered a visionary of a sort when the unemployment figure hit nearly 4 million. In the March 1930 election, the Nazis gained 19.2% of the vote.

On the onset of the Depression, the ruling coalition, led by Chancellor Bruning of the Center Party, tried to balance the budget, hold down wages and control prices to prevent a return to earlier hyperinflation when the new problem was deflation. His government refused to increase public works expenditure to boost the economy. The Great Depression deepened and by 1933, the unemployment rate reached almost 50%. It paved the way for Adolf Hitler to gain power. Hitler promised full employment and he delivered it whether by hook or crook. When he became Chancellor, he closed off imports, stopped the flight of the mark by a rigid exchange control, undertook massive public expenditure programs, abandoned the Treaty of Versailles, promoted rearmament, built up military-industrial complex, abolished trade unions and controlled prices to prevent hyperinflation. The government's public work s included digging ditches on farms to assist irrigation, building the new autobahns, creating new forests, etc.

Initially, his policies did not affect the lives of ordinary Germans unless they were Jews. Germans enjoyed more job opportunities and higher pays. In the summer of 1935, however, Hitler introduced Labor Service, under which all men aged between nineteen and twenty-five had to work for the government for six months. Later, women were also included in the. A person had to do whatever work is given to him or her. Otherwise the government classified the person "work-shy" and relegated him or her to a concentration camp. Initially, the government banned the introduction of labor-saving machinery to achieve full employment. The government gave work contracts to those companies that relied on manual labor rather than machines. This was especially true of the government's massive autobahn program. Employers had to get government permission before reducing their labor force. "By 1939, Germany faced the shortage of workers. The number of hours worked increased from 60 to 72 per week. The average factory worker was earning 10 times more than those on dole money and few complained—though to do so was fraught with potential difficulties."[3] Unemployment disappeared. Government revenues and expenditures soared.

Without Hitler's racism and the invasion of neighboring countries, he might have been remembered as a national hero. In the end, the Nazi racism and an attempt to create a self-sufficient economy by invading neighboring countries brought the greatest human tragedy and devastation in the history of the world. This is the model that Japan copied during the same time. The remnants of such policies are found in various other countries even today. It is nearly impossible to fire an employee in France. The most dangerous idea was to create self sufficient economy by invading other countries. The war it started killed four million Germans, six million Jews and as many as twenty-seven million Russians. The number of dead in combat includes over 400,000 British troops and about 280,000 American troops. At Dunkirk alone the British suffered 68,000 casualties.

The recovery of the German economy after World War II was miraculous. This was achieved under free-market capitalism. Although many German cities were destroyed, the war did not destroy German technology, or its management and organizational skills. Its labor force was willing to work hard without demanding excessive wages. It is also worth noting that although West Germany was part of a defeated country, it received a considerable amount of aid under the Marshall Plan, $1,448 million. It was directed to the re-industrialization of Germany. Germany has been grateful for this. Although it received smaller amount than other countries such as the UK and France, Germany "made better use of it" according to the German government. West Germany established the German European Recovery Program (ERP) Special Fund to make use of aid under the Marshall Plan. It lent money to its industries. The assets of the Fund have grown and it is now an integral part of Germany's financing of Third World projects. Germany has not only remained a partner in the Cold War but paid part of the money back to the U.S. in the form of the German Marshall Plan for the U.S., amounting to about DM 250 million drawn against the ERP Special Fund. Some of the money was used for a number of young East German leaders and academics to spend time in the U.S.

---

3.   ibid.

The main architect for the German free-market economic miracle was Ludwig Erhard. Between 1950 and 1960, industrial production rose "to two-and-one-half times the level of 1950 and far beyond any that the Nazis had reached during the 1930s in all of Germany." [4] The unemployment rate fell from 10.3% to 1.2%. "Along with such explosive growth, wages and salaries rose over 80 percent between 1949 and 1955 even without excessive wage demand from labor."[5] Those who do not believe in trickle down will find it difficult to explain how such a real wage increase was possible without labor activism and under Adam Smithsonian capitalism.

During the 1960s, the growth of the West German economy slowed down partly because the supply of labor from East Germany was cut off by the Berlin Wall and partly because the Bundesbank made several moves to slow down potential overheating. In 1966, Chancellor Ludwig Erhard was voted out of office. In 1969, a left-leaning coalition government was formed under the Social Democratic Party (SPD). It adopted the welfare socialism, which is the trade mark of the euro-economies today. It increased the cost of social security system by over 10 percent a year during much of the 1970s. Over time, the West German social welfare system has become one of the most expensive in the world. With it, the era of rapid economic growth disappeared in Germany. The problem was not only a slowdown in GDP growth, but also an alarming increase in unemployment rates. West German industries did not expand and create employment as they used to. To compensate for this, the government began to shelter and support some sectors and industries to maintain economic growth. Some large existing industries benefited but it did not help the economy by much. The West German economy slowed to 1% growth in 1980, no growth in 1981, and negative 1% growth in 1982. The people were not happy with the slow growth. In the fall of 1982, Schmidt's coalition government collapsed as the Free Democratic Party withdrew to join a conservative coalition of the Christian Democratic Union (led by Helmut Kohl) and the Christian Social Union.

Helmut Kohl tried to restrain spending in order to reduce the deficit and to make room for tax cuts. History has shown, however, once social welfare programs are in place, no government can really reduce them because the people come to depend on them. Kohl succeeded in marginally reducing income taxes during 1986–90. The overall tax burden came down from 38.2% of GDP in

---

4.   See "The Economic Miracle",
      http://www.germanculture.com.ua/library/facts/bl_economic_miracle.htm
5.   ibid

1980 to 36.8% in 1990. Kohl also reduced the government's ownership of the economy from 52% to 46% of GDP between 1982 and 1990 by carrying out a series of privatization measures. The new government also tried to reduce regulations and improve the flexibility of the labor market.[6] The German economy performed much better under Kohl[7] than 10 years prior to his government. However, he could not do much about the rising tide of strong unions. In this respect, his reforms did not quite measure up to those of Margaret Thatcher.

The German reunification in 1990 changed the dynamics of the German political economy drastically. The newly enfranchised voters from East Germany were accustomed to government welfare programs and demanded them from the unified Germany. The Kohl government had to increase taxes. The overall tax burden in the late 1990s increased to almost 40 percent of GDP. Social security contributions rose to 26% of GDP in Germany compared with 21% in the UK and 13% in the U.S. See Table 3. German central government's debt rose from 43% of GDP in 1990 to 76% of GDP in 1997. The German Central Bank was, however, firmly in control of the monetary policy. As a result, inflation was contained.

---

6. See Willi Leibfritz, Wolfgang Bütner, and Ulrich van Essen <u>Ken Messere, ed., The Tax System in Industrialized Countries (1998) pp. 128–130.</u>
7. Per capita GDP in constant 2000 US$ increased at the rate of 2.8% compared with 2.2% between 1971 and 1982

Table 3

Public Social Security Taxes as Percent of GDP
Selected OECD Countries *

Country	% of GDP ILO (1996)	% of GDP OECD (2001)
France	30.1	28.5
Germany	29.7	27.4
Japan	14.1	16.9
South Korea	5.6	6.1
Sweden	34.7	28.9
United Kingdom	22.8	21.8
United States	16.5	14.8

*   Source: (1) The International Labour Organization, World Labour Report 2000, Statistical Annex Table 14. (2) OECD Social Expenditure Database 2004 except for Japan. For Japan, it is calculated by the National Institute of Population and Social Security Research according to the OECD Social Expenditure definition. Notes: The scope of the OECD Social Expenditure is broader than that of the ILO, and includes the money equipping facilities.

Kohl's government fell in 1998 because of his party's financial scandal. This brought in Social Democrat government once again under Gerhard Schröder. History repeated again. He did little to restrain the strong unions which made the country an unattractive place to invest and do business. The German economy lost momentum built up during the Kohl government. Unemployment rates increased gradually. The growth rate of per capita GDP in constant 2000 US$ fell to a new low (0.8% between 1999 and 2003). The UK's per capita GNI surpassed that of Germany in the year 2000. [8] In 2004, *The Economist* posted a rather scathing article on the German economy with a provocative title of "How the mighty are fallen." The German economy was the envy of the world after World War II but "not any more, though. Today it is Germany that economists point to with a mixture of contempt and alarm."[9] The unemployment rate rose to 11.8 % in April 2005 in spite of Schröder's pledge in 1998 to cut unemployment. He, like many other politicians before him, raised false hopes to get elected but without any policies to achieve such a promise. Germany proves once again

8.   By applying the World Bank's Atlas method of calculation. This method smooths fluctuations in prices and exchange rates by applying a conversion factor that averages the exchange rate for a given year and the two preceding years,

9.   *Economist.Com,* May 19, 2004

that strong unions, high taxes and generous social welfare benefits are incompatible with a strong economy and low unemployment.

In 2005, facing worsening economic woes, the Schröder government introduced interesting measures to reduce unemployment, and save social security funds. The long-term unemployed would be penalized when job offers were refused. The so-called one-euro jobs pay €1 to €3 an hour on top of the welfare checks. The unemployed are supposed to work between 15 and 30 hours a week. There is a wait list of the job seekers now. Therefore, the has succeeded Another novel, called mini-jobs, pays €400 a month for part-time jobs. There is no evidence on the success of this program yet. Any that entices unemployed workers to work is the right thing to do. In 2006, conservative Angela Merkel of the Christian Democrats (CDU) formed the government but her winning margin was so slim that a coalition government was formed. However, within a couple months of forming government, she has clearly steered German foreign policy away from France and Russia. Even more amazing is that the Cabinet approved on March 15, 2007 to cut the company tax rate from 38.7% to 29.8%.

The German public and labor unions realize now that in this global economy, German companies would rather invest in China than in Germany unless the government and unions make it worthwhile to invest in Germany. German engineering is respected worldwide but its industries can no longer afford excessive union demands and taxes. The per capita GNI of Germany slipped from 95% of that of the U.S. in 1980 to 67% of the U.S. in 2003. It appears that Germany is onto something "new". It is called a supply-side reform. See Table 2.

Sweden

The population of Sweden is only 9 million, but its economic history has been closely watched by many people. If there was a welfare state that appeared to work, it was Sweden. A review of Sweden's economic performance shows that its economy grew at a brisk pace until 1974 but between 1974 and 1992, Sweden experienced high inflation and unemployment rates. Like in other euro-economies, its Achilles heel is a high unemployment rate. In the early 1990s, annual work hours in Sweden stood at about 1400, compared with about 1600 in the U.S./UK and about 2000 in Japan. The official unemployment rate of 7.1% in June 2005 is misleading. It failed to consider work sharing of a sort. The true extent of unemployment is also "masked by use of make-work s, further education, early retirement and sick leave—on as much as 80–90% of previous salary. Employers fearful of such costs are understandably reluctant to hire."

The inflation rate shot up to10% in 1989, and controlling inflation became an urgent task. Because of sluggish revenue collection, the government had to cut back its spending for public assistance. Like in Germany, public sector unions pushed wages too high for their own long-term good. In order for Swedish exports to remain competitive, the government was forced to devalue the krona and maintain high interest rates. Sweden had little choice "when the interest rate jumped within a few days from 16% to 500% [lasted only several days], forcing the Bourgeois government to get the huge public sector deficit under control."[10]

In September 1992, the government reached an agreement with the labor unions to reduce their demands. Sick benefits were cut and the groundwork was laid for sweeping reforms of the old age pension system even as the contributions of employees to their social insurance were raised. The agreement also put into effect a drastic reduction of the employer's contribution. This change was designed to reduce deficits in the pension funds. It is also important to note that some negative developments in the economy were unrelated to the excess demands of labor unions and welfare state. Swedish banks incurred massive losses in the 1990s in the European property market. However, by and large, the root cause of the lackluster growth of the Swedish economy, which led to a cut back in social welfare benefits, was excessive socialism and union wages.[11]

Raising interest rates in the hope of stemming currency outflows was unwise for Sweden. Such a move exacerbated the economic downturn and added to the banks' loan losses. All in all, in the three years from 1991 to 1993, Sweden's GDP fell by a total of around 6 per cent. Defending a fixed exchange rate is a common mistake that a country in a financial crisis makes.

In Sweden, the need to reform labor unions was accepted by most politicians, but carrying it out has been another matter. Swedish voters, accustomed to a-cra-dle-to-the grave welfare system, resented it whenever conservative governments cut social security benefits and put socialists parties in power (i.e., the oust of the Bourgeois coalition in the elections of 1994). Social Democrats which came back to power restored the double taxation on dividends in 1994. Along with their victory, Bourgeois coalition's ideas of lowering capital gain tax and abolishing the net wealth (worth) tax never saw daylight.

Once again, Sweden proved that reducing government benefits to those accustomed to such benefits was extremely difficult. In Sweden, the notoriously high

---

10. For a brief but accurate description of this even, see Nicole Faher, "Country Case Studies and Links : Sweden", http://www.pitt.edu/~heinisch/ca_swed.html

11. ibid

payroll taxes (33.06%) are paid entirely by employers and self-employed individuals. There is no income ceiling on such taxes in Sweden. In the U.S., 12.4% social security tax is collected on the first $90,000 of income (in 2005 but adjusted from year to year to reflect inflation). The Medicare tax of 2.9% has no upper income limit. But a direct comparison of the U.S. and other countries on healthcare can be misleading. European countries have national healthcare system but the U.S. healthcare covers only elderly and poor population.

Sweden collects more taxes for social security (as the percentage of GDP) than the U.S. government collects at all levels of government (federal, state and local). Generous social welfare benefits are a compassionate and humane thing to do in the short run, but they ruin a nation in the long run. Generous social benefits create temptation to drop out of the labor market and live off such benefits. Sweden and Nordic countries as a whole are often cited as the most dynamic and highly competitive economies. This is not true. See Table 2. In 1980 the per capita GNI of Sweden was 27% higher than the U.S., but in 2003 it was 23% below that of the U.S. (see Figure 2). There is no free lunch. Sweden may have looked like a workers' paradise, but the people do not work in a worker's paradise.

France

The French remedy for the Great Depression was similar to what is now a familiar pattern: spending cuts, balanced budget and inflation watch. France also prolonged the Depression by sticking to the gold standard when the UK and Germany abandoned it early. The gold standard kept the franc overvalued and slowed its exports. The Great Depression lingered on until 1939 when World War II started. The French reaction to the German invasion was a short confrontation, retreat and quick capitulation. The best spirit of defiance against the German invasion was embodied in Charles de Gaulle, but he could do little when his government abandoned resistance. Because France gave up fighting German invasion early, its cities and factories particularly Paris remained more or less intact.

After World War II, France also received generous assistance for redevelopment under the Marshall Plan amounting to $2.3 billion. France also borrowed from IBRD. In fact, IBRD's first loan was to France in the amount of $250 million in 1947. De Gaulle emerged as post-war leader and led France's economic recovery. He elevated the status of France as a world leader. The French economic recovery up to 1970 was almost as miraculous as that of Germany. In terms of GNI, the per capita income of France in 1975 was not only well ahead of the UK but also slightly ahead of West Germany. But Germany surpassed

France in 1990; Hong Kong surpassed France in 1998; the UK surpassed France in 2000; and Ireland surpassed France in 2001. Why? It is a familiar story which varies only by a degree. The socialist government of François Mitterrand came into power in 1981 and turned France into workers' paradise. The labor market became so rigid that firing an employee became nearly impossible. Such a policy discouraged French industries from hiring workers. France's unemployment rate hit 10.2% in 1985, 12.3% in 1994 (the German unemployment was 8.4% at that year) and now hovers around 10%. France spent about 27% of its GDP on social security and its overall tax burden was 45.2% of GDP in 2000. This was only surpassed by Sweden's 54% tax burden. See Table 4.

Table 4

Total Tax Revenue as Percent of GDP (Tax Burden)
Selected OECD Countries *

	1975	1990	2000
France	36%	43%	45%
Germany	33%	33%	38%
Sweden	41%	52%	54%
UK	35%	37%	37%
U.S.	27%	27%	34%

*   Source: OECD

Any attempt to introduce a marginally flexible labor market reform caused massive rallies and protests by the labor. To appease the militant labor unions, France tried to protect existing jobs by resisting globalization and practicing thinly-disguised protectionism. France says that it is protecting its "strategic" and "sensitive" industries from buyouts by foreign companies and is not practicing protectionism.[12] But the definition of such industries is fluid and expanding. They included food giant Danone, which Pepsi Co Inc. was interested in acquiring; supermarket chain Carrefour, which Wal-Mart was interested in; and engineering company Alstom, which Switzerland's Novartis was interested in.

The latest battle is France's attempt to block the takeover of energy group Suez by Italian firm Enel. Italy demanded for "Brussels to intervene, arguing that France's protectionist stance is unfounded." Italy's industry minister has been

---

12.   "Economic Brief: French Protectionism", *The Power and Interest News Report* (PINR); September 15, 2005.

quoted by *FT Europe* for saying: "If neo-protectionism prevails, the political and economic destiny of the European Union will be compromised." The E.U. Commission told the press that the E.U. does not "want to see any disguised protectionism". France also threw the final blow to the Hong Kong round of WTO talks in December 2005 by not willing to open its agricultural market to the world. Of course, France was not alone. Japan took a similar position. The U.S. also provides agricultural subsidies, although it is willing to give up them up in return for a more global open market.

To make the matter worse, France accepted a large number of foreign immigrants. About 11% of its population is foreign born compared with 9% in Germany and 7% in the UK. What soured the French attitude toward immigrants is that the second generation immigrants have turned restless and violent. The situation has caused the French population to elect a conservative politician Nicolas Sarcozy to presidency. He is pro-U.S., pro law-and-order and pro-capitalism. This is just another Euro country that has abandoned the welfare socialism in favor of capitalism and social order. It is better to be late than never.

France has been always nationalistic but has led a movement to create a European Union which would rival the U.S. It would have established an EU constitution and a president, but it was the French workers who rejected the proposition because they feared the invasion of cheap laborers from Poland and other East European countries would have taken their jobs away. That would jeopardize the hard won victories of French workers: 35-hour work week and six-week vacation. Since the rejection, Jacques Chirac has put his head in the sand and blamed Anglo-American sentiments for the failure. The French continue to reject globalization in the name of preserving its national and cultural identity.[13] Frenchmen have come to smash the windows of MacDonald restaurants and Target department stores to show how much they hate Americanization of the French way of life. If history has anything to teach, this will not help France in the long run. How much can Sarcozy change the French protectionism and socialism? Only time will tell.

Conclusions

The economies of Western Europe boomed after World War II but lost momentum after 1970. The growth rate of the most highly taxed economy, Sweden, was the slowest. The mistake that all of them have made was to continue with the

---

13. See Sophie Meunier, a lecturer in Public and International Affairs, Center of International Studies, Princeton University.

Keynesian economic policy and increasingly high taxes even after the war. Social security costs as percentage of GDP in 2001 was 28.5% in France, 28.9% in Sweden, 27.4% in Germany, 21.8% in UK and 14.8% in the U.S. The percentages have been decreasing somewhat in recent years. However, they are still too high (see Table 4). Some do not agree that high taxes and high social program expenditures have caused slow economic growth and high unemployment. However, evidence both in the U.S. and Western Europe is overwhelming. One has only to compare the economies of the euro-Zone, the U.S. and UK, and Asia (to be discussed later) to find this unmistakable correlation.

As shown in Figure 2, the per capita GNI of France, Italy and even Finland (Western Europe's strongest economy) have all slipped relative to the U.S. The per capita GNI of France went down from 98% of the U.S. in 1980 to 66% in 2003. Finland did somewhat better, but it went down from 84% of the U.S. GNI in 1980 to 72% in 2003. Sweden and Germany did even worse than France, Italy and Finland. Exception has been the UK, which has gone through supply-side reforms. Lately, there has hardly been any growth in the euro-economies. Italy and the Netherlands experienced negative growth between June 2004 and June 2005.

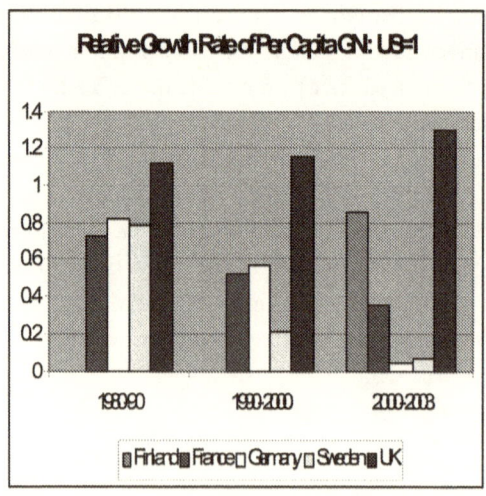

Figure 2

More importantly, this relative slide was accompanied by high unemployment rates. For all of Western Europe (excluding the UK), the unemployment rate in mid-2005 was 8.7%. The German unemployment rate stood stubbornly high at

11.6% in July 2005, even after a slight improvement over earlier months. See Figure 3. As in Sweden, the real unemployment rates of euro-economies may be even higher than the nominal percentage figures.

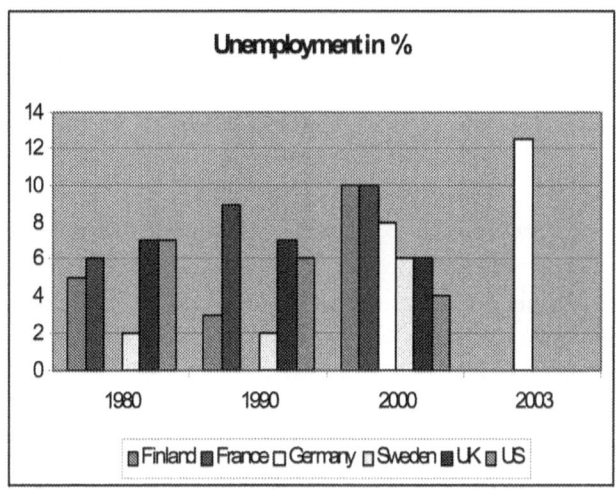

Figure 3

The euro-economies allowed the labor unions to go out of control, national-ized key industries and expanded welfare socialism enormously when their econo-mies were suffering from supply-side bottlenecks and high inflation. Margaret Thatcher of the U.K. reversed the trend but other countries did not. See Table 3 & 4 for social security and other taxes in Western Europe.

To contain inflation, the central banks tightened money supply. Such a policy kept inflation on check as it was designed to do, but low inflation per se was not sufficient to promote sustained economic growth. Even with such high taxes, the investment in the tertiary education has been low. Western European technology and engineering still mean quality, but its technology development from Internet to biotechnology has lagged behind the U.S. Japan by comparison had a much lower tax burden. So did the U.S. although it does not provide medical care other than for Medicare and Medicaid for eligible persons. In 2000, Americans spent 6.7% of GDP for private medical care services. If this percentage is added directly to the social security tax, the total social security costs come to 21.5%. This is in line with the UK rate. The only difference is that Americans have access to pri-vate practitioners. The Japanese government collected only 17% of GDP for social security.

Largely because of the high cost of social security taxes, Western Europeans pay far more taxes than other countries. In 2000, the tax burden was 54% in Sweden, 45% in France, 38% in Germany, 37% in the UK and 34% in the U.S. The U.S. tax burden is not as light as the percentage figure suggests because the U.S. government does not provide universal healthcare service that Western European countries do. If the private medical care cost, amounting to 6.7% of the GDP in the U.S., is added to the U.S. tax burden to make it comparable to those of Western European countries, the tax burden would become 41% of GDP, which is higher than the U.K and Germany. Germany, by the way, hardly spends anything for national defense. In recent years, tax burdens in Western Europe have not increased and some efforts are being made, for example in Germany, to provide incentives to work. The labor unions now understand that they cannot be overly militant because their corporations would simply cut jobs at home and build plants overseas. The global economy has a way to discipline national economies including labor unions.

The UK went through supply-side reforms in 1979 under Ms. Thacher. Two Labour governments in power since then have not turned the clock back. Similar but less far-reaching reforms are taking place in the euro-economies as well. The election of Nicolas Sarcozy of France and Angela Merkel of Germany are the latest and most important developments in this regard. A different set of reform policies was adopted by The Netherlands in 1982; by Ireland in 1987; and by Denmark, Finland, Sweden and Italy in all in the 1990s. They all have seen the light. The entry of China and India to the global economy and the integration of Eastern Europe to the European Union have curtailed the demands of militant labor unions and have made structural reforms imperative.

Chapter 3

U.S. Twin Deficits and the Global Economy

What Is Wrong With Twin Deficits?

The U.S. economy looks good in terms of growth rate and job creation but the fly in the ointment has been twin deficits—the simultaneous deficits in the government budget (fiscal) deficit and the balance of payment current account deficit. There are some $3 trillion U.S. "checks" out there held by China, Japan, Taiwan and others. They have not demanded cash for the checks to the delight of the U.S. government and consumers. Such debts have been accumulated by the U.S. government, corporations and individuals. A problem is that one day the creditors may want to exchange these debt instruments for other currencies if not for key U.S. corporations.

How Significant Are Twin Deficits and Why?

One cause of the twin deficits is that the U.S. government has been running on deficits as long as most people can remember except for a brief period in 1999–2000. While politicians were salivating how to spend it, the tech bubble burst and fiscal balance went once again to deficit the very next year. The collection of revenues has fluctuated with economic conditions, but government spending has always increased year after year. Government fiscal deficits do not always cause current account deficits, but they do in the U.S. because the non-government sectors do not save to finance government spending deficits.

Where is the government spending this money? It used to be for national defense, but the expenditures on national defense have plummeted sharply from 53% of government expenditures in 1960 to 12% in 2006 in spite of the Iraq and Afghanistan wars. The most expensive functions of government today are social services and the next to it is education. Expenditures on Education have increased from 15% of government expenditures to 20.2%. Expenditures for social programs are the fastest growing category of all government functions.[1] See Table 5 below. There is little chance that this trend will change any time soon. The aging of the baby-boomers alone will push up the costs of Social Security and Medicare.

Table 5

Government Expenditures for Selected Functions
U.S. Government at All Levels

(amount in billion $) *

	1960	1990	2000	2006
Gross domestic product (GDP)	526.4	5803.1	9817	13,253.9
Current Government expenditures	122.9	1872.6	2886.5	4308.9
% of GDP	23.35%	32.27%	29.40%	32.5%
National defense expenditures	53.4	374	370.3	516.9
% of current govt. expenditures	43.45%	19.97%	12.83%	12.0%
Government social benefits	24.6	574.8	1044.1	1397.5
% of current govt. expenditures	20.02%	30.70%	36.17%	32.4%
Education	16.1	280	474.1	870.0
% of current govt. expenditures	13.1%	15.0%	16.3%	20.2%

*   Source: Bureau of Economic Analysis, as revised on August 31, 2005.
Table 3.1 and Table 1.1.5 and Table 3.16 of National Income and Product
Accounts Tables, except percentages calculated by the author.

The expenditures on the Iraq and Afghanistan wars in the past few years have not helped the matter. The actual expenditures on the wars are not available year by year but Congress has so far appropriated about $100 billion per year for military operations, reconstruction, embassy costs, enhanced security at U.S. bases and foreign aid programs in Iraq and Afghanistan. The wars in Afghanistan and Iraq have been responsible for slightly less than 30% of the federal deficits.[2] This

1.   They comprise "Income security" in the National Account Tables of BEA and includes social security costs.

means that other government spendings have been responsible for the 70% of the deficits. Bush was elected under the slogan of compassionate conservatism. He has been more compassionate than conservative when it comes to spending. Not a single spending program prepared by Congress has been vetoed by Bush yet.

Not surprisingly, fiscal deficits under the Bush administration ballooned. The average government deficit during Reagan Administration's eight years was 1.93% of GDP compared with 3.33% during the Bush's first five years (2001–2005). It is unprecedented although not extraordinarily large compared with some other countries. The U.S. federal government debt in mid-2006 was 65% of GDP compared with 49% for the UK in 2000 (IMF data), 76% for Germany in 1997 (IMF data) and 160% for Japan in 2005 (the Ministry of Finance). However, the U.S. federal government debt is still increasing and the cost of money is higher in the U.S. Furthermore, Japan and Germany have current account surpluses. Therefore, they can borrow locally. For the US government, its deficits more or less add directly to foreign debts.

The good news is that the federal deficits declined rather substantially in 2005 and 2006 because of economic growth leading to higher tax revenues. This is happening in spite of the fact that Bush initiated huge additional spending programs under No Child Left Behind and the Medicare Drug Benefits for seniors as well as the Iraq War. Republicans have done nothing to curtail earmarks.[3] Bush spent lavishly on the victims of 9/11 and Hurricane Katrina. There have been many victims of disasters. Why should the policemen and firemen who died in the line of duty become multi-millionaires while U.S. servicemen who die in the battlefields receive a tiny sum in comparison? Why should the families of the unfortunate occupants of the Twin Towers become millionaires when the victims of other disasters do not? Can the U.S. afford to pay such a huge compensation if Los Angeles is wiped out in a nuclear attack? Bush attracted the ire of fiscal conservatives and did not even get any credit from the liberals.

Many observers and partisan politicians have also blamed the tax cuts for growing fiscal deficits, but that is only half true at best. Each tax cut has been followed by robust economic growth. As a result, government revenues have always increased in the years that followed. The main cause of fiscal deficits in the U.S.

---

2. The budget deficits, according to BEA, were $529.7 billion in 2003, $533.1 billion in 2004, $456.3 billion in 2005 and $312.5 billion in 2006 (based on the seasonally adjusted annualized rate of the first quarter 2006 deficit).

3. Congress obliging government agencies to spend a portion of the budget on special projects chosen by politicians such as $223 million for the so-called "the Bridge to Nowhere" connecting an Alaskan town of 8,900 to an island of 50 inhabitants.

has been increasingly high social spending. To deny that is either pure ignorance or partisan talking.

At the end of 2005, the U.S. owes over 100% of its GDP to other countries. In terms of the net international investment position, it was $2.7 trillion, about 21% of GDP.[4] The U.S. external debt increased by $333 billion between 2004 and 2005. See Table 6. It is this trend that is worrisome. In 2006, the first quarter deficit was running at the annualized rate of $868.6 billion, which amounts to 6.7% of GDP. By the end of 2006, the net international investment position may exceed $3 trillion. No other country can incur this kind of deficit without suffering a financial crisis.

Table 6

External Debt of the USA
(amount in billion $) *

Year	External Debt	GDP	Debt as % GDP
1980	$209.0	2,789.5	7.49%
1985	$451.1	4,220.3	10.69%
1990	$830.2	5,803.1	14.31%
1995	$1,209.3	7,397.7	16.35%
2000	$1,589.2	9,817.0	16.19%
2004	$2,867.0	11,735.0	24.43%

*   Source: The Department of the Treasury for external debt and the Bureau of Economic Analysis for GDP; % calculation by the author.

The Economist said the "current-account deficit is big enough to have bankrupted any other country some time ago." It asks, "Why should anybody invest in a currency that will almost certainly depreciate?" Will the U.S. be in trouble? Yes, if creditor countries want to cash in on American debts. Competitive economies such as China and Japan have huge savings, not huge debts. In 2003, Hong Kong's surplus was over 10% of GDP and Singapore's surplus was over 30% of GDP! This excellent magazine opined that the dollar's "dominant role can no longer be taken for granted. If America keeps on spending and borrowing at the present pace, the dollar will eventually lose its mighty status in international finance. And that would hurt: the privilege of being able to print the world's reserve currency, a privilege which is now at risk, allows America to borrow

---

4.   The source of the data on the external positions is Table 1. International Investment Position of the United States at Yearend, 2004 and 2005, BEA.

cheaply, and thus to spend much more than it earns, on far better terms than are available to others.... If you had been granted that ability, you might take care to hang on to it. America is taking no such care, and may come to regret it."[5]

Impact of Twin Deficits

With the ballooning twin deficits, the value of dollar plummeted to about half its former value against the Japanese yen (JPY), German mark and Swiss frank between 1968 and 1979. See Figure 4 for the long-term trend of the U.S. dollar against major currencies. This was the period when Japanese imports surged and American industries were in danger of being destroyed from electronics to automobile industries. The falling values of the dollar was the reflection of the weak U.S. economy. During the first term of the Reagan Administration, the dollar bounced back considerably because of the renewed strength of the U.S. economy but a strong dollar was practically "killing" U.S. corporations. Reagan chose a weak dollar policy, and pressured G5 (France, West Germany, Japan, and the United Kingdom) to revalue their currencies. They obliged through what is known as the Plaza Accord (9/22/85). The dollar dropped all the way to ¥84 in April 1995, a 76% drop since 1971. A weak dollar policy was the only way the U.S. corporations could survive.

The value of the dollar strengthened somewhat during the second term of the Clinton Administration because the U.S. economy strengthened and its interest rate was much higher than that of Japan, but during the Bush presidency, the dollar has been losing its value particularly against the euro and British Pound (BP) not necessarily because the U.S. economy was weak but because of the extremely high twin deficits. Just like anything else, the value of a currency is determined by the supply and demand of the currency. Obviously, it is determined not only by trade balance but also the movement of long-term investment capital and short-term investment capital in stocks, savings accounts and corporate and Treasury bonds. Between 9/11/2001 and 12/5/06, the dollar depreciated even against some Asian currencies (39% against South Korean Won and 14% against Singapore dollar) but not against JPY and the Chinese yuan, the two countries from which the U.S. imported most. A main reason why the Japanese yen has been weak is because of the low interest rate and the resulting carry trade (a currency trade where one borrows low-interest currency in order to buy high-interest currency). While these undervalued currencies are a blessing of a sort, China's currency manipulation has been threatening many American companies,

---

5.   "The Disappearing Dollar," *The Economist*, December 4th 2004.

if not driving them out of business. Weak Chinese and Japanese currencies have kept inflation low in the U.S.

The U.S. trade balance against China has been growing ominously: $162 billion in 2004 and $202 billion in 2005. The U.S. government has been pressing China to float the yuan and Congress has threatened to impose tariff on Chinese products. Fair trade depends on a free currency market although a significant and sudden revaluation of the yuan would make Chinese goods more expensive in the U.S. and cause inflation in the U.S. However, the longer the massive trade deficits continue, the greater is the danger of a financial turmoil later. China has now accumulated enough dollar to buy several crown jewels of American corporations such as Exxon-Mobil, Boeing and Microsoft corporations simultaneously if they can be acquired on the present market capitalization value and if the U.S. government allowed China to buy them. Another possibility is for China to dump dollar and start a financial earthquake. The U.S. is now a heavily indebted nation and it is vulnerable to such external shocks.

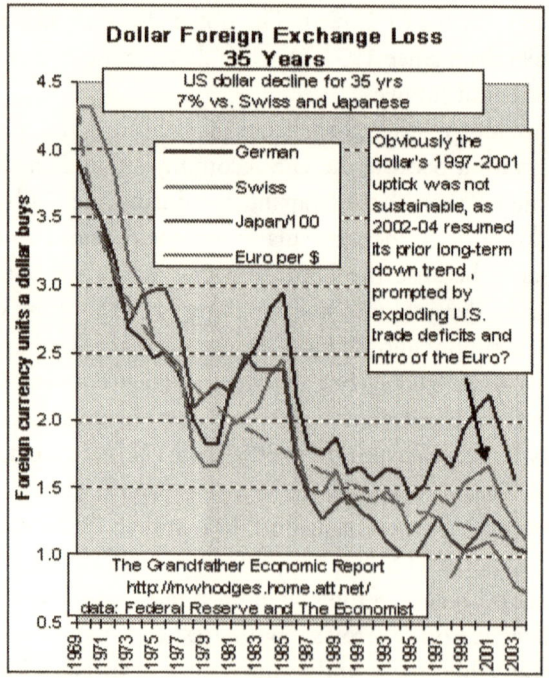

Figure 4
Source: Reproduced with the permission of Michael W Hodge.

The Global Economy

Today's global nature of the world economy is changing the ability of the Federal Reserve to control inflation. The U.S. economy does not dominate the world economy as it used to and cannot control the liquidity in the U.S. let alone the world. As a result, the Federal Reserve can no longer fine tune the inflation rate by raising or lowering the Fed Fund rates. The 17 consecutive interest Fed rate hikes in 2005–06 did not do much to bring down the inflation rate or raise the long-term interest rates. Greenspan called it a conundrum. If the Fed drives the short-term interest rates very high, it can still create a recession. It would be worthwhile to bring down a run away inflation rates like in the 1970s, but is it worthwhile to do so to bring the inflation rate from 2.5% to 2% because 2.0% is more in line with the Fed comfort zone? We doubt it.

With no tariff to speak of now, noncompetitive economies have few places to hide today. Free trade is good but is not necessarily a cure-all for all countries. Nazi Germany and Japan did well before World War II and Japan did well even after World War II with protectionism until the 1980s. China is doing well with protectionism now. George W. Bush sold the North American Free Trade Agreement (NAFTA) in 1994 on the ground that it would be good for the U.S. economy and create more jobs. Has it? Robert E. Scott of the Economic Policy Institute (EPI) said in 2001 that NAFTA promoters played "fast and loose with facts." NAFTA has been a net loss to the U.S. trade balance and and employment but net gains to Mexico and Canada. This trend has continued even after 2000.

Just as industrialization rewarded some more than the other, globalization rewards some more than the other. U.S. current account deficits against NAFTA partners were for every category of Standard Industrial Code (SIC) including the service sector, not just for the oil and gas sector. Losses to the auto sector, including auto parts, have been most significant. Government projections were wrong. This, however, does not necessarily prove that NAFTA was bad for the U.S. Without NAFTA, the U.S. might have imported more from China, the Middle East and other countries, and may have paid higher prices. A more reliable evaluation of NAFTA has to be based on with- or without-NAFTA assumptions. This is, however, not a simple task to perform. It, however, proves that government economists had a bad crystal ball.

The largest trade deficits is against China. To make the matter worse, China steals intellectual properties as well as manipulates its currency. It also provides massive subsidies to state enterprises. For the massive trade deficits, the U.S. is partly to blame. Japan, South Korea and Taiwan have been making trade surplus against China. U.S. industries as a whole lack competitiveness. Why? One has only to examine GM and Ford, which have been losing market shares even within the U.S. The Detroit auto makers are burdened with legacy costs due to concessions made to unions years ago. How can they compete with the likes of Toyota, which do not have such problems? On top of that, Toyota factories run on more than a full capacity but the Detroit companies run on far below their capacity and have to pay a full-time wages to laid-off workers for years to come.

The U.S. steel industry faced a similar problem from foreign competitors. The U.S. produced about half of the world's steel in 1945, but in 1999 the U.S. produced 12% of the world's steel. At one point, the steel industry appeared that it would go out of business like the garment and TV manufacturers. What has salvaged the U.S. steel industry from a total extinction has been going nonunion, becoming leaner and meaner and running "mini-mills" that recycle scrap metals and produce specialized products rather than iron and steel ingots.

The U.S. needs another round of reforms including the reduction of regulations (environmental and other), legacy costs, excessive and secretive executive compensations, AMA monopoly, the abuse of class action law suits and excessive jury awards. Some parts of the Sarbanes-Oxley Act of 2002 need to be repealed. The market economy does not work when certain professionals (whether physicians or trial lawyers) have a monopoly protected by laws and certain workers (such as union members) prevent a free labor market. Option backdating as well as situations such as the fall of Enron have occurred because of the lack of transparency or outright cheating. This may not call for more onerous regulations but more strict application of existing laws.

A belated but encouraging move by the Bush Administration is the emphasis on global competitiveness (State of Union message 2006). Global competitiveness has more than one definition. By one definition (sustained per capita income growth), the U.S. economy is ranked among the highest. The only problem is that the high living standard of the U.S. is based on its ability to write large checks without anyone demanding cash for them. The U.S. cannot have sustained prosperity without healthy current account balances and a stable currency.

Bush's strategy for increasing global competitiveness is better education, affordable health care and energy independence through the development of alternative energies. His goal is to replace more than 75 percent of U.S. oil imports from the Middle East by 2025! Energy independence has been a proclaimed goal by several presidents before him but the U.S. has become more dependent on foreign oil each year. What would solve the U.S. energy problem rather quickly is to reduce environmental controls over drilling and start the construction of nuclear power plants and expedite the development of clean coal and clean diesel. Unfortunately, that will not happen in the U.S.

Bush also proposed more federal support for the development of cutting-edge technologies and for making tax credits permanent. The U.S. is decades behind Japan, South Korea and Singapore in providing government support for technology development. However, it is better late than never. The U.S. should also support for the competitiveness of strategic existing industries including the auto industries. Why fight the EU on the Airbus subsidy? Join it. To fight off EU subsidy to Airbus, Boeing had to take in Japanese partners (Mitsubishi, Fuji and Kawasaki). The Japanese were eager to enter the aircraft design and production business and they would "design and build the box that ties together the wings in the fuselage—the largest structural part of the wing."[6] These Japanese firms will receive development subsidies from their government in the same manner as Airbus did. The net outcome is that Boeing will outsource American jobs to Japan. This is good in a short term. But one day Japan may create an aircraft industry of its own. The U.S. prosperity cannot continue without competitive industries. Once, Chrysler needed a government rescue and it did well after restructuring. Likewise, the U.S. government should provide R&D support for strategic industries including automotive, aircraft and steel industries.

The U.S. should also adopt EU-like value added tax (VAT) which exempts taxes on exported products. Otherwise, the U.S. should give tax credit for the goods and services exported to abroad by U.S. corporations. This will level the playing field with Western Europe and Asia and reward exporters. When American corporations are just trying to defend their domestic market shares, they will lose the market shares. The East Asia economies succeeded by promoting exports through the provision of financial and other incentives to export industries. The U.S. should do the same. This is also a time to fight protectionism and piracy abroad more aggressively. One estimate shows that the U.S. is losing approximately $200 billion a year because of piracy. The U.S. should be prepared to have a trade war with China if necessary to fix these problems. The U.S. holds the trump card because of its huge market.

American manufacturers are moving to foreign countries in a record number. They need more tax and non-tax incentives to stay put in the U.S. Many countries are enticing U.S. companies with such incentives—corporate tax exemption for a period of time, the relaxation of cumbersome labor and environmental regulations. Most Asian countries have export processing and other special zones

---

6.   "Boeing gets on track on track," *The Economist*, June 4, 2005.

ready to build on. Foreign investors do not have to wait five years to obtain build-ing permits or fight environmental and community activists. The exceptionally high cost of healthcare in the U.S. is acting like an extra 4%-7% taxes on corpo-rations and individuals, and class action lawsuits threaten to put every company out of business in the U.S. (see further discussion of these in Chapter 5). This is why American corporations are expanding plants in low-wage and business-friendly countries abroad while cutting jobs in the U.S. Americans rarely appreci-ate corporations for creating jobs or creating wealth in the U.S., but many foreign countries do.

A country goes through a cycle. Since the tech bubble burst, the U.S. has been in a relative down cycle compared with Asia and some European economies in spite of the fact that its economy has performed well. During the past 5 years (the first quarters of 2002 through 2007), the U.S. stock market, measured in S&P 500, has lagged miles behind not only the Emerging Markets but also Australia, Canada, Germany and the UK. The U.S. has become a sluggish giant trapped in its old habits, i.e., anti-corporate culture and "social causes" that border schizo-phrenia. For example, it is extremely difficult for scientists and engineers to obtain H1-B visas for work (temporary work permit) but anyone walking across the U.S. borders without any paper is being considered for U.S. citizenship. The West is now obsessed with the fear of man-made global warming. It is playing a havoc with energy policies of the West.

Part Two
Failed Values and Social Policies

Chapter 4

Failed Healthcare System

Problems

The U.S. has an outrageously high healthcare costs but the life expectancy is low and the infant mortality rate is exceptionally high compared with other industrialized countries. What is the cause of this problem? The access of the population to medical care is another issue. The problems in other industrialized countries are complaints against nationalized healthcare. What can the U.S. do about its problem and other countries about their problems coming from the opposite field?

Cause of Low Life Expectancy and High Infant Mortality in the U.S.

Table 7 provides cross-country data on healthcare costs per capita, life expectancy and infant mortality rates. The life expectancy of Americans in 2005 was 77 (rose to 77.9 in 2007 but the rank dropped a notch to the 42nd in the world), which was significantly lower than Japan (82); considerably lower other Canada and West European countries; and about the same with South Korea. The WHO cites various reasons why the U.S. ranks low in life expectancy among wealthy nations.

Native Americans, rural African Americans and the inner city poor have low life expectancy. These are well known facts. Other interesting points with ethical implications are: (i) the U.S. has a high incidence of HIV infection which shortens the life expectancy of male infants born in 1999 by 3 months and female infants by one month; and (ii) the U.S. has fairly high levels of violence, especially of homicides, compared with other industrial countries. This subject is discussed in Chapter 10. HIV infection in the U.S. is higher than in Western Europe and Asian countries, except India and Thailand. Interestingly, the life expectancy of Thailand declined from 70 in 1992 to 68 in 1997. The prevalence of AIDS and HIV infection among adults was 0.6% compared with 0.4% in France, 0.2% in the UK and Singapore and 0.1 in China, South Korea, Sweden and Japan. These percentages are from CIA Factbook 2005 but the data are for years 2001 or 2003.

Is the low life expectancy of the U.S. due to other American lifestyle issues? The U.S. is one of the leading countries for cancers in general and lung cancer in particular. What is odd about this is that Americans smoke much less than other nationalities (tested in 1991 and 2005). Independent data indicate that lung cancer and adult smoking are poorly correlated across different countries although physicians have clinical evidence on the relationship of smoking and lung cancer. Even among European nations, which are of a similar ethnicity, the prevalence of smoking and lung cancer are poorly correlated, statistically.[1] Another factor that could explain the incidence of lung caner is radon gas but there is no cross-country comparative data on this.

A large number of persons without health insurance may be another causal factor but the this assumption is more apparent than real because even the uninsured and illegal immigrants have access to free emergency room service and vulnerable age or income groups are covered by Medicare and Medicaid. Some blame the affluence and the easy life style of Americans for the relatively low life expectancy rate. Americans rank highest in obesity, and obesity has been increasing. What about the drinking habits of Americans as the cause of short life? According to an OECD study conducted in 2006, Americans consume much less alcohol per adult than West European countries, Mexico, Japan or South Korea.[2] A factor that the WHO does not report is the relationship of illicit drugs and death rate. There is a relationship but no mention of it is in the WHO article.

What do all these life style factors point to? HIV infection and a high murder rate are something definite, but physicians cannot do anything about that. Obesity may be a factor although obesity and death due to coronary diseases have been moving in opposite directions over years in the U.S. Another suspect for low life expectancy in the U.S. is poor healthcare. A Web article "Doctors Are The 3rd Leading Cause of Death in the US, Causing 225,000 Deaths Every Year" is worth reading.[3] This rather damning article against the U.S. medical profession is based on a July 2000 article in the Journal of the American Medical Association (JAMA) by Dr. Barbara Starfield of the Johns Hopkins School of Hygiene and Public Health.

---

1.   Visit http://www.kidon.com/smoke/percentages.htm for a display of these rather surprising cross-country data.
2.   http://www.irdes.fr/ecosante/OCDE/812010.html
3.   http://www.healingdaily.com/Doctors-Are-The-Third-Leading-Cause-of-Death-in-the-US.htm

A more serious evidence for poor health in the U.S. is in an exceptionally high infant mortality rate compared with other industrialized countries. See Table 7. China is an exception where infanticide of girl babies is an epidemic. The high infant mortality rate of the U.S. may be partly due to the prevalence of American mothers infected with HIV and the mothers who use drugs and alcohol during pregnancy. The prevalence of drug use in other countries is not available. The drug of choice varies from country to country. According to the National Institute of Drug Abuse, in the U.S., one in eight mothers uses alcohol, tobacco or other drugs during the week prior to delivery. Could there be under-reporting of such cases since some states have prosecuted the mothers of crack-babies, etc.? The answer may be yes on both. Babies of such mothers are often grossly underweight and their chances of survival are much less than normal babies. The lack of health insurance may be another factor.

Table 7

Health Expenditures, Life Expectancy and Infant Mortality
Selected Countries: year 2002 unless otherwise noted *

| | Health expenditures Per Capita | | Health Indicators | |
	in US$	as % of GDP	Life expectancy at birth 2005	Infant Mortality rate per 1,000 live births
Canada	$2,222	9.6%	80	5
China	$63	5.8%	71	30 (2003)
France	$2,348	9.7%	80	4.4
Germany	$2,631	10.9%	78	4.2
Japan	$2,476	7.9%	82	3.1
Korea, Rep.	$577	5.0%	77	5 (2003)
Sweden	$2,489	9.2%	80	3.3
United Kingdon	$2,031	7.7%	79	5.2
United States	$5,274	14.6%	77	7

* Source: World Health Organization (WHO) and OECD data compiled in World Development Indicators database, supplemented by World Bank poverty assessments and country and sector studies.
Note: Total health expenditure is the sum of public and private health expenditures. It covers the provision of health services (preventive and curative), family planning activities, nutrition activities, and emergency aid designated for health but does not include provision of water and sanitation.

Healthcare Costs

The U.S. spent 15% of GDP on healthcare; Germany 11%, France 10%; and the UK and Japan 8%. In dollar amounts, the per capita cost of U.S. healthcare was

$5,274 compared with $2,222 in Canada, $2,348 in France and $2,631 in Germany. By all means, the U.S. is the place to come, if a person needs to replace five organs simultaneously but it will be costly. The Japanese live five years longer than Americans and their infant mortality rate is less than half of the Americans but the cost of healthcare in Japan is 50% of the U.S. in percent of per capita GDP. Newt Gingrich predicted that health care costs in the U.S. would increase to 21% of the economy in a few decades—a terrifying thought.[4] This means one out of every five dollars that the economy produces will go to healthcare! Such a high cost is one of the reasons why many Americans do not have healthcare insurance. According to BEA time series (slightly different from WHO definition), the U.S. healthcare cost as percentage of GDP was less than 3.2% in 1950, but it increased to 4.2% in 1960, 12.4% 2000 and 14.3% in 2005. Extrapolate this trend. Then, 21%, which Gingrich cited, is not out of the question. As a percentage of personal consumption expenditures, the U.S. healthcare cost of 15.2% in 2000 was higher than the cost of housing, food, or the purchase of all kinds of durable goods such as automobiles and furniture. For most people, the healthcare costs are invisible, partly because not everybody pays for it out of pocket (such as Medicare, Medicaid and free emergency room services) and partly because the payment goes in form of insurance premiums paid by individuals and employers. If the cost of medicines, such as an average hospital cost per day, were posted along highways like the price of gasoline, people would be outraged.

The largest component of health care cost is "Hospital" at 32.5% and it has been growing at the rate of 10.7% per year between 1960 and 2005; and the next larges component is "Physician", 19.2% growing at the rate of 9.5% per year. The U.S. has taken many experiments to slow the accelerating medical costs but nothing has worked. Why? The monopoly of the American Medical Association (AMA) and the out of control class action suits by trial lawyers are the two biggest reasons. A good news is that Tort reforms are underway in a number of states and the tyranny of class action suites and unreasonable damage awards for plaintiffs may be waning now.

Another reason for rapid cost increase is that, in healthcare, the supply creates the demand because a patient is in no condition to know whether a procedure prescribed is necessary or not. Since medical and hospitalization costs come out of insurance companies, a patient does not care about the cost. Once a doctor refers a patient to hi-tech procedures, whether a newly installed MRA machine or a new catheter lab procedure, patients do not care. Americans demand the best

---

4.   See Newt Gingrich, *Winning the Future* (2005) p. 103.

and immediate treatment. Since physicians have to protect themselves from lawsuits, they have no incentive to save money. Therefore, a lot of inappropriate and unnecessary procedures are performed.[5] Medicare and Medicaid programs were supposed to have contained the cost of healthcare. But they did just the opposite. Since 1970, Medicare expenditure has grown at the rate of over 12% per annum. Medicaid (free medicine under federal and state governments) grew at the rate of over 16% per annum since 1960. When the Medicare program was instituted in 1965, it was projected to cost $9 billion in 1990 but the actual cost in 1990 was $67 billion. Medicaid's special hospitals subsidy was projected to cost $100 million per year by 1992, but the actual cost by then was $11 billion.[6]

The American Medical Association (AMA) does not censure physicians for providing unethical or unnecessary procedures. The main mission of the AMA is to increase the incomes of physicians. Those who work for medical insurance companies to approve or deny medical procedures are also the members of AMA. The AMA goes as far as reducing the supply of doctors to look after the welfare of physicians. It does so through its power to certify medical schools. It also protects physicians by limiting the public access to the professional records of doctors and hospitals.[7] As a result, the U.S. faces the shortage of doctors from primary care doctors to surgeons, cardiologists and neurologists. It has been alleged that before the AMA monopoly, American health care was better.[8] AMA also makes sure that foreign physicians do not come to the U.S. to practice medicine.[9] Foreign students are not even admitted to U.S. medical schools unless they have attended U.S. college beforehand.

With all that training, one might expect American physicians to know what they are doing but what they learn are costly procedures that often do not work. This is the main point of Dr. David Eddy the cover story in *Business Week* of May

---

5. See "Medical Guesswork,"A cover story of *Business Week,* May 29, 2006.

6. See Stephen Dinan of *The Washington Times,* January 30, 2004; Dale Steinreich of the Mises Institute in "100 Years of Medical Robbery".

7. See Joseph L Bast, the Heartland Institute; "How We Lost Our Health Care Freedom … And How To Win It Back"; April 1, 1998; http://www.heartland. org/Article.cfm?artId=736.

8. See Lawrence D Wilson, The Future of Freedom Foundation, "The Case against Medical Licensing," *Freedom Daily* January 1994.

9. An exception exists. If foreign doctors want to practice in rural areas where no American doctor wants to go, an exception can be made under the Nursing Relief for Disadvantaged Areas Act of 1999. Is the health of rural people less critical than urban people? No. AMA wants to make sure that its doctors have plum jobs.

29, 2006.[10] He was a former full professor at Stanford University before being recruited as chairman of the Center for Health Policy Research & Education at Duke University. He says: "From heart surgery to prostate care, the health industry knows little about which common treatments really work. He gives a list of such treatments. He concluded that only "15% of what doctors did was backed by hard evidence."[11] In short, physicians opt for expensive procedures rather than effective procedures. A problem for AMA is that a large number of doctors and health-care quality experts have now come to believe in Eddy's findings. Eddy says that what is required is a revolution called "evidence-based medicine."

American physicians earn several times more than their counterparts in other advanced countries. See Table 8. By specialization, they earned from $150,267 for family practitioners without obstetrics up to $306,964 for anesthesiology. According to the U.S. Census of 2000, other professionals with advanced degrees earned $55,242.[12] Doctors of science and philosophy spend as many years as most physicians to obtain their credentials.[13] "On the average, doctors in Canada and Germany earn about half as much as their U.S. counterparts; physicians in Austria, France and Britain less than one-third as much; and physicians in Finland, Norway and Sweden just one-fourth as much."[14] The people there may have to put up with delays but the irony is that they live much longer than Americans.

---

10. "Medical Guesswork", op. cit.

11. ibid

12. See U.S. Government census data, "Employment, Work Experience, and Earnings by Age and Education: Civilian Noninstitutional Population"; http://www.census.gov/hhes/income/earnings/call1usboth.html

13. See "Table P-18. Educational Attainment—People 25 Years Old and Over by Mean Income and Sex:1991 to 2001."

14. Devon Herrick, National Center for Policy analysis, "Would National Health Insurance Benefit Physicians?" August 31, 2001; http://www.ncpa.org/pub/ba/ba370/

Table 8

Total Compensation of Physicians by Specialty
USA 2002 *

Specialty	Mean Compensation
Anesthesiology	$306,964
Obstetrics/gynecology	$233,061
Psychiatry	$163,144
Internal medicine	$155,530
Pediatrics/adolescent medicine	$152,690
Family practice (without obstetrics)	$150,267

*   Source: Medical Group Management Association, Physician Compensation and Production Report, 2003.

American physicians have to put up with a ton of paperwork that "eats away at the time they might spend on other patients."[15] Insurance companies need documents to protect itself against multi million dollar awards for pain and suffering. The juries do not understand or do not care to understand the implications of a $100 million award for a single victim for pain and suffering.[16] Malpractice insurance premiums are dramatically higher in states without a cap on non-economic awards.[17] Ordinary Americans ultimately end up paying the excessive awards. In some states with no cap on the amount of malpractice awards, certain medical specialists cannot obtain insurance at any cost. This is the reason why there is no obstetrician, gynecologist or brain surgeon in some states. The irony is that injured patients receive a little or tiny compensation for their pain and suffering. Practically all the money goes to the trial lawyers who bring these cases and those who defend them.

Trial lawyers have put not only asbestos industry out of business, which is fine, but are now going after those companies which sold asbestos products not knowing its health implications. Sometimes the asbestos "victims" have included

---

15. Josh Fishman, *U.S. News & World Report*, January 31/February 7, 2005: 46

16. The problem of multi-million dollar jury awards has reached crisis proportions, such as $100 million to a litigant in Mississippi in 2002 and $100 million to a litigant in Pennsylvania in 1999. In New York State, there were three awards ranging from $80 million to $90.5 million in 2002.

17. The average highest insurance premium increase in 2001 and 2002 in states with a cap of $250,000 or less was 26% per annum, but in states without a cap, it was 45%. In 2001 and 2002, the rate increases went out of control.

those exposed to asbestos for just one hour in their whole lifetime and the "victims" who are not even sick.[18] Hundreds of thousands of claims are still pending and are clogging the courts with total costs and awards estimated to reach $200 billion. Of course, insurance companies will have to settle for a staggering amount of money and will eventually recover the losses by raising rates. The next such lucrative source of litigation is said to be common mold, which is already driving up the cost of homeowners' insurance and threatening to slow construction in some areas of the country. "The *American Bar Association Journal* is now predicting that mold could surpass asbestos in case volume and value of awards."[19] One bad drug or disclosure problems could risk the fortunes of a company and the assets of investors in the company. Merck's Vioxx is a good example.

Fraud is yet another critical problem in the industry. The California Chamber of Commerce cited a manager of a small construction company saying that "an individual who claimed to have suffered a back strain, had in fact a long-standing history of making back injury claims and was absolutely not injured while working for us.... what began as a good idea [workers' compensation] has been bastardized into a wasteful, expensive, useless, bureaucratic, mismanaged mess and employers and workers are paying the price."[20] Many California companies have seen their workers' compensation costs nearly tripling between 2002 and 2004. Its insurance rate was three times that in Colorado and twice that in Texas. Numerous documented cases indicate that California liberal judges reward liars generously and business owners are considered automatically guilty unless there are iron tight evidence and documentation.

Cases of collusion between the watchdog contractors, who are paid by the government to police Medicare, and the doctors and hospitals they are supposed to be policing is common.[21] Malcolm Sparrow, a health care fraud expert at Harvard University's Kennedy School of Government "estimates Medicare fraud at $50 billion to $75 billion a year." This amounts to 20–30% of the program cost. *Forbes* documented many disturbing fraud cases involving from small-time crooks to large corporations.[22]

---

18.   See *The Economist;* January 29th-February 4th 2005: 69.
19.   "A Report on the Lawsuit Industry in America, 2003: High-Growth Product: Mold"; Trial Lawyers, Inc. Com.
20.   See calchamber.com/CC/Headlines
21.   See Reynolds Holding of the *San Francisco Chronicle,* "Medicare bilked for billions in bogus claims, Private watchdogs rife with conflicts make system an easy target for fraud," January 12, 2003

The cost of medicines is extraordinarily high in the U.S. mainly because the pharmaceutical industry spends $500 million per drug and Americans are absorbing all the R&D costs. Foreign countries regulate drug prices through direct price control. As a result, foreign drug prices are generally 50%–60% of U.S. prices. The U.S. government should also negotiate the price so that drug companies will have to equalize drug prices on a global basis. Why should Americans subsidize the entire world? Democrats are right on asking the government to negotiate drug purchase prices for Medicare and Medicaid. The U.S. government should, however, protect American drug industries by retaliating against those countries that threaten to delist patented American medicines and steal intellectual properties. Gingrich says, "The Chinese and Indian governments turn a blind eye to outright theft of patents and production of counterfeit drugs."Some other countries do so more subtly: "The European and Japanese drug-purchasing systems are rigged to cheat American companies and to favor local companies. The French government, for example, threatened to steal American patents unless U.S. corporations sold drugs to France at very low prices."[23] The American public is increasingly aware that they can save huge amounts by re-importing medicines. They are doing so although the government has warned about the dangers of such practices.

Access to Health Care Services

The extremely high cost of healthcare notwithstanding, the U.S. does not even provide universal health care coverage. According to the 2005 U.S. Census, 46.6 million Americans (about 15.9% of the total population) did not have health insurance at least part of that year. This is an increase of about 1.3 million uninsured from the previous year. According to Wikipedia, most uninsured Americans are working-class persons whose employers do not provide health insurance but earn too much money to qualify for Medicaid. According to National Coalition for Health Care, 58% of the uninsured changed or lost jobs. About 20% of the uninsured used ER. Some of them are illegal immigrants and others are middle-income families who refuse to buy health insurance because the price is too high.

---

22. See John Simon, "Drug Fraud: Why Do Drug Companies Fear U.S. Attorney Michael Sullivan?" *Forbes*, Dec. 3, 2003. See also Nathan Vardi, "Rx for Fraud" *Forbes*, June 20, 2005.
23. ibid,. 127.

Does this situation call for universal health care coverage? That is not a bad idea if a price control is implemented like other countries together with a national healthcare. Without such a control, a nationalized health care system will take even a bigger bite out of the household budget. A previous attempt to introduce nationalized health care system failed miserably. Hilary Clinton's Task Force tried to pass a version of a national health care bill in 1993 without regulating the healthcare costs. One estimates indicated that it would have increased healthcare cost by over a trillion dollars to cover a relatively small proportion of the population which was uninsured. It did not address relief from huge malpractice damage awards. The plan was rejected by medical doctors, small businesses and even some labor unions which had a better deal already from large corporations such as the General Motors. Public opinion polls showed that only one in five supported the system, and the bill died. Massachusetts and California have launched what appears to be an innovative health insurance product that will allow thousands of uninsured persons to purchase private health insurance at affordable costs. None of these address the fundamental problem: the cost. Any state or national healthcare insurance that does not control healthcare cost will only line the pockets of medical doctors, trial lawyers and drug companies at the expense of American corporations and individuals.

An interesting idea, proposed by Steve Case's Revolution Health Group, is to provide consumers access to data on physician and hospital cost and quality, lower health insurance costs by streamlining the purchasing process, and enable consumers to rapidly access their personal health care data at convenient locations. Steve Case is the former founder of AOL and plans to invest $500 million in the new venture. This would encourage open clinics where one can step in for treatment without waiting days and weeks for an appointment. The U.S. is the only country where such open clinics are not available because of all the insurance paper requirements. Steve's system could possibly fix such a problem and make the health industry more transparent. Anything that brings transparency to healthcare costs and quality is good for patients.

Solution

Solutions to the high cost medicine require a series of steps to be taken in a logical sequence. First, federal and state governments should significantly limit non-economic awards for malpractice and pharmaceutical products in all states—including the amount of money that trial lawyers can take out of settlements, say, not more than 50%. Without this reform, nothing else will work. Second, the governments should chip away the AMA monopoly parading as an organization for the promotion of higher healthcare. This means (i) letting the market decide the number and standard of medical schools and students and (ii) allowing foreign doctors to take board examinations in the U.S. Third, the government should (i) let Medicare, Medicaid and any other bulk purchasers of medicines to bargain drug prices as foreign governments do; (ii) create an entity to police and certify that imported medicines are safe and genuine to prevent cheap copy cats in India and elsewhere from ripping off American companies; and (iii) allow the re-importation of genuine medicines sold by American companies oversea. This will protect American patients and level the playing field. Fourth, the government should (i) require insurance companies to provide in-between-job insurance coverage and (ii) allow emergency rooms of hospitals not to accept those without any proof of insurance or means of payment (credit card, checks, etc.) unless it is life threatening emergency. Finally, the government should allow the release of medical history to any licensed clinics and disclose the cost and quality of medical services in different medical facilities and individual practitioners. The market cannot perform its normal function without such knowledge and transparency.

An alternative is to have a universal healthcare system, where the government controls the cost as Canada does. It is not as bad as some Americans believe it is. An improvement over the Canadian system is to give the people the option of not paying for or being covered under a universal healthcare system and joining a private insurance with a higher price and standards of service (speed of service and coverage). For countries like the UK, the challenge is to introduce private medical practices to their government-monopolized systems.

Chapter 5

Failed Education Policies

Problems

The U.S. is the most powerful and wealthy country in the world but the academic standard of its students is dismal. A student must be able to read, write and work with numbers to become a productive worker, advance to the next level of education and eventually make a decent living. But this is proving to be difficult for American schools and students. American 8th graders were ranked 19th out of 38 countries on the most recent international mathematics comparison (1999) and 18th out of 38 countries in science. American 12th graders were worse: they ranked 19th out of 21 countries in both math and science general knowledge. Asian countries such as Singapore, South Korea, Chinese Taipei, Hong Kong and Japan have been on top of test scores whether in math or science.

What is Ailing K-12 Education?

The most popular theory among school teachers and their political supporters is that the government is not spending enough money for education. The truth is the U.S. government spends more per student in relation to its per capita GDP for primary and secondary students than most industrialized countries in the world. This is also true of the classroom size. It is small compared to other industrialized countries. The U.S. spends for primary and secondary education more per capita GDP than Japan, Germany and the UK. (see Table 9). Furthermore, there is no correlation between the spending per student and academic achievement. Japan, South Korea and Hong Kong spend much less than the U.S. in relation to their GDP, yet their students excel in all kinds of international competitive tests. Additional funds to inner city schools funded by the federal government have not brought about much improvement in the inner city schools, where the problem is most severe. The U.S. expenditures on education, at all levels of the government, have surpassed those for national defense since 1995. In 2006, 20% of the entire government spending was for education vs.

12% for national defense in spite of Iraq and Afghanistan wars. Bush's No Child Left Behind (NCLB) program has pushed up government expenditures for Education at all levels.

Table 9

Expenditure per Student
Selected Countries: In % of GDP Per Capita *

Year 2000

	Primary	Secondary	Combined
France	17.93	28.97	46.89
Germany	16.22	21.71	37.92
Hong Kong, China	12.92	18.75	31.67
Japan	21.53	20.91	42.44
Korea, Rep.	16.58	15.19	31.77
Sweden	23.24	26.62	49.87
United Kingdom	15.14	16.16	31.30
United States	21.18	24.46	45.64

* Source: United Nations Educational, Scientific, and Cultural Organization (UNESCO) as compiled in *World Development Indicators* database.

Note: Public expenditure per student (primary) is the public current spending on education divided by the total number of students by level, as a percentage of GDP per capita.

One primary contribution that federal government involvement in public education has made is that crime rates in schools have dropped considerably. The credit goes largely to the Educate America Act of 1994, which says, by 2000 "all schools in America will be free of drugs and violence and the unauthorized presence of firearms and alcohol, and offer a disciplined environment that is conducive to learning." Public schools, however, are far from being free of crime and drugs. The total nonfatal victimization rate for students aged 12 through 18 declined from 144 per 1,000 students in 1992 to 72 per 1,000 students in 2000. This decline was due in large part to the decrease in theft at school, which declined from 7 percent in 1995 to 4 percent in 2001. However, other more serious problems have increased. The incidents of school bullying increased between 1999 and 2001. Between 1993 and 2001, the percentage of students in grades 9 through 12 who were threatened or injured with a weapon on school property in the past 12 months did not decline.

The National Center for Education Statistics (NCES) concluded that the school safety picture is mixed. In 2000, there were 128,000 serious violent crimes (i.e., rape, sexual assault, robbery, and aggravated assault) at school. There were also 47 school-associated violent deaths in the United States between July 1, 1998 and June 30, 1999, including 38 homicides, 33 of which involved school-aged children.... more work needs to be done to address the issues related to school violence and safety."[1] The incidence of crime in school is unevenly distributed. City schools had a disproportionately higher incidence of crimes than small towns and rural areas. Principal Michael Durso of Springbrook High School summarized the situation well: "No matter where you are, parents want their students to be safe and secure ... that might even precede a quality education." [2] With drugs, gangs, and guns on the rise in many communities, the threat of violence "weighs heavily on most principals' minds these days ... Anyone who thinks they are not vulnerable is really naïve."[3]

School teachers' pet solution for education quality is to reduce classroom size. Experiments have shown that smaller class sizes have done little to improve the quality of education in the U.S. The National Center for Policy Analysis (NCPA) said that there is no conclusive evidence that reducing class size would improve the quality of education. According to World Bank data in 2000, pupil-teacher ratios were 29 in Japan, 32 in South Korea, 18 in the UK and 15 in the U.S. Even between Japan and South Korea, similar in education culture, South Korean students perform as well as Japanese students in spite of its larger class size. Americans may protest: "Asians are different." The optimum size of classroom boils down to the ability of teachers to control the class. Even a small class encounters a problem when one or two students disrupt the whole class. A rotten apple in a class of 15 is just as likely to pollute the entire class as in a class of 25 according to NCPA. It is all about how to maintain classroom discipline.[4]

Another theory, heard often, is that a problem is in low pay for teachers. Kafer says, "teachers earn more on an hourly basis than other educated professionals, including accountants, computer programmers, engineers, and architects."[5] However, teaching in a school with discipline problems is hard work, and good teachers spend long hours checking homework and preparing for classes. Teachers also have limited opportunities to make huge salaries. As a result, schools lose some teachers to other occupations. A school district which pays less than other

1.   "Indicators of School Crime and Safety, 2002," NCES; http://nces.ed.gov/pubs2003/schoolcrime/
2.   "Violence and Discipline Problems in U.S. Public Schools: 1996–97" op. cit.
3.   ibid
4.   "Student Misbehavior Solves Classroom Size Mystery," National Center for Policy Analysis; August 08, 2002.

school districts nearby does have recruitment problems also. It might surprise some people, however, that good American teachers go to private schools for less pay because there are fewer discipline problems in private schools and students have better learning motivation. Some teachers avoid inner city schools even at a higher salary because of safety and discipline problems.

There is no overall shortage of teachers, but there is a shortage of science and math teachers in public schools. For such teachers and for inner city schools, a higher pay, signing bonus and housing subsidy would be helpful. An even better idea is to hire non-union and not-accredited persons to teach such subjects provided that they have appropriated degrees in science and mathematics. At present, real scientists, engineers and mathematicians with an advanced degree (PhD or master's degrees) cannot teach in public schools. They go to private schools to teach. This raises the question about the role of teachers' unions. They restrict the supply of teachers and deprive the principals of schools the power to hire and fire. They look after the seniority system rather than performance.

The performance of U.S. public schools varies a great deal from school to school even within a school district. The most severe problem is in the inner cities. That is where discipline problems are most severe, particularly in neighborhoods with gang culture and a large proportion of single parent household heads. Single parents have less time to get involved in their children's education at home and with school. Schools with a concentration of "Hispanic" students have another kind of problem, i.e., language. Take San Rafael, California (a northern suburb of San Francisco) as an example. Glenwood Elementary School is a Blue Ribbon K-5th school. It receives some Hispanic overflow students from other neighborhoods, but the majority of its students are either Caucasian or Asian-American students from middle-class families. Its fourth graders scored 86% proficiency in English and 76% proficiency in Math in the 2005 California Standardized Testing and Reporting (STAR) tests. In close proximity in the same school district is San Pedro Elementary School attended primarily by Hispanic

---

5.   In 2004, Krista Kafer, of the Heritage Foundation, said that test scores have been improving somewhat but in 2003 only 16% of the Hispanic and 10% of the Black 4th graders achieved proficiency in mathematics, compared with 43% of the White students. The Asian/Pacific Islander group did somewhat better than the White group. This holds true for 8th grade math as well: 37% of the White group achieved proficiency, while only 12% of the Hispanic group and 7 % of the Black group did. The National Assessment of Educational Progress (NAEP) data shows that these patterns hold true for 4th grade reading, science, and American history.

students. In the same tests, the school tested 18% in English and 17% in Math (*Marin Independent Journal*, August 16, 2005).

The teachers of course matter. It is not a question of whether a teacher has a master's degree or bachelor's degree. It is the ability to control students. For example, the principal of the Glenwood Elementary School is a take-charge type of lady who does not let even a small disciplinary problem slide by her. She even stands at the school parking lot in the morning and makes sure that parents stop and park cars correctly. She also demands parental involvement, and she gets it. This is an example of a good teacher that goes well beyond classroom or office.

Lessons from Other Countries

Asian students outperform all other racial groups in international academic achievement tests. Why? Asian students from Confucian background grow up in families that place education above other things. Asian students who have migrated to the U.S. recently have language problems just like the Hispanic students, but Asian students overcome the language barrier more quickly than the Hispanic students because their parents do not insist on educating their children in their native languages. Asian students (particularly from Japan, Singapore, South Korea or Taiwan in alphabetical order) graduate from high school with American college level calculus. Some private schools in the U.S. offer similar advanced courses. In most Asian societies, parents accept teachers' authority over their children and support it. Asian parents motivate and encourage their children to spend longer hours on homework and even send them to tutorial schools after regular school hours. The University of California system, particularly UC Berkeley and UCLA, practices discrimination of a sort against Asian students because they are "over-represented" in the universities.

Asian schools have a different kind of problem. Many Japanese and South Korean parents spend thousands of dollars per year for such lessons. Students often do not come home until late in the evening. The whole purpose is to prepare for the next big entrance examination. Japanese and Korean parents now believe that there is too much pressure on students to have a life of their own. Furthermore, those families who cannot afford tutorial schools are placed at a disadvantage. In South Korea, the government banned such schools but the U.S. government has the opposite problem. Education is clearly far more than about a school or a teacher. It is about the home and the community (particularly school board) as well as school. Improvement in American education must deal with all these elements. The school board tends to lower the academic standard of the school district than fail students. This sends a wrong message to students. Discipline and values (whether family or religious) have become dirty words. Parents are its customers of public schools but they seem to have no say on what their children learn. No business in the U.S. can survive by treating the customers in this manner except government.

Milton Friedman was the first person to advocate a voucher system for the U.S. in the 1950s. The progress has been slow and the experiment has been limited largely to low-income or inner city students whose schools are failing them badly. The logic of the voucher system is compelling: "Competition and the profit motive must be reintroduced into education so that teachers and school administrators will once again have a powerful incentive to meet the needs of the children and parents they serve."[6] The first voucher system started in Milwaukee in 1990. This controversial experiment was last evaluated more than ten years ago. The program has, however, been politically popular, and has been expanding. Unfortunately, the voucher program could not be used for parochial schools because of court intervention on the basis of the separation of church and state. Since Milwaukee, ten states and the District of Columbia have experimented with some forms of voucher program. They all ran into legal challenges.[7] Yet, the freedom to choose is making progress. Ohio recently joined other states working to implement statewide programs. In June 2005, Governor Taft signed the state's budget bill opening scholarships (vouchers) to students statewide. [8] Cleveland has been experimenting with the Scholarship and Tutoring Program for 10 years. The Cleveland program has been evaluated annually since 1998 by the University of Indiana. Its conclusion on the voucher program is mixed by subject category but the overall improvement was considered insignificant.[9]

---

6.   See "Markets Versus Monopolies in Education: The Historical Evidence," *Education Policy Analysis Archives* 4.9 (June 12, 1996). Coulson is a senior fellow in Education Policy for the Mackinac Center for Public Policy.

7.   In 2003, Colorado adopted a statewide voucher program, but it was quickly ruled unconstitutional by the Colorado Supreme Court. Florida is attempting to expand the nation's first statewide school voucher program, but the Florida State Supreme court is taking up the legality of one state program (Opportunity Scholarships) which allows students in failing public schools to attend private schools at the state's expense.

8.   Gary T. Henry and Craig S. Gordon, Andrew Young School of Policy Studies, Georgia State University, 2003; "Can Competition Improve Educational Outcomes?"; http://aysps.gsu.edu/ar2003/annual_report_2003.pdf

9.   The study points out that there is some evidence that benefits of the voucher program are showing up in junior high school grades and emphasizes the need to continue with evaluation.

Yet, "Every socioeconomic sector has parents clamoring to get their kids out of government schools and into alternatives. Indeed, when philanthropist business-men Ted Forstmann and John Walton set up the Children's Scholarship Fund offering 40,000 partial scholarships to inner-city children whose families earned less than $22,000 per year, they were overwhelmed by the response. Even though each low-income family had to contribute an average of $1,000 per year, the fund received 1.2 million applications."[10] According to the study, minority students make up 23 percent of enrollment in nonpublic schools and the proportion is growing. The non-public schools emphasize academic performance. Students are better motivated and understand that they will be expelled if they do not meet the standards of the school. Some of the schools teach moral, cultural and even religious values (as in parochial schools) and some parents choose independent schools precisely because of this.

Recently, the success and failure of voucher programs have been studied on a multi-locations and international bases and have been positive.[11] A Brookings Institute and other studies have shown that voucher programs have reduced the black/white achievement gap and promoted racial integration. G. T. Henry and C. S. Gordon of Georgia State University provide strong and non-ideological evi-dence indicating that school vouchers and competition among public and private entities benefit all students, regardless of race or family income. The voucher sys-tem has now gone international.

The socialist haven of Sweden has a lesson to teach on it. It adopted the voucher system more than ten years ago. The system allows parents, regardless of their income, to use their share of public education funds "to send their children to a school of choice, whether that school is public, private or religious."[12] It sep-arates the government financing of education from the government operation of schools. The Swedish non-state schools must accept students, regardless of their academic or other background and must not charge tuition beyond the value of the voucher. Yet, the private schools now educate more than ten percent of school-age children and are increasing rapidly. According to Swedish journalist Kristian Tiger the private schools have not harmed municipal schools. *The Econ-*

10. "Martha Naomi Alt and Katharin Peter, "Private Schools: A Brief Portrait," *The Condition of Education 2002*, National Center for Education Statistics April 1, 2003.

11. See Andrew J. Coulson, "Market Research: A Quick Guide to the Scholarly Litera-ture on School Choice"; http://www.cato.org/research/education/marketresearch_coulson.html#1a

12. See Alliance for School Choice, "School Vouchers", http://www.advocatesforschoolchoice.org/home.aspx

omist (May 5–11, 2007) says that parental choice raised standards of education in Sweden and Columbia. In Sweden, independent schools have also increased the level of socio-economic diversity and the voucher system is popular.[13] Caroline Hexby, an economist, at Harvard University says that the standard of public schools improves. The essence of the voucher system is to give parents their share of school taxes so that they can take their children to whatever school they want to. This would solve the school busing problem, people moving residence to go to better school districts, unequal tax resources among school districts, etc. Most public enterprises have been privatized. Why not education?

The voucher system is gathering momentum because a school choice is not only about academic scores but also about the safety of children, drug, gang culture and discipline and family value. Parents should have a say whether second graders receive education on sex or family values. Some families may or may not want their children to hear the Pledge of Allegiance and "under God". Some families send their children to parochial schools because they believe that schools should teach religious values. Others take an opposite stance. One size fits all does not work in the U.S. In an increasingly radicalized society, the freedom of choice may be the only answer.

University Education

American universities and colleges are the envy of the world. The admission is determined by supply, demand and cost. Inclusiveness and racial balancing acts are corrupting the system somewhat but the situation is not out of control yet. Students come from all over the world to learn in American universities. Being admitted is no guarantee for graduation. Fierce competition goes on for four or more years. The cream of the crop goes on to graduate schools. Research programs are the incubators of hi-tech industries and innovation. A large number of new companies spring up around leading research universities such as Stanford University vis-à-vis the Silicon Valley, the Massachusetts Institute of Technology (MIT), etc. vis-à-vis Cambridge and Boston industrial and research parks, and Duke University, etc. vis-à-vis the Research Triangle Park. In tertiary education, students choose university, majors and minors, courses and professors. University fees vary. Even the regent of a university or the board of trustees cannot tell professors what to teach and what not to teach. Theology is even taught in most universities.

---

13. Frontier Center for Public Policy, "Sweden's School Voucher Program"; 5/16/2005.

America's free and creative university environment has attracted a number of famous professors, including Albert Einstein, and students from all over the world. The U.S. leads in science, technology and economics. Since 1950, Americans have won approximately half of the Nobel Prizes awarded in the sciences. Most of Nobel laureates in economics have been Americans in recent years. But a serious flaw in U.S. universities is in softer social sciences such as sociology, African American studies and history. Left-wing professors make a living by expounding their ideologies rather than science. A University of Wisconsin lecturer, Kevin Barrett, appeared on several talk shows saying that the U.S. government used "controlled demolitions with explosives" on Sept. 11 to bring down the World Trade Centers and said that the idea of a hijacked plane hitting the Pentagon was "preposterous." University of Colorado professor Ward Churchill stated that the victims of 9/11 were not innocent and called them "little Eichmanns", a ridiculous accusation coming from an impostor and plagiarizer.

Conclusion

The poor performance of American public schools is the result of uniquely American phenomena such as the inner city culture, the large Hispanic population which demands bilingual education, the culture of permissiveness rather than discipline, and atheism as the dominant value of public schools. Teaching religious or moral values is for all practical purpose banned. Changing these practices and the laws associated with them will be very difficult if not impossible. Given this situation, the voucher system seems to be the only solution in order to to give Americans the choice.

Chapter 6
Lies About Poverty and Racism

The Nature of the Problem

In 2004, 12.7% of Americans fell below the level of poverty threshold income. It seems high, but it is not much higher than the unemployment rates of some euro-economies. Has it been increasing as some newspaper and magazine articles suggested? It all depends on which two years are compared because the incidence of poverty has fluctuated. See Figure 5. Since 1959 when the measurement first started, the incidence of poverty has declined almost 10%.

It is important to understand how the poverty threshold is measured. In 2004, the poverty threshold for a household of four was a cash income of $19,157, not counting Food Stamps, the value of Medicaid, public housing and other welfare assistance. This definition makes it impossible to eliminate poverty by more generous public assistance programs. The method of calculating poverty threshold was first determined in 1964. Scholars went out and conducted a survey and found out that low-income people spent about one-third of their income on food. So they multiplied the necessary food budget times three and came up with a poverty threshold income. The government later revised the food budget from 30% to 27%. The revision took place in 1969 and 1981.[1] This obviously increased the number of poor people. None of these revisions took into consideration the Food Stamp Program. Today, spending for food is basically irrelevant as a yardstick to measure poverty. Obesity is the real problem among the poor in the U.S. than undernourishment.

---

1. In the original calculation, families of three or more persons were assumed to spend approximately one-third of their after-tax money income on food; accordingly, poverty thresholds for families of three or more persons were set at three times the cost of the economy food plan. For two-person families, the cost of the economy food plan was multiplied by a factor of 3.7. http://www.census.gov/hhes/income/defs/poverty.html

The Heritage Foundation pulled together some facts on the conditions of the poor household in the U.S. from various government Census reports.[2] The facts are:

- Forty-six percent of all poor households actually own their own homes. The average home owned by the poor is a three-bedroom house with one-and-a-half baths, a garage, and a porch or patio.

- Seventy-six percent of poor households have air conditioning.

- More than two-thirds have more than two rooms per person. The average poor American has more living space than the average individual living in Paris, London, Vienna or Athens,

- Nearly three-quarters of poor households own a car; 30 percent own two or more cars.

- Ninety-seven percent of poor households have a color television; over half own two or more color televisions.

- 62 percent have cable or satellite TV reception.

- 73 percent own microwave ovens, more than half have a stereo, and a third have an automatic dishwasher.

- In short, being poor in the U.S. is not that bad.

The author has surveyed and studied more slums of Asia than practically anyone in the world. I have walked through the Calcutta*bustees and* the slums of Bangladesh, the Philippines, Indonesia and Thailand. Some of the common characteristics of these slums are not only the poor physical conditions of shelters but also the stench from open sewers, skin diseases and the signs of malnutrition. What the U.S. has in the inner city and public housing projects are are none of such conditions but a dangerous living condition created by criminals and drug dealers.

---

2.   See Robert E. Rector and Kirk A. Johnson, PhD, "Understanding Poverty in America", 1/5/2004

Income Distribution and Taxation

Do not expect more social welfare to bring down the incident of poverty because the strange way that the U.S. calculate poverty does not take into account the benefits of Food Stamp, Medicaid, etc. A problem in the U.S. as in Western Europe is that it is better to be welfare eligible than being marginally above the poverty line and have to buy one's food and health insurance. A country should be compassionate to those who cannot help themselves such as the sick and the old but not to those who would rather depend on welfare programs, the alcoholics and substance abusers. The only way to dissuade such persons to get off welfare is to cut down the size of benefits benefits. If a government's welfare and unemployment insurance benefits are adequate for a "dignified" living standard which the Left seeks, there could be 50% unemployment rate in the country.

Is it fair for everyone to earn equally? Some work harder than others. Some have saved money while others have just spent it. Some invested money and took time to go to college and other have not. An income distribution is equitable if it has resulted from fair opportunities for all. A statistical indicator that measures income distribution, without asking the question of fairness, is the Gini coefficient. A coefficient of zero means everyone is earning the same amount and an index of 1 means one group takes all.

The Gini coefficients of the U.S. over time increased from 0.394 in 1970 to 0.462 in 2000. The income gap widened although it went down to 0.408 in 2004.[3] Often, the coefficient rises during a period of dynamic economic growth and social changes such as rural-urban migration, industrial revolution and technology changes. Poor and stagnant economies based on agriculture or Mao's egalitarianism (the era of poverty for all) usually have a low Gini coefficient such as .32 for Bangladesh and .33 for Pakistan. China, Singapore and Hong Kong have a high Gini coefficient now but everyone became wealthier. A question for the Left is: would you rather have equity than prosperity for everyone?

One may assume that welfare socialism may decrease the Gini coefficients. But this is not necessarily so. West European countries have lower Gini coefficients than the U.S., but comparing the Gini coefficients of the U.S. with Denmark or Sweden is meaningless. In Europe, the Gini coefficients of Denmark and Spain are measured separately, but the coefficients of the U.S. from Louisiana to California are measured together. If the entire European Union is considered a country, its Gini coefficient may be higher than that of the U.S. A skewed

---

3.   The 2004 data is from the UNDP *Human Development Report* while other years are from the U.S. Census.

income distribution is bad if it is caused by immoral and dysfunctional capitalism resulting from corrupt dictatorship, nepotism, crony capitalism, monopoly or oligarchy. Capitalism is not necessarily against charity. In fact, the U.S., private charity is much more strong and growing than in euro-socialist countries. Charity has been part of human society taught by Christianity, Islam and Buddhism for thousand years. Modern governments also understand the need to help out the victims of disasters as well as those who have fallen to hard times because of temporary unemployment and other circumstances. Capitalism does not work if able-bodied persons would rather depend on hand-out than work.

All modern governments have tried to make the tax system progressive[4] to ensure that the rich does not get richer and the poor do not get poorer. But each time a tax cut was made, its fairness was questioned. Democrats have argued that tax cuts by the Reagan or Bush (II) administrations benefited the rich. Is this true? No. Reagan's tax cuts benefited the lower 50% of the income groups more than the upper 50%. How is this possible when the marginal rate of the top income-tax bracket came down from 70% to 28%. A marginal tax rate does not mean much if no one pays the marginal tax rate because of so called tax "loopholes" or tax deductions provided for in the tax codes such as deductions for mortgage interest payment. After Reagan's tax cuts, the income tax system became more progressive. See Table 9. In 1979 (during Carter's presidency), the top 5% of the taxpayers paid 37.6% of their income as income tax, but in 1989 (just after Reagan's presidency) the top 5% paid 43.6%. Additional taxes have been collected mostly from very high income bracket households.

Table 9

Percent of Federal Individual Income Taxes Paid by Income Brackets
The U.S. *

Income Group	1979	1989
Highest 5%	37.6%	43.6%
Highest 10%	49.5%	54.5%
Highest 25%2	73.1%	76.5%
Highest 50%	93.2%	93.9%
Lowest 50%	6.8%	6.1%
Lowest 25%	0.5%	0.7%

*   Source: *Information Please Almanac, 75 (1991)*

4.   Under a progressive tax system, tax rates increase as the incomes of a person increases.

The Reagan tax reform eliminated many tax loopholes for the rich although they still have the ways to reduce tax payments. The Kennedy families still have domestic trusts, and George Soros have set up foreign trusts to reduce tax payment. Some people reduce tax payments by giving generously to charity. Bill Gates have donated $30 billions—larger than GNP of some countries—to his foundation to spend on education and public health including the reduction of HIV infection in Africa. Buffet donated $30 billion to the Gates foundation rather than setting up his own foundation. Americans as a whole donate several times more money for charitable organizations than other industrialized countries. On average, conservatives and church-going Americans give far more than the progressive secularists. This has nothing to do with how rich the person is. Low-income households donate more than high income households. The Bible Belt states donate more than rich coastal states in the east and the west. Liberals are not compassionate for the poor; they just want other people to pay taxes.

George Soros has given generously to tax-exempt foundations but to promote his political agenda rather than charity. Peter Schweizer discusses sophisticated tax shelter used by the rich and famous left-wing Americans to avoid paying taxes while demanding the government to raise tax rates.[5] Schweizer's book goes beyond the matter of taxes and discusses how the super rich progressives preach but do not practice their slogans such as the protection of the environment, the use of alternative energy and the protection of the civil rights of others. The philosophy of the Left is not about the compassion to the less fortunate but to tax the rich to create a welfare society.

After the Reagan's tax cuts, federal income taxes become more progressive. The Congressional Budget Office (CBO) for the year 2000 found that the lowest 20% income group earned 4% of the total income but did not pay any income tax. In fact, they received 1.6% of their income through the earned income credit. The top 5% of the income group earned 40.6% of the total income but paid 67.7% of Federal income taxes (see Figure 5).

---

5.   See Peter Schweizer, *Do As I Say (Not As I do): Profiles in Hypocrisy* (2005).

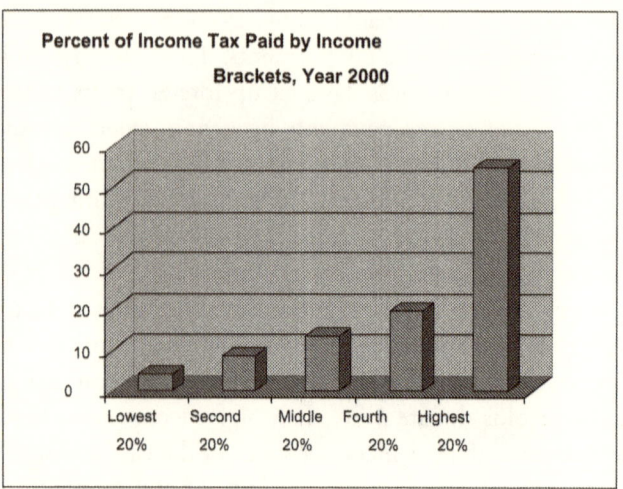

Figure 5

That is for income taxes. What happens to the progressiveness of taxation when other federal taxes such as federal excise taxes and custom duties are combined? According to CBO, federal taxes on the whole have become more progressive. An independent study by the National Bureau of Economic Research also confirmed that income taxes at all levels combined are progressive. See "The Distribution of Payroll and Income Tax Burdens 1979–1999".[6]

What happened to the progressiveness of taxation after the Bush Tax cuts? Steve Moore of the Cato Institute summed up the situation based on the latest IRS data: "The Bush tax cuts have been routinely assailed as multi-million dollar giveaways to the Rolls Royce owners of America at the expense of the middle class. But new IRS statistics on the taxes Americans pay show that George Bush's tax policies actually soak the rich. It turns out that the income tax burden has substantially shifted onto the wealthy. The percentage of federal income taxes paid by those who make more than $200,000 a year has actually risen from 41% to 47% in recent years ... The IRS data show that the share of all income earned by the wealthiest 10% of Americans has actually fallen since 2001. The rich are earning less of the total income but paying more of the total taxes."[7] In short,

6.   Andrew Mitrusi and James Poterba, "The Distribution of Payroll and Income Tax Burdens 1979–1999," **subscription service,** http://www.nber.org/papers/w7707.
7.   Steve Moore, "Rich pay more taxes" April 26, 2006; http://marketplace. publicradio.org/shows/2006/04/26/PM200604264.html

those who argue that the Bush tax cuts benefited the rich are either misinformed or are engaged in political demagoguery.

When state and local sales taxes and property taxes are combined, the progressiveness of taxation changes. State and local sales taxes and property taxes amounted to about 23% of current receipts, and payroll taxes 22 %. One such study concludes that the U.S. tax system for all taxes at all levels of government combined is marginally progressive.[8] This being the case, the U.S. can virtually eliminate IRS, tax lawyers and tax accountants by adopting a flat tax rate or a consumption tax, replacing all other taxes including the payroll tax. A consumption tax has other benefits such as encouraging exports and balancing the current account. It would also discourage conspicuous consumption. For example, the present tax-break for mortgage interest payments encourages the rich to build enormous houses and owning a second or even third home. Living large is fine, but it should not be for tax avoidance. Unfortunately, a radical reform to the tax codes has little chance of passing Congress. What would all the politicians and lobbyists do if the tax codes are thrown out of window!

Race, Poverty and Politics

The U.S. is unlike any European country. It is far more ethnically diverse than a European country. In 2000, the African American population consisted of 12.7% of the U.S. population, Asian Americans, 3.8% ; and the Hispanic, the fastest growing U.S. population, made up 14% of the population in 2004. The Hispanic can be of any skin color—varying from 100% white to 100% native South American Indians. In 2005, the average household income of the Asian Americans was $57,518, the white (non-Hispanic) $48,977, the Hispanic $34,241 and the African American $30,134.[9]

Liberals and black leaders are quick to draw attention to such facts as if they indicate injustice. The solution to income disparities is in eliminating causal factors such as education. The Asian Americans are earning more money than the whites not because they are held in a higher esteem than the white but because they are better educated. Some of prestigious universities in California, such as the UC-Berkeley and UCLA, in fact turn down Asian students even when their academic standards are superior than others, on the ground that Asians are over

---

8.   Brian Roach, Global Development And Environment Institute of Tufts University, 2003, "Progressive and Regressive Taxation in the United States: Who's Really Paying (and Not Paying) their Fair Share?"

9.   United States Census Bureau, 2006.

represented in their universities. The percentage of African Americans graduating from university is low and, by and large, they major low paying fields such as African American studies or other liberal arts fields. They are also under represented in top universities such as MIT or Stanford.

Today, the real problem is in reverse discrimination, not discrimination against African Americans. Liberals and African American leaders want to perpetuate Affirmative Action Program and more entitlement programs because they have built their political careers on black privilege and the expansion of entitlement programs. Entitlement programs are, of course, the main political tool of politics used by the Left all over the world. To most of them, government expenditures on these programs are never enough. To do otherwise would be a political suicide for a liberal political party such as the Democratic Party in the U.S. U.S. expenditures on social welfare are well below the level of euro-economies. The U.S. was racing to catch up with the euro-economies before the Welfare Reform Act of 1996 slowed the race toward a welfare nation. But even after 1996, spending on social programs has been increasing much higher than the growth rate of government expenditures as a whole.

Racism, in form of legal discrimination against colored people, is a red herring today although racial prejudice is common. There are many white supremacists and black racists such as black panthers and many so-called black leaders who rose to national prominence by spewing out hatred against the white. Racial prejudice is common even between the people who look alike such as the Japanese toward the Koreans in Japan although the prejudice is on decline now that South Korea has become a prosperous country. What the U.S. has today is not legal discrimination against the black but the race industry that exploits the Affirmative Action Program. If there is any doubt, one should read Ken Timmerman's *Shakedown: Exposing the Real Jessie Jackson.* He says, "Jesse Jackson is a modern day highway robber … who uses cries of racism to steal from individuals, corporations, and government, to give to himself. Until now, however, no one has been brave enough to say it and diligent enough to prove it. But Ken Timmerman has cracked Jackson's machine, found Jackson cronies willing to break ranks, and uncovered a sordid tale of greed, ambition, and corruption from a self-proclaimed minister who has no qualms about poisoning American race relations for personal gain."[10] O'Reilly has been fearless in criticizing Jackson for some time now, but some black scholars and journalists are also critical of Jackson. William Raspberry, journalist, and Thomas Sowell are a couple of them. Sowell is a black

---

10.　A blurb written on the book in Amazon.com

economist and accomplished scholar who graduated from Harvard University in 1958 with magna cum laude. This was before the era of Civil Rights. His believes that it is wrong to think that the black can succeed only with the Affirmative Action. The Affirmative Action program must go and discrimination against white males must stop if the U.S. really wants equality among races and genders.

A person like Sowell and many other accomplished black persons including Bill Cosby, General Colin Powell and Condoleezza Rice should be hailed as role models but they are marginalized by so-called black leaders and the Left. America should stop playing race politics and move on. Republicans also make a feeble attempt at it without scoring many points. In a speech to the nation delivered from Jackson Square New Orleans on Sept. 15, 2005, George W. Bush said, "some deep, persistent poverty in this region has roots in a history of racial discrimination ... So ... let us rise above the legacy of inequality." His speech sounded like a paragraph out of Lyndon B. Johnson's speech on War on Poverty. The U.S. cannot eradicate poverty among African Americans unless government and black leaders emphasize education and individual responsibility rather than providing them excuses for failure, such as the history of slavery. Bush should have told the displaced New Orleans citizens to take advantage of job opportunities created in the rebuilding of New Orleans rather than waiting for the federal government to fix their homes. Bush should have talked about reestablishing the law and order that broke down in the city. But politicians today cannot speak straight for the fear of being branded racists.

More compassion or handout are not the answer for the African American community. A dynamic economy, work and self improvement (education, training, etc.) are the only answer for poverty. A dynamic economy is created by well functioning capitalism. Adam Smith's capitalism conjures up an image of economic Darwinism, but that is for those who do not understand capitalism. Smith was a moralist who wrote *The Theory of Moral Sentiments* (1758) before he wrote the *Wealth of Nations* (1776). Capitalism cannot flourish in a nation without moral values, fairness and equal opportunities. Racketeering (such as the Mafia), slavery, corrupt dictatorship and monopolies destroy capitalism. Racism, secrecy and any barriers to economic freedom are incongruous with capitalism. The rule of laws that promote fair competition is critical for capitalism to flourish. The U.S. capitalism is functioning well but is far from being perfect. The government has recently going after crooks in corporate executive suites (Enron, Tyco, Worldcom and Adelphia) and the greedy executives and corporate board members who allowed options backdating as if their compensation packages were not big enough.

Even with a robust economy, the incidence of poverty may not go down if the labor market is not open. Strong unions, minimum wages and a massive number of illegal workers, who flourish in the underground market, prevent the trickle down to take place. No wonder that the working class Americans feel that their living standard has not improved. The liberals blame this to the conservatives but the opposite is true. On the individual level, education and work ethics are important prerequisite for success, but many youth in the inner city do not even have a chance to succeed because of poor education. Many of them end up in prisons or fall into the life of the under-class by getting addicted to drugs or becoming unwed mothers.

Poverty and Economic Growth

The incidence of poverty indicated in Figure 6 is inversely correlated with the growth rates of the economy. During the years of stagflation and recessions, the incidence rose. Whenever the real per capita income growth rate was roughly 2.5% per annum or above, the level of poverty declined. Whenever the growth rate was lower than 2.5%, the incidence of poverty increased. It proves the point that robust economic growth is necessary to bring down the rate of poverty. It also proves that trickle down works in the US although it might not in some other countries.

During the economic doldrums of the Carter Administration and the first two years of Reagan Administration (recession years), the rate of poverty increased. This was followed by 6 years of an increasingly lower rate of poverty during the Reagan economic boom. The rate of poverty increased again during the slow growth period of the Bush (41st) Administration. It was followed by a sharp decline during the Clinton Administration's economic boom. During the first four years of the Bush (43rd) Administration, the rate increased once again. The fact is clear. When the economy expands and there is a labor shortage, the wages and benefits go up even when the minimum wage does not change.

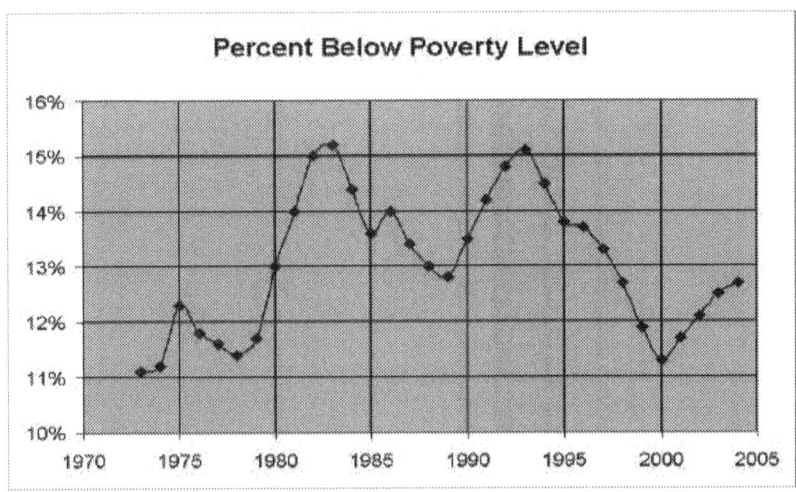

Figure 6

Source: The chart is based on Census Bureau data, the U.S. Poverty Rate from 1973 to present, released into the public domain by Richard Mathews.

Chapter 7

Failed Immigration Policies

Problems and Opportunities

President John F. Kennedy opened the U.S. immigration door ajar, and each succeeding president, whether Democrat or Republican, opened it wider. Today, over a million legal immigrants come to the U.S. annually, mostly based on family ties or so-called "chain migration" rather than based on U.S. economic requirements. On top of this, some 500,000–1,000,000 persons supposedly enter the U.S. illegally. Estimates for illegal immigrants in the U.S. are between 10 and 20 million persons although no one knows the exact number. A positive side of illegal immigrants is that it supplies inexpensive workers in agriculture, construction, meat packing, janitorial service, etc. where the industries face the shortage of labor and a labor cost squeeze. Most consumers, whose jobs are not taken away by illegal immigrants, benefit from illegal immigrants although the majority of them reject it for other reasons. An irony is that even work permits for highly trained engineers and scientists are very difficult to obtain. That is why Bill Gates and other hi-tech company executives want the federal government to issue more visas for such skilled- or knowledge-industry workers. But these pleas are falling in deaf ears.

Major problems with illegal immigration are many. American workers in the industries hiring illegal immigrants have a hard time finding a job and getting decent living wages. Something like Gresham's law (bad money drives good money out of circulation) applies here. Many illegal immigrants do not pay any payroll taxes. American workers cannot do that. Therefore, low wages in such industries drive out tax paying workers.

Illegal immigrants cost the government or other institutions a large amount of money. Industries and individuals hiring illegal immigrants simply shift the cost to taxpayers. Most of them without medical insurance have turned hospital emergency rooms into free clinics. The federal government does not allow the emergency rooms (ER) to turn away patients even when they do not have insurance or identification. The ER in states with a large illegal immigrant population are packed with patients with non-emergency conditions because they are used as free clinics. True emergency patients have to wait hours to get treated. As a result, many hospitals have closed down emergency rooms to avoid financial losses. To make the matter worse, all the illegal immigrants enter the U.S. without health checkup, posing additional public health threat. Illegal immigrants have placed a tremendous burden on state government budgets on education. Schools cannot turn away any student simply because he or she does not any document for being in the country legally. Many of them do not speak English and demand bilingual education. Traffic courts in California are full of illegal immigrants caught driving recklessly without a driver's license or automobile insurance, but judges do not ask whether they are in the U.S. legally or not. They just ask the illegals to pay fines.

The porous borders through which so-called "coyotes" smuggle in human beings also allow drugs to be smuggled in. U.S. border guards who have shot and wounded drug smugglers are in jail while the very same drug smugglers continue to smuggle in drugs. Lawlessness is not limited to the southern borders of the U.S. alone. Chinese crime syndicates, such as Snakeheads (human smuggling and prostitution rings), are a multi-billion dollar industry. Ms. Cheng Chui Ping, once called the Mother of all Snakeheads, collected "more than $40 million from such rackets by charging upwards of $40,000 a person. Once in the U.S., these smuggled human beings were held and threatened with violence until the balance is fully paid. The illegal immigrants are creating a culture of lawlessness and double standards. Every opponent of illegal immigration has his or her reason. To me, the erosion of law and order is most important. Law and order are the foundation of U.S. prosperity. It is being eroded, among other things, by illegal immigration. The height of hypocrisy is that some local and state governments refuse to enforce the existing laws for political reasons (Latino votes). Some mayors have issued specific orders to the police not to arrest illegal immigrants or report them to the Immigration and Customs Enforcement (ICE). The Federal Government has promised to build security fences at critical locations to protect the southern borders but construction is slow in coming, if at all. Such fences will be costly and ineffective unless the existing laws are also implemented.

National security is also an issue associated with illegal immigration. This is conservative talk-show host Sean Hannity's principal concern. The solution is relatively simple but thee political will is not there. In the U.S., a driver's license is the only ID that an adult carries around as a proof of citizenship or residency. Yet, some states do not check whether a person applying for a driver's license is a legal resident of the U.S. or not. All the 9/11 hijackers had a driver's license. Hijacker Hanni Hanjour and Khalid Al-Midhar obtained Virginia licenses by hiring an illegal alien to co-sign their residency forms and listing his address as theirs. "The day after they got their licenses, they sponsored two other hijackers, Salem Al-Hamzi and Majed Moqed, to get licenses, too."[1]

The U.S. legal immigration program is as irrational as the illegal immigrant policy. Through chain migration, old or welfare dependent immigrants enter the U.S. for welfare or medical benefits and end up receiving Medicare or receive Medicaid, which are going bankrupt. This is not only for direct members of an immigrant but also relative. The annual number of legal immigrants tripled since chain migration began in the mid-1960. FAIR says, "The illegal aliens given amnesty by Congress in 1986 are now fueling naturalization in record numbers. As these former illegal aliens become citizens, all of their immediate relatives qualify to come immediately to the United States, and start new migration chains of their own."[2]

How Other Countries Deal With Immigration

The movement of labor to high-income economies is a worldwide phenomenon, although nowhere is it as large a problem as in the U.S. With falling birth rates, aging population and cushy welfare systems in the West, there is the shortage of those willing to do hard, "dirty" and low-paying work. This is true in euro-economies even with their double digit unemployment rates, Japan with its aging population, Hong Kong, Singapore, South Korea and Malaysia. However, Asia and Western Europe, except Spain, enforce immigration laws. It is not as difficult as the likes of Senator John McCain make it out to be.

The EU has its own unique problem. Because the EU is integrated now, the problem in one country such as Spain is a problem for all EU member countries. Spain has been the favorite destination for illegal immigrants because it has given one amnesty after another. They are mostly from Latin America and Africa. Some Chinese also enter the EU through the Balkan countries. According to the Statistical Office of the European Communities (1999), most EU member states had an average of 10–15 % non-White population in 1994. They are not necessarily illegal immigrants. This figure has been doubling every fifteen years. In Western

---

1.   See "Driver's License Security," Federation of American Immigration Reforms (FAIR), 10/05 update. http://www.fairus.
      org/site/PageServer?pagename=iic_immigrationissuecenterse1df
2.   ibid

Europe, most numerous non-White groups are Turks and other Muslim populations. France has an estimated 12 million non-white population, mostly from
North Africa (particularly Algeria, Morocco and Tunisia). There were 100,000
North African immigrants to France in 1946, but it increased to 1.4 million in
1990. Cumulatively from 1946 to 1990, a total of 6.95 million persons migrated
from North Africa.[3] These figures do not even include illegal immigrants. The
non-whites now represent about 20% of the French population. High unemployment and violence instigated by the black and the Muslims youth in France have
become the front page story in 2005, and that may have done more to elect
Sarkozy than any other factor.

The German constitution adopted immediately after World War II compelled
the country to accept virtually any refugee who was fleeing political or social violence in their home countries, but this changed in the mid-1990s after public
resentment rose to the level of national crisis. There were an estimated 7 million
"foreigners" (the Germans codeword for non-Whites) at the end of the 20th century and most of them were Turks.[4] This is about 8.5% of the German population.

EU member countries are now actively restricting the entry of immigrants
partly because of diminishing job opportunities and partly because of terrorism.
The Netherlands began to tighten immigration after filmmaker Theo van Gogh
was murdered in November 2004 by a Muslim extremist. The Netherlands
began requiring foreigners to pass language and cultural-awareness tests before
applying for immigration.[5] Germany's 16 regional states would require immigrants to pass language-proficiency tests and take citizenship classes if they wished
to become Germans. It is love-it-or-leave-it policy.

The continuous expansion of EU member countries is creating another kind
of complexity. Germany, France and Italy say that they have trouble finding jobs
for those who are there already and continue to shut their job market to workers
from newer East European EU member nations. The UK, Ireland, Sweden,
Greece, Spain, Portugal and Finland still accept workers from other EU member
countries; but this is creating resistance from the local population. As the mem-
bership of the EU expands further, it may become even more of an issue than
now. "In Britain, lorry drivers are now fined £2,000 for each illegal found hidden
in their vehicles, and the Prime Minister and his Italian counterpart have called

---

3.   See BBC News website www.bbc.co.uk, 13 March 1998,"France Tops Europe Rac-
     ist Poll"
4.   *Ostara Publications,* op. cit.
5.   See Jeffrey Stinson, USA TODAY, op. cit.

for 14-year prison terms for persons profiting from the trade in people." The EU governments, however, are dealing with illegal immigration problems far more intelligently than the U.S., by controlling the employment of illegal immigrants. Some EU member countries have also restricted the access of illegal immigrants to public services such as social security, health care and education. This method costs far less than building double-layered security fences.

Japan, Hong Kong, Singapore and South Korea as well as oil producing Middle East countries find the solution to labor shortage by issuing work permits. Filipinos go all over the world as contract workers (the Middle East, Japan, Hong Kong, South Korea, etc.) without any intention or hope to become citizens of these countries. Hong Kong, the freest economy in the world, is full of foreign contract workers from the Philippines and other countries, but it does not accept a single Chinese from the Mainland for the fear of being inundated by cheap workers who would take jobs from the locals. Contract workers from overseas are required to return home upon completion of their contracts and reenter if they get contract extension or find a new employer. The Hong Kong police and immigration officers require a person to carry an ID or work permit at all time. This does not make Hong Kong a police state. If anything, the opposite is true.

The U.S. has to overhaul the legal immigration policy as well as stop illegal immigration. The policy should be tied to national interest. Priorities should be given to scientists, engineers, business entrepreneurs with money to start job-creation, nurses and physicians, farm workers, nannies and other jobs in short supply in the country. Most of them should be given temporary work permits without any guarantee for citizenship. Citizenship should be awarded for those those who have been in the U.S. for a period of time without committing any crime, those who are financially independent—not welfare dependent—and those in a job market that has a long-term demand for their skills. What is the point of giving citizenship to those illegal immigrants who do not speak English, do not understand of agree with the constitution of the U.S., commit crime or occupy the positions that Americans want? Hoe can the trickle down take palace if the labor market is flooded with illegal immigrants who do not even pay taxes.

The Refugee Act of 1980 should be amended, if not suspended altogether. Even the U.S. is neither big nor rich enough to accept all the hard luck people and the politically oppressed around the world. In reality, the Refugee Act has been used to smuggle prostitutes, sweatshop workers and other economic opportunity seekers. Most of all, the U.S. should not accept those who do not value the U.S. Constitution or culture or who pose a security threat to the U.S. such as Wahhabi clergies. The U.S. government should protect its citizens from potential terrorists, criminals, American haters and welfare system exploiters. Rational reform is needed but the government has to prove that it has the will and capacity to implement the existing immigration-related laws before concocting more laws that will be abused. This is where George W. Bush had a disconnect with Americans. He like most politicians was born with a silver spoon in his mouth does not understand the plight of some Americans. The so-called "comprehensive" approach of Bush, Kennedy and McCain tries to rationalize illegal immigrants in spite of the fact that all that the government has to do is to implement the existing laws. The U.S. government should make greater use of work permits to meet periodic or seasonal labor shortages.

What every country needs is an immigration policy that would benefit it. Some does this better than other. In 2001, Germany announced that it was creating a special "skilled worker" visa while it was curtailing a compassion-based immigration policy. This was aimed at bringing in Indians from India's IT technicians from India. Even France is opening a special immigration window for talented workers from abroad. France would no longer let illegal foreigners apply for citizenship simply because they have been in France for 10 years or more. It requires the long-term residents to speak French and respect French values.

The Democrats have been least willing to restrict the entry of illegal immigrants to the U.S. The conservatives should know better, but they are too eager to play a catch-up game with the Democrats on Latino votes and look after business interests. The true fiscal and economic impact of illegal immigrants is difficult to measure because most illegal workers cannot and are not in the open economy. A Columbia University research has shown that illegal immigrants cost the government about $68 billion a year. But the true cost to the U.S. is in the erosion of its values. The notion that everyone who enters the U.S. is entitled to become a U.S. citizen is a foolish notion. Citizenship should be earned. It is not the right of everyone who has entered the U.S. by hook or crook.

Solution

Before creating more complex immigration policies that may never be implemented, a sequence of steps should be undertaken. First, the federal and state government should build the security fences and increase the number of border guards as promised by the president and provided for by Congress. Second, only after the above program has been implemented, the federal government should (i) issue an identification card to those without any document and those who over stayed their vista limit, (ii) issue temporary social security numbers and an ID, (iii) require employers to report anyone without such ID. Third, the federal and state governments should deport those without an ID immediately and those with criminal records and occupying the positions where there is no shortage of American workers at a reasonable pay. Even those who passed the screening process should be treated as temporary workers with no automatic pass to a Green Card or citizenship. Finally, the federal government should overhaul the legal immigration programs to give preference to those with skills that the U.S. needs rather than chain migration. The employers, who hire those without an ID, Green Card or proof of citizenship should be vigorously prosecuted.

Chapter 8

Failed Energy and Environmental Policies

Problems

Each time oil and gasoline prices shoot up, there is a hue and cry about the "evil" oil industry monopoly and price gouging. The U.S. Senate passed a bill requiring an average 35-mpg fuel economy (CAFE) standard for cars and sport-utility-vehicles by 2020 mainly because of the fear of global warming. A filibuster (i) prevented additional taxes on the oil industry, which would have meant a higher gasoline price at the pimp; and (ii) defeated the attempt to curtail the production and use of coal and nuclear power. What is wrong with this picture? Such irrational policies are all mixed up with the theory of global warming. Is a man-made global warming real and, therefore, should everyone drive around in an electric car? Should the U.S. government impose price control on gasoline?

Facts

The price of oil is not outrageously high as populist politicians and the media believe. This includes the populist talk-show host Bill O'Reilly. He earned the bragging right to being the most-watched cable-television host but he is no better than his arch enemy, the main line media, when it comes to economics. His instinct is usually correct on what is right and wrong but economics is often counter intuitive. He should let his colleague Neil Cavuto do the talking on the subject but O'Reilly is a fearless warrior on any subject whether he knows any fact or not.

The fact is that the price of oil has lagged well behind the inflation rate for decades. The talk about record highs is based on a failure to adjust the price of oil for inflation.[1] After adjustment for inflation, the gas price is significantly below the level that prevailed during 1979–1985. Furthermore, if the price of gasoline relative to wages were comparable today to what it was in 1920, we would be paying almost $10 a gallon for gas.[2] The expenditures on energy (gasoline, fuel oil, and other energy goods plus electricity and gas services) in the U.S. comprised 4.2% of GDP in 1965 and 5.7% in 1980 but 3.6% in 2004. The populist view that large international oil companies are a monopoly and the OPEC is a powerful cartel that can charge any price that it wants is wrong. Oil companies compete against each other as furiously as companies in other industries and the OPEC cartel is not powerful because it needs money just as urgently as large oil consuming countries need oil. They don't have the luxury of sitting back and stop the production and export of oil. Capitalism is working well in the energy market. It is the fault of the U.S. Government, especially Congress, for not allowing the exploration of domestic resources and to prepare and implement a long-term plan for energy supply. A private company reacts to a short term energy market signal but energy is one sector that requires a long-term plan.

In 1972, my colleague in Baltimore had only a four letter word for large oil companies for reaping excess profits off Americans. I said, "Why don't you buy Exxon shares then?" He gave me a dirty look. On May 21, 2007, I looked up the price earnings ratio (PER) of Exxon-Mobil. It was 12 compared with 15 for S&P 500 and 47 for the Research in Motion. If Exxon-Mobil is a monopoly, which can rip off the people at will, how come its shares are so unpopular with a PE ratio of well below other big companies? The answer is simple: Smart money knows that oil companies are not such a great business with so many restrictions on exploration and drilling, difficulties of building refineries and the risk of doing business in such countries as Venezuela, Russia and Nigeria. In addition, the profits of oil companies are unpredictable because they cannot control the crude oil price and the government is promoting alternative energies. The more the U.S. government fiddles with excess profit taxes or the like for the oil industry, the higher will be the price of gasoline.

It is also wrong for Congress to impose a CAFE standard of 35 mpg by a date certain because such a technology does not exists at this time. Unless there is a technological breakthrough, all Americans may end up driving tiny tin can cars. This is not in the best interest of Americans. Leave the technology and auto designs to the private sector. It is also wrong for Congress to try to suppress the use of nuclear energy that really reduces greenhouse gas emission and discourage the use of coal. Coal gasification and liquidfication are far more promising than

---

1.   Stephen Moore and Phil Kerpen, "Historically, Gasoline Prices Are Not Expensive," September 6, 2003

2.   ibid.

corn based ethanol as an alternative fuel and for the purpose of achieving energy independence.

The fear of global warming in the West will bring down the living standard of the people without affecting the global level of CO_2 because of China, India and other developing countries will make up more than what the West can cut. The earth has warmed and cooled several times before without automobiles or power plants. If everything else remains constant, a higher level of CO_2 in the atmosphere increases the earth's temperature as proven by science. But this does not mean that the world will have a disastrous global warming because the earth's temperature is determined by far more complex factors than CO_2 buildup because of the sun, oceans, vegetation and other chemicals in the atmosphere such as aerosol (airborne solid particles). The earth's ocean has warmed a fraction of centigrade in recent years. What is causing it? Some scientists are certain that it has been due to the temperature of the sun which affects the temperature of Mars as much as the Earth? The Earth has experienced the Ice Age, the Great Flood and the periodic cooling and warming of temperature even before cars and electricity were invented. So why is this tiny rise in the temperature is causing all the hullabaloos? It is a mass hysteria and a tiny bit of science.

Many respectable scientists, who do not take any research grant from oil companies or environmental organizations, have said that the premise of Al Gore's *An Inconvenient Truth* is ridiculous. See the Web site of U.S. Senate Committee on Environment and Public Works for the names and views of some of these dissenters who spoke out against the avalanche of global warming alarmists.[3]Richard Lindzen, the Alfred P. Sloan Professor of Atmospheric Science at MIT, said, "Don't believe the hype. Al Gore is wrong. There's no 'consensus' on global warming." His article was disseminated widely including in *The Wall Street Journal* (7/2/2006). "Gore's circumstantial arguments are so weak that they are pathetic," says Professor Bob Carter of the Marine Geophysical Laboratory at James Cook University, in Australia. "The man [Gore] is an embarrassment to US science and its many fine practitioners, a lot of whom know (but feel unable to state publicly) that his propaganda crusade is mostly based on junk science." (6/12/06) More than 60 leading Canadian and other international climate-change experts asked Canada's new prime minister to review Canada's global warming policies. (See The Next Ice Age-Now, 4/4/06). Recently, Russian scientists came up with the theory that the earth's temperature change is due to the

---

3.   Http://epw.senate.gov/pressitem.cfm?id=257909&party=rep

level of the sun's irradiation. These alternative theories make a point that there is no consensus on global warming even among academics in the field.

In addition to the sun as a factor, the earth is a complex living organism. Trees, the oceans and soils absorb CO_2 and use it for productive purposes. CO_2 in the atmosphere also enters the ocean through rain water, whose absorption rate varies by the temperature level, and helps shell fish to grow. The ocean has vents and ridges that clean the ocean from excess sediments and salt buildup. Volcanic activities undersea have something to do with sea water temperatures also. There are hot spots under the Arctic Ocean, the western Pacific Ocean, near Sicily and the southern Atlantic Ocean. Some of them have been unusually active.[4] The undersea activities may explain why icebergs are melting in some places and thickening in other places. The CO_2 based theory cannot explain why the temperatures of the Mars, Pluto and other planets have been increasing at the same time the temperature of the earth has been increasing a bit, which some scientists believe is the sure sign that it is the sun that dictates temperatures of different planets. The inability to resolve such disputes suggests that the theory of man-made global warming is far from established. We do not have to turn the world upside down on the basis of such a flimsy theory.

Kyoto Protocol

The UN sponsored Kyoto Protocol of 1997 is based on such a flimsy theory and global warming can be stopped if the rich countries reduced CO2 emissions. Among other things, the Protocol excludes China and India altogether. Even the signatories to the Protocol have not been reducing CO2 emissions. Europe is just buying carbon offset under a CO_2 trading known as the Clean Development Mechanism (CDM). It provides billions to China, India and other developing countries for air pollution abatement projects. Most of the money has gone to China although it has more foreign currency reserves than any industrialized country. With such money coming from developed countries, because it pollutes the air, some observers have pointed out that China has no incentive to shut down old factories spewing HFC-23 (the most potent greenhouse gas) although such factories were supposed to have turned into a scrap under the Montreal Protocol of 1987.[5]

---

4.   See Hydrothermal "Megaplume" Found in Indian Ocean, *National Geographic News,* 12/12, 2005.
5.   See Bart Mongoven, "Industry's New Stake in Kyoto", Public Policy Intelligence Report of Stratfor 11/15/2006.

Even without any cheating, the Kyoto is hardly going to make any difference to the level of greenhouse emissions. *The Christian Science Monitor* reported, "The official treaty to curb greenhouse-gas emissions hasn't gone into effect yet and already three countries are planning to build nearly 850 new coal-fired plants, which would pump up to five times as much carbon dioxide into the atmosphere as the Kyoto Protocol aims to reduce ..."[6] The article goes on to say that by 2012, China alone will add between 844 and 1,926 tons of CO_2 emissions per year, and India will add between 179 and 486 million tons per year. By comparison, the Kyoto Protocol is supposed to cut CO_2 emissions by some 483 million tons by 2012, just a fraction of additional greenhouse gas emissions to be produced by China alone.

To its credit, China also plans to build 30 nuclear reactors by 2020. India has nine nuclear power plants under construction. They are not doing this because they believe in global warming but because nuclear power is the cheapest source of energy. The nuclear power plant technology has made a huge progress since the U.S. built the last one. U.S. environmentalists do not support the nuclear power plant although it is the cleanest generator of energy. Why? Could it be that they bask in the image of saviors to an imminent disaster to the planet? The fear of environmental disasters fills the coffers of green organizations and increases political supports to the Democratic Party, the self-anointed champion of the environment. Ironically, ordinary Americans can drive mini cars or bicycles while the big chiefs of green organizations and green politicians travel in private jets and live in 20,000 sf plus mansions. They include Al Gore, the Kennedy, Hilary Clinton, Barbara Streisand and John Edward.

Michael Crichton's novel, *State of Fear*, is a page turner. Although it is fictional story, it is full of factual data on global warming and references to scientific studies in footnotes and appendixes. His point is that a widely-held belief is not necessarily true. How can that happen? Simple: the media hype, research papers sponsored by green organizations (the UN, EPAs of the world, Sierra Club, etc.) and green politicians. A medicine man loses his power if nobody believes in his magic; environmentalists lose their power if nobody believes in their diagnosis of an impending global disaster and their remedies that will save humanity. The environmentalists have convinced most government of rich countries to sign the Kyoto Protocol except the U.S. Those industrialized countries which truly turn

---

6.   Mark Clayton, Staff writer, "New coal plants bury 'Kyoto'", *The Christian Science Monitor*, December 23, 2004.

the CO_2 clock by decades will suffer job losses, high energy costs and low living standards.

This is neither the first time nor would it be the last when the prophets of dooms would drive the people to panic. Remember the DDT ban which killed millions based on *Silent Spring written by* a pseudo-scientists Rachel Carson. She argued in 1962 that "pesticides, and especially DDT, were poisoning both wild-life and the environment. Remember the Kool-Aid served by Jim Jones to his fol-lowers in 1978. Remember the Y2K phobia which kept computer software firms on a hyper drive.

Having said these, let me make it clear that global warming may be a hysteria but the adverse impact of pollution on human health is real. Air pollution is believed to cause 300,000–700,000 premature deaths annually in addition to causing millions of cases of respiratory disease.[7] Tropical forests are being cut at an alarming rate in Brazil, Indonesia, Malaysia, and other developing countries. We know that trees clean the air. Poverty in Nepal caused deforestation and the erosion of soil on the Himalayan mountain slopes. Lawlessness in the Philippines allows fishermen to use dynamite fishing which has destroyed coral reefs as well as everything that lives around them. It also allows loggers to denude forests thus causing soil erosion and landslides. Air pollution originating from China is caus-ing significant levels of air pollution in Korea, Japan and beyond. Most of the mercury pollution on the West Coast of the U.S. comes from China. Dr J Win-ston Porter, who was an assistant administrator of the Environmental Protection Agency and is now a consultant, says: "it is China that loads the atmosphere with the largest share of the airborne mercury that is transported and deposited around the world; the United States is just a tiny player in the global pool … China alone accounts for about 1,000 tons of the toxic metal emitted annually." In short, China's economic growth polluted the entire world.[8] "There is no point in com-mitting the nation to a new regimen of costly restrictions—not when a multitude of emission sources in China and other countries escape scrutiny largely for polit-ical reasons."[9] This is the kind of problems that the UN should attack.

Wisely, the U.S. Senate resolved by a vote of 95–0 not to ratify the Kyoto Treaty unless China is subject to the same Protocol. What makes the U.S. differ-ent? Part of that answer is in the talk radio and the Internet which effectively

---

7.   Refer to this and other related discussion in "Overview: Development and the Envi-ronment," *World Development Report 1992* of the World Bank (New York: Oxford University Press, 1992) 1–15.

8.   "Mercury Emission From China Exceed USA," *The Virginian-Pilot;* 8/10/98.

9.   ibid

counter the views of the main line media. What matters is not what any person or institutions believe in but the truth. The truth that I believe in is that a man-made global warming is a myth but the level of air and water pollution should be brought down for health reasons. China and India are major polluters today. Pressure should be applied to these countries to reduce the emission of toxic chemicals and metals, and reduce CO_2 emission so that neighboring countries do not suffer ill health. A good news is that when the per capita income of a country increases, a country spends more money to clean its air and water for the health of its own people. This will also be the case in China and India.

I have personally led several missions to study the environmental conditions of big cities in developing countries. I have always had a team of experts with me. It was easy to find what needed to be done. A tougher question was how much money to spend on environmental cleanup vs. economic development. In the final analysis, poverty is the main reason for environmental degradation such as cutting down trees as firewood, discharging dirty water directly to rivers without treatment and using coal to create electricity rather than cleaner fuel.

Jobs, Living Standard and the Use of Energy

Cutting down the use of energy means lowering the standard of living because they are closely correlated. An American uses 19 times more energy than an India and 9 times more than a Chinese.[10] However, per $2,000 GDP-PPP, the U.S. and China both use 0.58 Kg oil equivalent in energy and India is not far behind at 0.44 Kg oil equivalent. See Table 10 for detail. It is true, however, even in terms of GDP-PPP, Americans clearly use more energy per capita than Japanese, German or other Europeans because Americans have bigger houses and cars, own more cars per capita and depend more on cars than other modes of transportation. American cities are more spread out than European or Asian cities. It is, however, in developing countries where the consumption of energy is shooting up because of their new prosperity. Good for them as long as they take care of air quality for the health of their people and other countries. Air pollutants circle around the globe.

---

10. World Resources Institute. 2003.

Table 10

CO2 Emission, Energy Consumption and GDP
Selected Countries *

Country	CO_2 emissions per capita (MT)	Energy consumption (kg oil equivalent) Per $2000 GDP-PPP	Energy imported (%)
China	2.21	0.58	3
Germany	9.55	0.37	61
India	1.05	0.44	19
Japan	9.34	0.36	80
UK	9.64	0.39	-17
U.S.	19.85	0.58	27

*   Source: WBDI; May 1, 2005.

Energy is what creates jobs and makes living convenient. Consequently, China is desperately searching to secure stable sources of oil and gas whether from Iran, Venezuela or South China Sea. It has tried to buy Unocal although the Chinese government abandoned the plan when it realized that U.S. Congress would not approve it. Between 1970 and 2000, the consumption of energy went up by 39%, in the world, 27% in the U.S., 15% in the UK and only 5% in Germany. It went up by 91% in China and 113% in India. Their consumption of energy will certainly increase further. Furthermore, the developing economies use mainly coal for the generation of electricity. They may go increasingly nuclear but not soon enough. Nuclear energy supplies 20% of electricity requirements in the U.S., 25% in the UK, 30% in Japan and one third in Germany. France gets 77% of its electricity from nuclear power plants and the remainder from hydro-electric power plants.

Increases in the use of energy in the world are inevitable as long as the world economy expands. The only way to cut down greenhouse gas emissions is to use cleaner energy. The oil price has gone up high enough now to make many alternative energies economically viable. Such alternative energies are necessary because the amount of available oil reserves in the world is limited. There are those who believe that the world has plenty oil reserves to last centuries and those who believe that oil production in the world is peaking. *Hubbert's Peak: The Impending World Oil Shortage* predicts that the peak production will occur between 2004 and 2010.[11] They have made a strong case that there is far less oil reserves in the world than the OPEC claims it has. As a result, the oil price will shoot up to $150 per barrel.[12] The truth is buried deep underground.

Some of the confusion over oil reserves is over the meaning of the <u>proven</u> reserves, which are determined by economically recoverable deposits. New technology of drilling changes the amount of proven reserves all the time. Notwithstanding that fact, OPEC members have a motive to lie about the amount of proven reserves because an OPEC member country's production quota is determined by the amount of proven reserves. Every OPEC country needs money badly and wants to sell more oil. Therefore, it exaggerates the amount of proven reserves. Of course, new oil and gas fields are discovered every year. The proven reserves do not include the vast quantity of Venezuela Heavy Crude, Canadian Tar Sand, or the U.S. oil shale. They will all come into play one day depending on the price of crude oil. However, it is only a matter of time before good quality and easy-to-explore oil becomes more scarce. Therefore, the development of alternative energy is a must.

Necessity is the mother of invention. In Europe, the number of clean diesel passenger cars is about to exceed gasoline cars. Diesel cars get 40% more miles per gallon than equivalent gasoline cars. European diesel is as clean as gasoline and diesel does not have to be derived from oil. It can be derived from coal and other fossil fuel. Natural gas cars, which are already in Europe (e.g. Volvo V70), pollute less and would increase fuel efficiency even further. Every government, particularly the U.S. government, needs to invest in the development of alternative energies. The U.S. has a considerable amount of untapped oil and gas deposits, abundant coal deposits and advanced and safe technology on nuclear power plants Yet, its dependence on foreign oil has increased from 20% in 1970 to 42% in 1980 and to 52% in 2000. It is now projected to grow to 70% by 2020, thanks to the coalition of the environmentalists and the Democratic Party which has blocked every attempt to explore for more oil and natural gas in the U.S. And offshore and build nuclear power plants in the U.S.

The Bush Administration did the right thing to pass the Energy Bill in August, 2005 but it did so only after dropping the provision for drilling at Anwar and other places. The answer to energy self-sufficiency may be in coal (in cleaner forms, liquefied, etc.), solar energy and wind power based on more cost-effective

---

11. An overview of the of the book (2004) by the author Kenneth S. Deffeyes who retired as <u>Princeton University professor.</u>

12. *Outstanding Investments.* The ranking is provided by an independent company, a subsidiary of CBS.

technologies. The corn-based ethanol is not an economically viable alternative to oil because it requires a heavy subsidy and increases the price of corn, which in turn increases other agricultural commodities. Unless an alternative form of ethanol is developed, this is not the way to go.

Saving Endangered Species

The Endangered Species Act (ESA) of the U.S. is another holy cow of the tree huggers. Preserving national parks and forests is one thing but saving fairy shrimp in seasonal rainwater puddles is another matter. If the government must take someone's property to preserve a particular species of insect, it should pay landowners for it. Not to do so is to violate property right provided for in the Constitution, but this is what has been happening. Environmental activists ask the government to add more species to the endangered species, and the U.S. Fish and Wildlife Service (USFWS) and the National Marine Fisheries Service (NMFS) are more than willing to comply. Government bureaucrats love regulations. It means more money, more staff and more power for them. The constitutionality of the ESA has been challenged although the Supreme Court refused to consider the case! However, the legal challenge is not over yet.[13] The Supreme Court has been asked to consider new cases, including the importance of preserving the "fairy shrimp" that thrives in seasonal pools and puddles in the Central Valley, California.

The USFWS aggressively protects endangered species and bars land use changes. Harold Johnson, an attorney with the conservative Pacific Legal Foundation, has said that "Hurry up and build" has become the property owner's mantra, lest an endangered creature show up and trigger regulations that prohibit changes in the use of the property.[14] The Bush Administration "reportedly will try to curb the ability of independent groups to sue to get more plants and animals added to federal endangered lists", but in Johnson's opinion what the U.S. needs is to overhaul the Act, not just trim it. Johnson told a story of an elderly lady in Santa Barbara County who dreamed of transforming 500 acres of unprofitable cattle land into a vineyard. But her dream ended abruptly when she did not hurry up before the Fish and Wildlife gave a 6-inch salamander an endangered

---

13. M. Reed Hoppe, a principal attorney with Pacific Legal Foundation (PLF) filed an amicus curiae brief in support of GDF Realty at the Supreme Court. The following commentary appeared in the October 7 issue of TownHall.com.

14. See Harold Johnson, the Pacific League Foundation, "The Endangered Species Act Threatens Our Environment and Property Rights," April, 2001.

designation. Robert K Best, president of the Pacific Legal Foundation, wrote in September 2001, that four firemen died while battling the Thirty Mile Fire in Washington because of delays in obtaining permission from the U.S. Forest Service to draw water from certain rivers, lakes and streams where there might be fish protected by the Endangered Species Act.[15] What is even more outrageous is that a species designated as endangered is not always endangered. One such case involved the Oregon coast Coho salmon. The zeal to keep every insignificant species and subspecies has gone too far. Nature eliminates those that cannot adapt to the ever-changing environment. There is no harm in not saving every subspecies of fry.

---

15. M. David Stirling of the Pacific Legal Foundation, "A New Endangered 'Species': The Principle of Human Dignity," November 2002.

Chapter 9

Failed Policies on Crime and Values

Problems

The U.S. total crime index (number of crimes per 100,000 inhabitants) has been increasing continuously from 1960 to 1991 by 213%. During the same period, the violent crime index (murder, rape, robbery and assault) went up by 471%. There was one murder every 22 minutes, one rape every 5 minutes, one robbery every 49 seconds, and one burglary every 10 seconds.[1] The total crime rate has dropped since 1973 because an increasingly large number of criminals have been incarcerated. In 2002, 1 out of every 143 U.S. residents was in prison. The U.S. prison population was around 22% of the total world prison population although the U.S. population was 4.3% of total world population. The number of prisoners in the U.S. is increasing while this is not the case in most other countries.

The cost of crime is estimated from a low of $674 billion (*U.S. News and World Report*, 1994) to over $1.7 trillion if one includes all direct and indirect cost including the opportunity costs of time lost by victims, criminals and prisoners, as well as the cost of private deterrence and losses due to the fear of being victimized.[2] Drug abuse and alcoholism are other serious problems. According to the National Institute of Drug Abuse, the estimated economic cost from alcohol and drug abuse was $246 billion then. It has been increasing further since 1992. This cost does not even include death and suffering. It is estimated that "more than 17,000 people were killed in alcohol-related crashes in 2002. That's an average of one every half-hour. It made up 41 percent of the 42,815 total traffic fatalities in the U.S. In comparison to these mind boggling costs, the U.S. national defense budget of $374 in 1990 appears small.

---

1.   See Kerby Anderson,"Crime in America";
     http://www.leaderu.com/orgs/probe/docs/crime.html
2.   David A. Anderson

Causes of Drug Abuse and Crime

Drug addiction has serious repercussions on crime, health, education and social order. The situation is very serious in the U.S. The incidence of drug abuse and crime has come down as discussed above because an increasingly large number of drug users and dealers and criminals have been locked up in prison. There is no doubt that the crime rate would drop more dramatically if the country put away a larger number of drug-related criminals for a longer period. But, the U.S. is now running out of prison space and the rate of violent crime is on the rise again (2004–2006). An attempt by the State of California to transfer some prisoners to Tennessee was blocked in 2007 by public employee unions. The ACLU, the champion of criminals, is also blocking such attempt everywhere. As a result, too many dangerous convicts are released prematurely and too many gangs and drug dealers are out loose in the streets.

A question is why are there so many drug users and criminals to begin with? Some people have tried to link high crime rates to poverty and racism. There may be those who steal because they are hungry or their children are sick and need medicine. But they are few and far between. The liberals and populists such as Bill O'Reilly link crime in industrialized countries to poverty, but they are ill informed according to many international studies conducted. Crime rates are poorly correlated with poverty whether cross-countries in industrialized world in general or across cities within the U.S. as well as within the U.S. over time. The crime rate began to soar when the U.S. became more affluent than ever before and the civil rights movement reduced racism in the U.S.

The U.S. government recognizes that illicit drugs are largely to blame for rising crime rates, but it was wrong to think that it could solve the problem simply by cutting down the supply of drugs entering the country. The coast guard and military confiscated tons of drugs, and U.S. troops even invaded Panama and arrested its leader, Manuel Noriega, who was believed to have been the kingpin responsible for channeling illegal drugs to the United States. His arrest solved nothing. The routes for the shipment of drugs simply shifted to Mexico. A measure of success came when the police put away an increasing number of gangs that sell drugs in the street. In 1990, the total number of prison population in the U.S. was 773,905 but by 2002 it rose to around 2.1 million, and about 57 percent of those incarcerated were drug offenders. Most younger addicts are still not caught. Most of the increase in drug-related ER visits is for those between age 12 and 25. Hispanic youths have accounted for much of the increase.[3]

Cross Country Comparison

Once again international comparison is useful but one obstacle is that cross-country crime data are notoriously unreliable. Many countries do not report all crimes, and others do not even bother to investigate and record property crime or theft. The International Crime Victimization Survey (ICVS or the Survey hereafter) by the Dutch Ministry of Justice is the best source of data for international comparison although its coverage is limited to industrialized countries. It does not rely on the police records of different countries but on household surveys, which eliminates a major source of discrepancy among crime data of different countries.[4] According to the 1999 Survey, the U.S. crime rate stood somewhere in the middle of industrialized countries after the steady decline in the crime rate since 1978–79 for reasons discussed above.

Although the U.S. belongs in the middle of the ranking, the homicide rate in the U.S. is much higher than the EU average.[5] For the period 1998 to 2000, the number of homicides per 100,000 people was 1.7 in EU member states compared with the 5.9 in the U.S. Some countries had a much higher homicide rate than the U.S.: 64.3 in South Africa, 11.4 in Estonia, 8.9 in Lithuania and 6.5 in Latvia. The homicide rates within the U.S. cities vary considerably from city to city. The incidence of homicides in New York City was 8.77 but it was 45.79 in Washington, D.C. A person is five times more likely to be killed in Washington, D.C. than in New York City. The saying that Washington is the murder capital of the world rings true although South Africa as a whole had a higher homicide rate than Washington, D.C. Another interesting fact among EU member countries is that Amsterdam, where drugs are legal, had a high incidence (4.09) compared with other Northern European cities such as Oslo, Norway (1.51), Stockholm, Sweden (2.97). This makes one to think twice about the argument for legalizing drugs to cut down crime.[6] Australia, England and Wales, The Netherlands and Sweden, all rich countries, have the highest overall crime rates (above 24% in 1999). This proves wrong the notion that prosperity and generous social programs would reduce crime rates. Japan was in a class by itself with

3.   Drug Abuse Warning Network (DAWN) for 2000, the Substance Abuse and Mental Health Services Administration (SAMHSA)
4.   See Gordon Barclay and Cynthia Tavares for the RDS, "International Comparisons of Criminal Justice Statistics 2000", 12 July 2002.
5.   ibid
6.   Asa Hutchinson, <u>European Experience Shows Legalizing Drugs Doesn't Work</u>, St. Paul Pioneer Press, Oct. 11, 2002.

exceptionally low crime rates. This is mored or less true for Singapore and south Korea. Values and social order are decisive factors that determine the crime rate of a country but none of the crime studies ask proving questions on these.

A near unanimous conclusion from these country studies is that the fear of punishment is the single most important deterrent to crime.[7] It had a 93% positive correlation with crime rates and the severity of punishment had a 58% positive correlation. The Australian study found that teenagers living with a single parent are more likely to commit crime. Divorce is positively associated with crime. Increases in female participation in the labor force, as well as increases in the length of the full-time working week, were positively associated with crime rates. In the Netherlands, the proportion of unmarried young males in the population contributed significantly to theft rates. The U.S. Justice Department reported that 70 percent of all juvenile delinquents grew up in single-parent households. This reinforces the Australian survey. High divorce rates and single motherhood all have contributed to the increasing use of illegal drugs and high crime rates. Some people have suggested that pornography and violence on television in the U.S. have contributed to the breakdown of families and the increase in crime rates but the surveys have not investigated these variables.

Children are better off to grow up under the supervision of responsible adults who can teach them right from wrong, impose discipline and provide morality by example. Discipline needs to start at home. The type of punishment to be used should be left to parents including reasonable corporal punishment as is permitted in Connecticut. The notion that only positive reinforcement works is wrong. Unless corporal punishment involves pathological parents and serious injuries, government should stay out of family affairs. The government does not know how to raise children.

The level of poverty showed no significant correlation with the crime rate in international studies also. It reinforces the U.S. study. Alcohol consumption was not correlated with robbery, assault and burglary. Perhaps, drunks have money and do not necessarily rob houses or cars. Alcoholism is, however, a factor for the breakup of families. Therefore, it may indirectly contribute to drug abuse and crime. Another interesting finding in the Netherlands is that violent offenses were positively correlated with the numbers of second generation migrants.

7.	David P Farrington, Patrick A Langan, and Michael Tonry (eds.), the Department of Justice, "International comparisons of criminal justice statistics 2000", *Cross-National Studies in Crime and Justice*, 2004.

This cross-national survey did not explore some other critical factors, namely the use of illicit drugs. In some cities such as Amsterdam, drugs are legal. An attempt to crack down hard on drug users and drug dealers in the U.S. usually runs into race politics because a disproportionately large number of offenders is African Americans. Instead of receiving a praise for making their communities safer, the law enforcement system is blamed for incarcerating a disproportionately large percentage of African Americans. The spokesmen of the race industry routinely accuse the criminal justice system of racism without asking who commit crimes. By making such accusation, they make it difficult to get rid of gangs and drug dealers from the inner cities.

Today, schools cannot teach good vs. bad. Mentioning the Bible or Ten Commandments on which Western values are based is banned from schools and public places. But public schools cannot remain silent on sexual preference: they must teach that homosexuality is an acceptable life style. Every religion, particularly Confucianism, emphasizes family values. Islam is harsher against disobedient children than Christianity. Whenever, I had harsh words to my teenage children, they accused me of imposing Korean ways and reminded me that this is the USA. I searched Bible on how to raise children, the following verse was revealing: "Chasten thy son while there is hope, and let not thy soul spare for his crying" (Proverbs 19: 18). There are many more like this in Proverb and even in the New Testament. The West has done well by bringing children by the standard of the Bible but this has all but disappeared now. Parents are confused on how to raise children. A family is a molecule that makes up society. When it is decaying, the whole society decays. Purging God and family values out of the West has left a spiritual vacuum in Western men and women with nothing else to fill it except the pursuit of money, hedonism and selfishness. Social order, discipline, respect for others and personal responsibility are dirty words in the West. My right is the only value that matters. One can be critical of smokers but not about someone's life style or unwed mothers. Why? The "flower power" and "Just Do It" are the new philosophies today. Fear and love for God and family values have all but disappeared from the consciousness of Western men and women. Respect and love for other human beings are also fast disappearing. Legalism and looking after #1 are new gods.

Dr Benjamin Spock wrote the best seller *Baby and Child Care* in 1946. Some 50 million copies of the book were sold and became the Bible for raising children. The book became part of a massive paradigm change in America: the permissiveness culture became a good thing. Lately, however, Dr Spock began to send out different messages to the distress of his once faithful followers.[8] He said, "I have come to realization that a lot of our problems are because of a dearth of spiritual values." The later edition of his book *The Common Sense Book of Baby and Child Care* stresses that children need standards, and parents also have a right to respect. In 1994, he said, "I think that the children and adults in families that adhere to a specific religion (as I do) or a firm set of moral standards (as I do) are fortunate. Most human beings, by their nature, want to live by some set of spiritual beliefs, whether or not they're part of a formal religion." Unfortunately, he was a generation too late to come to that realization.

He also came to realize television can be a bad influence to the youth. He said, "Many children and young people get their standards primarily from movies and television. These media are so powerful that only forceful parents with firm beliefs can counteract the amoral or immoral values they often present. Yet, objections to the glorification of violence and casual sex in television and the movies are met with protestations by civil rights activists … To reduce violence in our society, we must eliminate violence in the home and on television. Parents should stop their children from watching inappropriate sex and violence—no excuse by parents is really valid."

Today, Church attendance has been in steep decline in Europe. Christian churches in the U.S. rarely speak of the Devil and Hell (except in fundamentalist churches) and do not belabor on Ten Commandments. The people do not want to hear about them. Many people go to the church to feel good and for social contact. Some politicians such as John F. Kerry go to church every election year for a photo opportunity. Atheism is the fastest growing religion in the U.S. It is a religion because it is a belief system without any proof.

The founder of CNN, Ted Turner, divorced Jane Fonda in 2001 because she turned Christian. How Hanoi Jane (once a pacifist and feminist) became a Southern Baptist fundamentalist is a mystery too. Perhaps she did not study the Bible. God is neither a feminist nor a pacifist unless she cherry picked only several verses out of the Bible. For Ted Turner to divorce his wife of nine years just because she turned Christian is also unreal. Does the wrath of a secularist against a Christian run that deep? Why so many billionaires such as Ted Turner, Jon Corzine (the former chairman and CEO of Goldman Sachs and current governor of New Jersey) and George Soros (hedge fund manger best known for currency speculation) become liberals is another mystery. It could be the life long thirst for money and power, hatred against Christianity and the passion for unlimited freedom that they worship. Certainly it cannot be because of the American economic

---

8.   See John Mullins, the Associated Press, March 16, 1998.

system unless they are ashamed of the way they made money. A big government is no problem for them. They know how to legally avoid paying taxes and that money in any case is irrelevant to them.

Secularists feel superior intellectually and they believe that they are more scientific than theists because they would not believe in something not proven by science. A belief system of an individual is an entirely personal matter since the existence of God cannot be either proven or diaproven. Yet, the animosity and contempt of the atheists toward Christians are unprecedented in American history. I heard Chris Mathew say in his Hard Ball TV program something like this: "Christian fundamentalists are those who believe in Genesis and Revelation." How is he so sure that God did not create the universe and Darwinism is not a garbage science? They believe in the Big Bang theory, as most modern men do whether religious or not, but they cannot explain how an infinitesimally compact spot with no space or time at all, called singularity by scientists, exploded to create so much energy and masses. It defies physics including the law of relativity and the conservation of energy. Secularists are so scared of any challenge to Darwinism that they do not allow any alternative views to be discussed in public schools such as how come paleontologists could not find any half fish and half fowl, a half fowl and half four-legged animals, etc? Secularists cannot even begin to answer whether a human being has a soul or spirit. Atheists are insecure human beings. Even a mention God in the Declaration of Independence drives them to anger. The ultimate avatar of a liberal belief in the West is that worldly pleasure is the only sure thing that matters, and that the ultimate mission of human being is to look after #1 even if it destroys the institution of marriage, children and social order. How have the Western governments come to overturn traditional values in schools and public places and come to side with atheists? The answer is yes.

The Values of the Supreme Court

The Supreme Court of the U.S. (the Court hereafter) does not interpret but reinvents the Constitution all the time. It has now replaced God as the final moral authority. The Supreme Court had no business to rule on the legality of abortion because the Constitution has no clause remotely related to it. However, it took the Roe v. Wade case in 1973 and decided in favor of the right of women to abort the unborn child for any cause and at any time until the until fetus become viable, that is, potentially able to live outside the mother's womb. I have no view on when life begins. If life begins at the point of conception, the logical conclusion is that even taking a morning-after pill is an attempted murder. I would rather leave it to God to punish sinners than the government to decide when it is a murder and what should be the punishment. A third tri-semester abortion is unacceptable to me as it is to most Americans. I object even more strongly that the basis of the Court decision was "privacy". The decision has created a whole string of permissive laws based on privacy. Privacy is not mentioned in the Constitution but that did not matter to the Court.[9] The case should have been sent back to the State where it belongs. Since the Supreme Court elevated privacy to a de facto article of the Constitution, a Washington State court ruled that privacy is so important that parents cannot eavesdrop on children's conversations even when they are talking about committing a crime. The court decided that criminal information gathered from this eavesdropping was inadmissible to the court. Such decisions will go a long way in destroying the family which is precisely where morality should be taught in the first place.

The Court has made law enforcement very difficult by striking against Anti-Loitering Law aimed at gangs. It also raised the standard of convicting a drug kingpin by requiring that jurors must agree unanimously that the drug kingpin committed each drug offense. In 2000, the Court limited the power of the police to search for the guns of suspected criminals, ruled that highway checkpoints with the primary purpose of detecting illegal drugs was unconstitutional and in 2004 rejected the police tactic of questioning suspects twice. In 2005, it overturned the death sentence of Ronald Rompilla saying that his lawyers failed to provide him with a defense that met minimum constitutional standards against execution of juveniles. They explain why it is so costly and difficult to apprehend and convict criminals, wipe out gangs off the streets of inner cities. In every broken system, there is a wrong court ruling which by fiat becomes a national policy. Americans are paying dearly for the rights of criminals. In the meantime, thousands die in the hands of criminals and become the victims of illicit drugs.

The Court has also weakened the President's ability to conduct war efficiently by ruling in 2004 that the detainees at the Guantánamo Bay have the right to appear in court when they believe they are being held illegally. It also declared that Yaser Esam Hamdi, a U.S. citizen, was illegally detained. The Court rejected the Bush Administration's claim that the executive branch has unreviewable authority in time of war. It also ruled in 2006 that it was against military commissions to try suspected terrorists detained at the Guantánamo Bay. These deci-

---

9.   See Mark R. Levin's *Men in Black: How The Supreme Court Is Destroying America* and Robert H Bork's several books including *Coercing Virtue: The World Wide Rule of Judges.*

sions were just icing on the cake. The decision to give the terrorists, not wearing uniforms, the protection of the Geneva Convention was a critical mistake. Congress and the President agreed to fight a conventional war when the enemies had no such intention. In the final analysis, politicians handcuffed the generals and fighting men in Iraq and deprived the means of striking back against twhenhose terrorists using ordinary houses as military barracks and bomb factories.

On God and morality, the courts at various levels have used the First Amendment to destroy religion and traditional values. The Court invented the phrase "the separation of church and state" although there is no such wordings in Constitution. Judges conjured up this phrase out of the First Amendment clause: "Congress shall make no law respecting an establishment of religion, or prohibiting the free exercise thereof." What the Supreme Court has done is to suppress traditional religions and establish atheism as state religion. The courts forbid the use of school vouchers for parochial schools. The Court ruled in 2004 that states can deny aid to divinity students. In Lee v Weissman (1992), "a six-justice majority held that a short, bland, non-sectarian prayer at public school commencement amounted to the establishment of religion."[10] A California court ruled that the Pledge of Allegiance was unconstitutional because it had the words "under God". What are these decisions if not "establishing" atheism as the state religion. Why not let the people celebrate the religion of their choice, whether it is the birthday of Jesus or Buddha? The Court is denying the people the Free Exercise clause of the First Amendment.

The Court outlawed a line-item veto of President in 1998, thus eroding the power of the president and making every Congressman an agent of special interests. The Court upheld the right of City of New London, Connecticut to use the power of eminent domain to acquire private properties for private developers to build improvement on (2005). Eminent domain has never been used before to increase property tax collection. This decision has greatly undermined the property right provided for in the Constitution. No property is safe any longer.

Every empire or kingdom in the history of mankind has fallen for one reason or another. Democracy is supposed to be a self-renewing political system but the U.S. Supreme Court is not a democratic institution. It is a tyranny. Supreme Court Justices and all important Article III Federal Judges are appointed for life and they are not accountable to anyone, once sworn into office. The Court has overturned the decisions of Congress and the Executive Branch often without any foundation in the Constitution. The Supreme Court has become absolutely

---

10.   ibid, p.87

powerful. "Absolute power corrupts absolutely." If anything destroys the U.S. as the greatest economic and military power, it will be the Supreme Court.

Chapter 10

Wars

Problem

Should a nation wage a war against another country? If yes, when and how?

Approaches of Two U.S. Presidents

Bernard Goldberg said in his bestseller *100 People Who Are Screwing Up America* that Arthur Sulzberger, Sr. (then the publisher of *Times*) asked his son Pinch (the current publisher of the *The New York Times*: "If a young American comes upon a young North Vietnamese soldier, which one do you want to see get shot?" Pinch replied, "The dumbest question I have heard in my life ... I would want to see the American get shot. It's the other guy's country." The basic premise of the liberals is that the U.S. is imperialistic, and it has no business meddling in foreign countries. This was also the mindset of Jimmy Carter, with which he won the election in 1976. True to his words, Carter avoided confrontation not only with the USSR but also with Islamic fundamentalists. He watched the fall of Shah Mohammed Reza Pahlevi and the rise of Ayatollah Ruholla Khomeini as a bystander. But that did not keep the U.S. out of trouble. In November 1979, a group of Iranian students overran the U.S. embassy and took everyone inside hostage with Khomeini's blessings. Carter practically begged Khomeini Ayatollah to release the hostages on humanitarian ground. This brought nothing but contempt from Ayatollah Khomeini.

Carter once again did nothing when the Soviet invaded Afghanistan in 1979. He pleaded to the Soviets to free the Soviet dissidents but such a plea brought nothing but contempt from the Soviets. The peanut farmer from Georgia was not a good student on the history of war. Neville Chamberlain's appeasement policy begot the most devastating war in the history of the world. To paraphrase John Stuart Mill, war is an ugly thing but to believe that nothing is worth war is to let evil to rule the world. Pacifism is what the Devil wants others to believe in. In 763, Tibet was powerful enough to invade and seize the the Chinese capital,

Xian. Since adopting the pacifist practice of Buddhism, it became defenseless and lost the country and freedom. It is the military power that guarantees freedom, independence and justice but Carter showed no inclination to use the power it had and develop new weapons. Carter decided not to support the development of the B-1 bomber or the neutron bomb. Jimmy Carter assumed that every country would respond to the goodwill of the U.S. However, he found it out a hard way that other countries did not share his view. Seeking peace through moral persuasion did not work in the real world, and it only delayed the solution and enlarged the problem. His reelection campaign in 1980 was overshadowed by the unresolved hostage crisis in Iran. By the end of his first term in 1980, Carter was seen as a failed president.

Even after his retirement from politics, Carter was handpicked by Kim Il Sung to come to Pyongyang in 1994 and discuss a solution to the brewing nuclear crisis. This visit eventually led to the Framework Agreement to freeze the North Korean nuclear development program in exchange for oil, food and nuclear power plants for the generation of electricity. Neither Carter nor Clinton was able to prevail upon North Korea on on-site verification. An agreement with a loophole as big as that had the predictable outcome. The North Korean nuclear and missile programs have grown bigger than ever before.

Reagan won a landslide victory in 1980. Iran released the hostages without delay. Iran knew that it was dealing with a different man. On the 69th day after his Inauguration in 1981, he was shot several times by a lone gunman. One of the six bullets was within an inch of his heart. Although he was hospitalized as a result and suffered excruciating pains from a .22 caliber Devastator designed to explode on impact, Reagan said, "I realized I couldn't ask for God's help while at the same time I felt hatred for the mixed up young man who shot me … We are all God's children and therefore equally beloved by Him. I began to pray for his soul and that he would find his way back into the fold."[1] Reagan was as a fundamentalist Christian, who became even more so after the near death experience. To him, God was a real, living and personal God rather than deification of the philosophy of love and forgiveness.

Reagan asked to see a minister and ended up declaring to Cardinal Cooke of the Archdiocese of New York: "I have decided that whatever time I have left is left for Him." What this exactly meant in his mind is unclear but his subsequent actions show that he dedicated his life to fighting the "evil empire" which had no regard for individual liberties or the opinion of the majority. At that time, the

---

1.   Edmund Morris, op. cit.

Soviet Union was still a mighty military power although it could not afford it. The Soviets still occupied Afghanistan and exported Marxism to the Caribbean islands and Nicaragua through Cuba. The ancient warrior Sun Tzu taught that a greatest military victory is one that a country does not have to send an army to win. Reagan simply cut off U.S. aid to Nicaragua. Reagan then mounted a major campaign to overthrow the Sandinista by supplying weapons, money, and training to the Contras. Reagan also sent arms and advisers to the regime in El Salvador.

When Reagan did not get the money for covert operations to assist the Contras in Nicaragua, he appears to have undertaken the operation in secret. The Reagan plan, according to some observers,[2] was "to sell arms to Iran as a first step to restoring close U.S.-Iran relations" and the arms would serve as "ransom for hostages held in Lebanon" according to his critics. The proceeds were then used to support the Contras, which was categorically denied by Congress. If it was really the work of Reagan, he could have faced impeachment but Colonel Oliver North took the fall. The operation eventually enabled the Contras to overthrow the Sandinista government.

Reagan also sent sophisticated weapons to Mujahideen rebels fighting against the Marxist government in Afghanistan which was backed by Soviet tanks and troops. This covert operation conducted by the CIA eventually helped the Mujahideen guerrillas to break the back of the Russian military. The war turned out costly to the Soviets both in terms of the number of Soviet troops killed (15,000) and equipment loss. The ten-year war nearly bankrupted the USSR. Its defeat and pullout from Afghanistan was the beginning of the end for the USSR.

Reagan's first deployment of Marines in a foreign war (excluding the Lebanon mission under the UN flag) was to remove Granada's Marxist leader who was building an air base with Cuban help. When completed, it "would provide a direct link in the supply of material to Nicaragua and El Salvador."[3] It would also have posed a potential threat against the Panama Canal. The final decision to invade Granada was made when six East Caribbean states requested American assistance in restoring democracy in Granada, fearful that if the Cuban-instigated revolution succeeded, it might spread to their island states. This successful preemptive action was the first clear-cut U.S. military victory in the Cold War

---

2.   "Reagan's Foreign Policy: an Overview," President Reagan and the World, Eds. Eric J. Schmertz, Natalie J Datlof, and Alexej J Ugrinsky (1997) pp. 5–6.

3.   Edmund Morris, op. cit.,483.

although it was against a tiny island nation. Reagan, however, sent the clear message that he would use force to prevent the spread of communism.

Another brilliant victory without shedding the blood of American soldiers was the attack on the palace of Libyan strongman Moammar Kadafi in March 1986. The bombs missed him but killed some of his family members. After that, Kadafi was no longer the same man. This is the way to win a war—by destroying a few evil persons rather than killing many innocent persons. Reagan was deadly with words as well as action. On March 8, 1983, Reagan delivered a speech to the National Association of Evangelicals in Orlando, Florida, which became known as the "evil empire" (referring to the USSR) speech. Few world leaders dared to utter such words. It rattled many Americans, who believed that such harsh words would harm détente. But Reagan's words had a powerful impact in the USSR, which maintained communism through words, intimidation, murder and gulags. His speech at the Berlin Wall in 1987 also resonated around the world, especially when he proclaimed: "Mr. Gorbachev, tear down this wall!" Words can bring an evil empire down.

Reagan then authorized the production of B-1 bombers which Carter stopped, a hundred MX multiple-warhead intercontinental ballistic missiles, second-generation Trident submarines, and stealth warplanes. More bad news from the point of view of the USSR was his intention to build the Strategic Defense Initiative (SDI), which if successful, would intercept and destroy Soviet intercontinental ballistic missiles before they reached the United States. The Soviet Empire, based on a "command economy", could not match the arms race with American capitalism and sustain costly foreign military operations. Reagan's hard line was increasingly worrisome to other world leaders and the liberals of the world. When the USSR fell, the same people said that the Soviet Union would have fallen with or without Reagan because of its crumbling economy. But if the U.S. were still led by Jimmy Carter, the Soviet Union would have grown fat by devouring one country after another.

Middle East Wars

A day after the independence of Israel on May 15, 1948, the Arabs attacked Israel and they have been at war more or less continuously since then. Having failed to push Israel out to the Mediterranean Sea, Arab extremists then decided to attack the U.S. The U.S. was the country behind the creation of Israel and the power behind Israel economically and militarily. The Clinton Administration treated the first attack on the Twin Towers as a routine law enforcement matter and did not pursue who were behind the terrorist act. His administration made a hasty retreat from Somalia, and made a wrong response to the 1998 attacks on the two U.S. embassies in East Africa, which killed more than 220 people and wounded over 4,000. In response, the Clinton Administration lobed several missiles to the suspected training camps of Al Qaeda in Afghanistan, but for reasons still unclear to the world, it bombed the Al-Shifa pharmaceutical factory in Khartoum on suspicion that it was producing precursors for chemical weapons (CW).

Immediately after the Al-Shifa bombing, the government of the Sudan proposed that the U.N. Security Council conduct an on-site inspection of the Shifa facility to determine whether or not the facility produced precursors for CW. The UN member countries supported an investigation but the Clinton Administration blocked any investigation. The U.S. was clearly afraid of the truth to come out. The right thing to do was to investigate and pay compensation if the U.S. indeed attacked a genuine pharmaceutical factory. The arrogance of the U.S. must have enraged the Muslims and helped Osama Bin Laden recruit more terrorists.

Al Qaeda then attacked the USS Cole in 2000 under Clinton's watch. The response was again muted. When Al Qaeda brought down the Twin Towers on 9/11 with a few thousand people in them, Americans asked "why"? The answer was in the Islamic ruling (Fatwah) issued by the Saudi Salafist Shaykh Hammoud al-'Uqla al-Shu'aybi: "America is a kufr [infidel] state that is totally against Islam and Muslims. In fact it has reached the peak of that arrogance in the form of open attacks on several Muslim nations as it did in Sudan, Iraq, Afghanistan, Philistine, Libya and others ... America expelled the Palestinians from their homes and housed the 'brothers of pigs and apes' in them; and stood firmly in support of the criminal Zionist state of the Jews, giving them all they need in the form of wealth, weapons and training."

According to a Congressional Report October 2002,[4] the U.S. has been providing $3 billion in grants annually to Israel since 1979, as provided for in the Camp David Accords (approximately 4% of Israeli GNI) and about $1 billion in philanthropy from the U.S. The Camp David Accords has also been paying off $2.1 billion to Egypt annually to buy peace for Israel. Yet, the U.S. has only limited leverage against Israel. Clinton almost clinched a peace agreement between Israel and Palestine but the deal collapsed when Israel refused to withdraw some die-hard settlers from the occupied territories. A deeper question is whether a peace agreement with PLO would have held, considering that Hamas was not agreeable to any form of peace agreement.

---

4.   Clyde R. Mark, "Israel: U.S. Foreign Assistance"

The Bush administration's response to the 9/11 was the invasion of Afghanistan. The invasion went far more smoothly than most people predicted although Bin Laden and his associates escaped into the mountains. The Bush Administration then invaded Iraq. Practically all Congressmen supported it then. The CIA and other intelligence agencies around the world believed that Saddam had a stockpile of the weapons of mass destruction (WMD). The invasion's primary objective, as most Americans and the world understood, was to get rid of that WMD. The only problem was that no new WMD was found. It appears to be another war triggered by intelligence failure. The invasion was swift and painless but establishing a democracy friendly to the U.S. has not been. In hindsight, it would have been better if Bush pulled another Reagan's act on Kadafi: bomb all Saddam's palaces where he was suspected of hiding WMD. If such bombs got Saddam, so much the better.

This war has taught the U.S. other bitter lessons. The CIA was degraded very seriously because of political correctness and the wall created between CIA and FBI. Democratic Senator Joseph Biden, a member of the Senate Foreign Relations Committee, proudly mentioned during his 1988 campaign for president that "he had threatened to 'go public' with covert action plans by the Reagan administration, causing [the Reagan Administration] to cancel the [covert] operations.... Senator Robert Torricelli of New Jersey ... led the charge in the mid-1990s to prevent the CIA from hiring unsavory characters [and] rallied to the defense of State Department employee Robert Nuccio, who leaked classified material dealing with CIA operations in Guatemala to Torricelli, who in turn held a press conference and revealed the information to the media. It was these revelations that led to congressional restrictions on the ability of agents in the field to deal with 'bad people.' Torricelli is now calling for a 'thorough inquiry' [in the aftermath of 9/11] into what he calls the intelligence community's 'stunning failure.'"[5] What good is a large spy agency if it is prohibited from spying and carrying out covert operations?

Even when intelligence was available, Clinton did not use it to the advantage of the U.S. According to reports, he had more than one opportunity to arrest or kill Bin Laden but he did not. What good is good intelligence if leaders do not act on them?

According to the Democrats, George W. Bush deliberately "lied" although that accusation makes a liar out of every Congressman and intelligence agency

---

5.   Stephen F. Knott, *History News Network*, "Congressional Oversight and the Crippling of the CIA" 11/04/01

around the world. But suppressing insurgents in Iraq has turned out very difficult because he did not and he was not allowed to use his military assets aggressively. What good are well trained soldiers and sophisticated weapons if they cannot be used? What good are national intelligence capabilities if secrets are leaked to the press with no fear of someone going to jail?

He could not secure a semblance of law and order in Iraq even after the deaths of 3,000 plus American soldiers and tens of thousand wounded. The number of casualties on Iraqi soldiers and policemen is far greater. When the Coalition including the Iraqi troops could not suppress the insurgents, Muqtada al-Sadr created an independent militia. Can one blame Shi'ites with the help of Iran? Iraqi Shi'ites refused to be massacred by the Sunni insurgents. Americans would not ask Israelis to take terrorist attacks sitting down. Reportedly over Iraqi 100,000 civilians have died in Iraq and neither the Americans nor Iraqi soldiers can protect them.

Anti-war groups blame Bush for this murderous war. But they should blame themselves first for not allowing brutal forces to be used against the terrorist. They practically tied the hands of the President and American soldiers in Iraq. They made a mountain out of the Abu Grab incident, however wrong it was, while they remained as silent as mice when the Al Qaeda slit the throats of American soldiers and civilians and hung them out to dry on a bridge or in the streets. The situation in Iraq calls for giving the soldiers an unusual latitude to deal with potential dangers than asking them to fight enemies like American soldiers fought Germans armies in WWII.

The problem is not about the number of boots on the ground but the rule of engagement. The Democrats won the mid-term election in 2006 largely because of the rising anti-war sentiment. Should the U.S. cut losses and pull out of Iraq?

Lee Kuan Yew, the Minister Mentor under his son Prime minister Lee Hsien Loong, remarked recently on the Iraq War. His views on geopolitical matters are worth to listen to. He is not a clueless talking head on television but was the architect of defeating Communists in Singapore and has built a most prosperous, stable, socially progressive, racially mixed and free economy in the world. He remarked that his Muslim neighbors (Indonesia and Malaysia) have turned hostile against the U.S. and its allies. Nevertheless, he says, "If the U.S. were to make a precipitous exit from Iraq, the Shiite and Sunni militias would be left to battle it out. Iraq's neighbors would likely join in, destabilizing the region. No American President—Republican or Democrat—can afford to let this happen."[6] He

---

6.   "Muslim Anger on the Rise" 10/16/06; www.forbes.com/currentevents.

said further, "the United States was not wrong to have removed Saddam Hussein" and believes that success in Iraq "is still possible—if Washington takes a page out of its Cold War playbook."[7] He believes that American policy makers did not realize "the depth of the fault lines in Iraqi society—between Kurds and Arabs, Sunnis and Shiites, and the members of different tribes and local religious groups" He believes that the westward movement of Shiite Iran and its Hezbollah and Hamas cannot be controlled if the U.S. moves out prematurely, which would bring America's traditional Sunni Arab allies, such as Egypt, Jordan, and Saudi Arabia to the Middle East conflict. If the U.S. cuts the loss and pulls out, jihadists everywhere would take the battle to Washington and its friends and allies. "Having defeated the Russians in Afghanistan and the United States in Iraq, they will believe that they can change the world."

The U.S. must also learn from Lee on how to govern and live in peace with moderate Muslims. The Dubai Ports World (DPW) matter is a good example of what not to do. The Bush Administration had decided that the management of ports by DPW would not pose any security threat to the U.S. Yet, both the Left and the Right rejected the DPW deal. The UAE is a vibrant and free economy that has been friendly to the U.S. It has allowed the U.S. warships and fighter planes to be based there and has been a U.S. partner in fighting terrorists since 9/11. To reject the Dubai Port deal because the UAE does not recognize Israel is just as stupid as asking Muslims to denounce their faith in Islam before buying any business in the U.S. The UAE is the kind of country that the U.S. hopes that Iraq would become one day. The U.S. cannot win the hearts and minds of moderate Muslims if Americans are fundamentally Islamophobic.

The U.S. was drawn into the Middle East conflict because of Israel. The Muslims hatred toward the Jews goes back to the days of Prophet Mohammad. The Koran considers that anyone who does not believe in all the Messengers infidels.[8] The Messengers include Moses, Jesus and Mohammad. While this is comforting to Jews and Christians, the difficulty about this is that one must also accept Mohammad, His "last prophet". Bible readers know that God was not pleased with the Jews and scattered Jews all around the world because the Jews did not obey God's command to "utterly destroy" idol worshipers. Mohammad dedicated his life in doing this. God, however, promised that one day He will bring his chosen people to the Promised Land from around the world. This promise

---

7.   "The United States, Iraq, and the War on Terror", *adapted from a speech he delivered when accepting the Woodrow Wilson Award for Public Service in October 2006. Foreign Affairs*, January/February 2007

8.   There are many references to this in The Koran. See Chapter 4:150–152.

was fulfilled on May 15, 1948. The Muslims should also accept this prophecy as the fulfillment of the words of God but they do not. What aggravate them most is that America has not been neutral in the fight between the Jews and Muslims. Why? American Jews and Christian fundamentalists in the U.S. are friends of Israel. The Old Testament says, "I [God] will bless them that bless thee [Israel], and curse him that curseth thee: and in thee shall all families of the earth be blessed." (Gen 12:3) Muslims do not have to believe this verse although it was conveyed by one of their prophets, Moses. Mohammad would be turning over in his grave if he knew that the modern day Imams are promising would-be-suicide bombers virgins in heaven. Suicide (qatlu nafsi-hi) is not referred to in the Koran but is forbidden in the Traditions (Hadith).

Purely from the point of view of American self-interest, there is no reason for the U.S. to align itself with Israel so tightly except that American Jews are powerful political force to contend with. Christian fundamentalists, the conservative political base of the U.S., support Israel. They believe that at the end of the Tribulation about one-third of the Jews would turn to Jesus and be saved. They also believe that Jesus will return and establish the Kingdom of God here on earth in Jerusalem. Yet, American Jews are practically all Democrats, they have not supported Bush's war efforts, and have been the harshest critics of Christian fundamentalists including George W. Bush. Increasingly the world including Western Europe does not share the pro-Israel view of the American conservatives. The U.S. has now lost its most staunch ally in Europe, Tony Blair, although France and Germany have elected pro-American leaders. The troop surge is the last ditch effort to convince the American public that the war can be won.

Wars That America Fought After WWII

Going to war is the most critical decision that a nation makes. The rise and fall of a nation depends on such a decision. Yet, sometimes, a war starts because of wrong intelligence. The premature withdrawal of American troops from Korea, based on faulty assumptions, in 1950 precipitated the Korean War. The Vietnam War started as a result of the Bay of Tonkin incident, whose factual accuracy has been disputed. The Iraq War started largely because of suspected stockpile of WMD but such a stockpile has not been found yet. This is not to deny that there were other valid reasons for the Vietnam and Iraq wars. A bigger problem in these wars was not winning the war although the outcome of the Iraq War remains to be seen. Why did the U.S. not win the Korean and Vietnam wars? In Korea, the liberals in the State Department turned Truman into a pussy cat and British socialist Prime Minister Clement Attlee convinced Truman to denounce the use of atomic bomb in public. Truman, who once used two atomic bombs to conclude World War II swiftly and with less casualties on both sides, fired General Douglas MacArthur for wanting to bomb Manchuria with <u>conventional</u> bombs and for wanting to cut off the bridge between Manchuria and North Korea. MacArthur believed, "There is no substitute for victory" but Washington no longer believed in it. A lot of water passed under the bridge in the five years between WWII (1945) and 1950.

Western intellectuals were fascinated with communism. After seeing what two small atomic bombs did to Japan, the world was gripped with the fear of a nuclear war that will end the world. In 1950, the old USSR detonated an experimental atomic bomb but was years away from developing a nuclear war capability. But the the West was paralyzed with the irrational fear of a nuclear holocaust.

The first mistake that the U.S. made in Vietnam was to stage a coup against Ngo Dinh Diem based on the recommendation of a bleeding-heart liberal in the State Department from Harvard, who though that South Vietnam was not worthwhile to support because several monks set themselves on fire. The second mistake was to allow too many American soldiers to be killed and take too long to fight the enemy. Against the Vietcong then and the Iraqi terrorists now, the U.S. government accorded the terrorists the benefits of the Geneva Convention when they wore civilian clothes and were irregular armies A "moral high ground" is the reason why the wars were fought in such a wimpy manner. This proved to be poor consolation to for the soldiers whose lives were taken by "invisible" enemies in civilians clothes. In Iraq, most Democrats and many Republicans including John McCain have tied the hands of CIA and the Commander-in-Chief by defining "torture" to include loud music, "waterboarding" and sleep deprivation. Such restrictions and the rules of engagement designed to fight the German armies in WWII condemned American soldiers to die. Many more of them will continue to die because Washington (Congress more so than the Administration) and anti-war/humanitarian groups have not allowed the U.S. troops to take gloves off for in kill-or-be-killed battles. If the battles are not worth for taking gloves off, it is better to return the troops home.

The irony of the Vietnam War was that American troops were in fact winning the war in spite of the wrong rules of engagement but the press and TV talking heads such as Walter Cronkite (and his cohorts in the media and politics) convinced the world and Congress that the U.S. had no chance of winning the war. We now know the reality because of declassified documents and facts flowing out of Vietnam. The ultimate act of the foolish Congress was to cut off war funds rather abruptly. Neither Walter Cronkite nor the New York Time reported the aftermath of the sudden withdrawal. The cost was horrendous in human sufferings and lives in the Indo-China region.

Khmer Rouge Communists killed between 1.7 and 2.3 million Cambodians out of a population of around 7 million, more or less 30% of the population. According to Montagnard Foundation, Vietnam Communists have killed and worked to death over 160,000 people and imprisoned over one million of its people in forced labor camps called re-education camps since the end of the war. The conditions were so brutal that starvation, executions and torture were common. A Montagnard hill tribe suffered the worst calamity because they rebelled against the Communists and collaborated with Americans. They were rounded up and shot to death or forced to slavery in labor camps. The Montagnard Senator under the South Vietnamese government (Mr. Ksor Rot) was publicly executed with a bullet in the back of his head in 1975. This was done as a warning to the Montagnard hill tribes. The Montagnard Minister Mr. Nay Luett was killed in a North Vietnamese prison camp. It is rumored that a North Vietnamese camp commander cut the top of his head off with a saw while he was still alive. About 3,000,000 million Vietnamese tried to escape Vietnam after the war but about 25% of them were lost in high sea.

While Hanoi Jane, John Carey, Walter Cronkite and other "humanists" were bringing down their government for Milay massacre and other "evil" deeds, Communists massacred 3,000 Vietnamese people and buried them in a mass grave during the siege of Hue in 1968 alone. The Viet Cong assassinated 33,052 village officials and civilians for not collaborating with them. Over 250,000 Montagnard hill tribe people were killed by the Communists. This was one of the main reasons why over 40,000 Montagnards joined with the US Army in the fight against the Communists to begin with. Since 1975 the Communists have systematically persecuted the Montagnards by execution, torture, religious repression, confiscated their ancestral lands, forced and coerced sterilizations.[9]

I wonder whether the likes of Jane Fonda, Senator John Carey and the Congress which cut off the funding for the war abruptly feel any sense of responsibility? Mt guess is that they have not lost a single night' sleep over it.

Do I believe in all these stories and numbers collected by an anti-Communist foundation. Yes I do. I was born in North Korea and saw what the Communists were capable of doing while the outside world was obsessed with Senator MacCarthy's "witch hunt"rather than thinking about millions people dieing and suffering from Communists. When I tried to say what was happening in North

---

9.   http://www.montagnard-foundation.org/opinion.html

Korea after coming to the U.S., nobody was interested in hearing the accounts and looked at me as if I was brainwashed by Senator McCarty. I stopped telling stories after a while.

A lesson that the Vietnam has taught the world is that in this day and age of televised war and intolerance toward casualties, an American president has a limited window of time and a limited number of casualties to win a war. A communist country, whether the former USSR, China or Vietnam, had all the time it needed to win a war but a U.S. president does not have such a time. The next Congressional or presidential election is always around the corner.

Once it is decided that a war must be won, a nation must go all the way. A quick war, even with the use of atomic bombs in WWII, saves lives in the end. Inability to defeat enemies quickly whether in Korea, Vietnam or Iraq has been largely because of political correctness. The outcome of a war hangs on the rules of engagement and the use of appropriate weapons, not on providing more men and money. The use of atomic weapons were surely not necessary either in Vietnam or Iraq. The U.S. government now has an awesome arsenal of weapons, but the U.S. military cannot use them for the fear of civilian casualties. Congressional politics and the Court have now placed further restrictions on how to fight a war, treat the prisoners of war and interrogate them. What can highly mechanized American brigades do to suppress insurgents in civilian clothes? To fight such a war according to the conventional rule of engagement is the dumbest idea. It did not work in Vietnam and it may not work in Iraq. Fallujah was a turning point. If the Coalition forces have tightened the noose around the city and eradicated the terrorists—after evacuating as many civilians as possible—even if it meant substantial collateral damage, the war could have come to a quick end and sent the terrorists the right message. But Bush did not want to face the cries of massacre from the Left. The Marines were told to back off. The war has now degenerated into body armor for men and vehicles rather than killing terrorists by preemptive strikes. I wish the Bush Administration to succeed in Iraq but I am uncertain that it will. The political war has to be won also. If Shi'ite politicians want to take forever to decide to share oil revenues equally among all Iraqis, let them die in sectarian violence rather than Americans.

In more than one way, the present war against the fanatic faction of the Islam is a global war against false teachers of the Islam. The Free World won the Cold War by discrediting the ideology of communism. The world can only defeat Islamic fanatics by exposing their perverted view of the Islam. The West must study and expose why those who recruit suicide bombers with a promise to send them to Heaven, where 72 virgins await them and all the sins that the Muslims are forbidden to enjoy in this world are provided, is wrong. I wonder how many Pentagon and State Department strategists have even read the Koran let alone studied the nuances of the Islam. It is time to consult Islamic scholars who teaches the Islam in its totality.

Part Three
Emerging Asia

o o o o o o o o o o o o o o o o o o o o o o o o o o o o o o o o o

Emerging Asia is now the center of dynamic growth. It has been providing enormous economic opportunities and fierce competition to the West. The GDP of the region has been growing much faster than the West (North America and Western European countries). In terms of cost of living adjusted GDP-PPP, its economy is far more affluent than in straight GDP. China's GDP-PPP was 4.6 times larger than its GDP and India's GDP-PPP was 5.2 times larger than its GDP in 2003. In terms of GDP-PPP, the Chinese economy is ranked 2nd in the world now, ahead of Japan; and India is ranked 4th in the world ahead of Germany.

Japan is the first country to emerge out of the ashes of WWII and became an affluent country. Although "Asia excluding Japan" is often used to describe the Asian economy, the level of Japan's industrialization today is no longer very different from some other Asian countries. Hong Kong's per capita GDP-PPP has surpassed that of Japan and the per capita GDP-PPP of Singapore is approaching that of Japan. South Korea and Singapore have more computers and Internet connections per 100 persons than Japan. China is now a major engine of growth in the world economy. What is happening in China now and in future is of an immense interest to the world. India now has changed from the largest pool of poverty stricken and illiterate population in the world to the most rapidly growing economy after China. Asia has many success stories but there have been exceptions also. Some of these countries merit detailed analyses.

Chapter 11

Japan: The Aging Sun

Focus

What were the reasons for the miraculous growth of the Japanese economy after WWII, slower growth between 1974 and 1989, and semi-recession since 1989? How did Japanese imperialism play out during WWII and how is it affecting Asian diplomacy today? The Japanese value system needs to be understood because it has contributed enormously to the economic success and in recent years acted as a liability.

The Post-War Prosperity

Japan was the first economy to take off in Asia after WWII and became a model for several Asian economies to follow. What were the factors? The U.S. did not plunder Japan as the old USSR wanted to do. After the war, the U.S. provided foods and economic assistance to Japan, amounting to about 15 percent of Japan's imports and 4 percent of GNP. Even more importantly, the U.S. brought about far-reaching political and economic reforms to Japan through the breakup of the military-industrial complexes, the establishment of democracy and the adoption of a new constitution. It forbids the rearmament of Japan. This turned out to be an advantage for the Japanese economy because Japan hardly spent any money for national defense but had the protection of the U.S. as West Germany did. Japan spent under 1% of GDP for national defense against 7.7% in the U.S. between 1952 and 1986. The money saved went into industrialization, manpower development, research and development and infrastructure development. Another factor which jump-started the Japanese economy was the Korean War (1950–53). The U.S. military purchase orders for the war reached 7 percent of Japan's GNP in 1953. Japan also benefited from other Cold War procurements of the U.S. such as the U.S. spending for the Vietnam War.

However, the growth of the Japanese economy owes much to the Japanese way. The Japanese saved and invested in new plants and technology. Investment in modern capital equipment averaged more than 11 percent of GNP during the prewar period, but it rose to some 20 percent of GNP during the 1950s and to more than 30 percent in the late 1960s and 1970s. During the late 1980s, the rate dropped somewhat, but it was still around 20 percent. With such domestic savings, Japanese businesses imported the latest technologies to make their industries super-modern without incurring external debt. Japanese corporations became the leaders in electronics, steel, shipbuilding and automobiles.

Furthermore, Japanese workers have been reasonable with wage demand, while remaining disciplined and highly educated. The Japanese valued hard work, thrift, and self-discipline like Max Weber's version of Protestant doctrines in the early stages of European capitalism (See *The Protestant Ethic and the Spirit of Capitalism:* 1904–05). Labor unions were generally satisfied to keep wage increases within the range of gains in productivity. In the end, the workers and industries prospered together. Unemployment hardly existed in Japan. It is also important to mention that Japanese corporate executives are not paid anything like American corporate executives. Their remuneration is not tied to quarterly or annual profits. Japanese business owners and executives try to achieve long-term growth through a larger market share. Ezra Vogel, the author of the 1979 best seller, *Japan as Number One: Lessons for America,* pointed out other factors such as the way the Japanese manage their corporations, educate their children, keep he crime rate low and save energy, which have all contributed to the meteoric rise of the Japanese economy.

Another important factor for Japanese prosperity has been that Japan has been politically stable. Except for a brief period, the conservative Liberal Democratic Party has been in control of the government in the post-war era. The notion that two political parties should be in close contention for power for progress has been proven wrong in Asia. The countries under one political party for a long period such as Japan, Singapore, Malaysia and South Korea have done much better than a country where the power shifted back and forth frequently. In Japan, the government has been a partner of the private enterprise rather than an adversary, as in the West. The Japanese modernization, industrialization and accumulation of wealth have come about as a result of government intervention in industrialization starting from the Meiji Restoration (1868–1912) when the government built factories and shipyards and sold them to entrepreneurs at a fraction of their value.[1] These entrepreneurs grew gradually into *zaibatsu,* which mean "wealthy

---

1.   "Patterns of Development," *Japan: a country study*; Ronald E. Dolan and Robert L. Worden, eds., Library of Congress; January 1994.

clique" in direct translation but they refer to large family-controlled banking-industrial combines which were nurtured by the government.

The Japanese government used these giant conglomerates for industrialization and war preparation as Nazi Germany did. Although they were dissolved after the war, the close ties between the government and corporations (including successors to the *zaibatsu*) have continued. This is why Japan is often called Japan, Inc. The Japanese people belong to a corporation almost for life in the way the samurai (those who serve) did to *daimyo*. The Japanese economy had very low taxes during its rapid growth phase and it still has relatively low taxes today; it has had business-friendly governments; healthcare costs are low and its standard is high; and the public education system is second to none. Protectionism was another way that the government has tried to protect domestic corporations.

By the mid-1950s, Japanese production matched the prewar level. Between 1953 and 1965, Japan's GDP expanded by more than 9 percent annum and the manufacturing and mining sector by 13 percent annum. In the mid-1960s, Japan ventured into heavy and chemical industries and succeeded spectacularly in the manufacture of automobiles, ships and machine tools. Between 1960 and 1970, GDP in current US$ grew at the annual rate of 16.5%. This was followed up by an 18% annual growth rate between 1970 and 1980. As a result, Japan's per capita GNI exceeded that of Germany by 1983 and that of the U.S. by 1988. Japan had merely 40% of the U.S. per capita GNI in 1970 but the U.S. was in danger of being overtaken by Japan in the 1980s.

At the height of the Japanese economy, 1989, Shintaro Ishihara (the governor of Tokyo now and a well-known nationalist accused of being a racist) and Sony Corporation Chairman Morita co-authored *The Japan That Can Say No: Why Japan Will Be First among Equals.* This best seller in Japan was translated and published in the U.S. in 1991. Shintaro claimed: "the 5th generation [of ICBM], can be developed by American know-how. However, to use this know-how across diverse applications, including weapons, requires a country with dramatically advanced production management; it is only Japan that can deliver on it."

General Douglas MacArthur was extremely lenient against Japanese war criminals compared with the American practice in Europe. It saved the Japanese the face but the downside of this policy has been that Japan has yet to apologize officially to China and Korea.[2] The Japanese remind the world that the Japanese and the Japanese government are not one and the same. Yet the Japanese keep elect-

---

2.   Historian Chalmer Johnson has written "The Germans killed six million Jews and 20 million Russians; the Japanese slaughtered as many as 100 million" Asians.

ing the leaders who pay tribute to the Yasukuni (Shinto) Shrine where war criminals are buried, in spite of outrage expressed in China and Koreas. The government revised textbooks to rationalize killing some 20 million Asians and hide ugly truths. Shintaro Ishihara became controversial again by making racist remarks directed against the Chinese and Koreans. This is not helping Japan's diplomatic relationship with its neighbors and its status in the world.

Morita's chapter in the book, "The Decline of an America Which Can Only See 10 Minutes Ahead", actually offered some sound advice to Americans. "Americans make money by playing 'money games,' namely M&A (mergers and acquisitions), by simply moving money back and forth." He goes on to say, "A ten-minute profit cycle economy does not permit companies to invest in long term development … I assume that the Bush [the 41st President] administration will take steps to tackle the present [economic] problems, but the country as a whole seems to be extremely nonchalant about the so-called twin deficits: budget and trade … There seems to be the feeling that Reaganomics raised the standard of living, taxes are relatively low, and they can buy goods from all over the world." He went on further, "The collapse of the American economy would cause a worldwide disaster. 1987's Black Monday chilled all nations momentarily. I am not a pessimist, but I cannot help thinking that unless the Bush administration handles economic issues very seriously, a worldwide collapse is not just a worry, but also a very real possibility. The ever-growing American inflation and thus its economic crisis will not only make other nations catch cold, but bring their economies into crisis as well."

Unraveling of the Japanese Economy

In spite of such concerns, the U.S. economy came out of stagflation in the 1980s while the Japanese economy began to tank precipitously in the 1980s. The Japanese economy showed the first sign of vulnerability in the 1973 oil shock. In 1974, the GNI per capita using the World Bank Atlas method posted a decline of 3%. Between 1973 and 1990, the growth rate of Japan's GDP per capita income in constant 2000 US$ came down to 2.9% from 8.5% between 1960 and 1973. It was still better than the U.S. whose per capita income grew by 2%. Yet, the Japanese economy after 1973 was a different economy from the earlier period: 1945–1973.

Oil price was just one factor. Another problem was the strength of the yen. During the 1970s, the Japanese yen appreciated dramatically from about 370 yen to a dollar to 180 yen to a dollar—an appreciation of about 100%. This appreciation of yen slowed down Japanese exports and the economy in the coming decades. Furthermore, the Japanese economy in the 1980s was churning out more bubbles than improving the living standard. Protectionism was a factor in this. The GDP-PPP was lagging far behind GDP.[3] The export economy was still doing well but in GDP-PPP, Japan's per capita income peaked at 82% of the U.S. in 1990 and declined to 74% in 2003. Finally when the property market bubble burst in 1990, the Japanese economy and stock market were sucking air.[4] This is the conundrum of the Japanese economy. A thriving export economy pushed the value of the yen high, but the living standard was mediocre. The costs of services, agricultural products, properties, rent and even the goods manufactured in Japan were and still are extraordinarily expensive because of tariff and non-tariff barriers and the inefficient service sector, which has been protected from external competition. Japan was so successful with export-driven economy and protectionist policy—both tariff and non-tariff barriers—that it decided to continue with it, illustrating a basic human fallacy.

Most Japanese live in tiny condominiums, not even as spacious as the South Korean counterparts. The cost of food is extraordinarily high. Some Japanese travel to South Korea just to eat. Japan still imposes some 500–1000% tariff on rice imports, depending on the variety of rice, and has restricted the importation of U.S. apples. Although Japan opened its apple market officially in 1971, U.S. apple growers could not export a single apple to Japan. Japan used non-tariff barriers to restrict the importation of "ridiculously cheap" U.S. apples. The WTO ruled against the Japanese practice in 2005. As U.S. apple growers have been saying, it is all about protectionism. It remains to be seen what effect WTO ruling will have on U.S. apple export to Japan. The mad cow disease gave Japan another excuse to shut the import of beef from the U.S. Japan has applied other non-tariff barriers to limit agricultural imports on a wide range of products: meat, poultry, vegetables, oranges, and other fruit products.

In addition to protectionism, the high cost of land is the underlying cause for the high cost of everything. Construction costs are extremely high because Japanese contractors prevent foreign construction companies to build in Japan and rig the bids. South Korean contractors used to build a large number of big projects in the Middle East and all over Asia including the state-of-the-art second Changgi Airport, ports and highways, but had no business in Japan. U.S. Trade Representative Robert B Zoellick complained about rampant bid-rigging and use of dis-

---

3. GDP-PPP data are not available for years prior to 1980.
4. Between 1990 and 2003, the Japanese GDP per capita in constant 2000 US$ grew at the rate of 1.08% per annum; GDP-PPP per capita grew at 0.99% per annum.

criminatory qualification and evaluation criteria[5] but it did not help. This pattern is carried on to Japanese foreign aid projects also. Japan provides low interest loans—by the international standard—under the Overseas Economic Cooperation Fund to developing countries. The loans are to be repaid in yen, and therefore, borrowing countries bear the currency risk. Biddings were often restricted to Japanese companies and the winning bid price could come 100% higher than what an international competitive bidding would bring. Japan called it foreign aid.

Japanese property values increased continuously without any dip between 1950 and 1991. A myth was created that one can never lose money in real estate. In the late 1980s, Tokyo businessmen boasted that land in Tokyo was worth more than the entire State of California. Land prices in Tokyo were 30 times higher than in New York City in 1995—even 5 years after the property market peaked. Tokyo was not an isolated case as land prices in Osaka and other cities were not much cheaper. A house and lot cost about 15 times the average annual income of a household in Tokyo and 13 times in Osaka, compared with 2.9 times in New York. A steep drop in the property market since then has brought about a sustained economic stagnation.

The process through which urban land is developed in Japan is called *Kukaku-Seiri,* although it is known as land consolidation or land readjustment in other countries where such practices are used for special purposes. In Japan, this is practically the only tool available to create more than several building or housing lots. Land development under the system is carried out either by government agencies or private associations following specified government rules. Such systems eliminate housing and land subdivision and development as we know them in the U.S. and make urban land scarce. In addition, the central government's strict control over the conversion of agricultural land for urban uses (for greenbelt and food security) has made urban land even scarcer. Beneficiaries were large Japanese landowners and real estate companies which amassed valuable rental properties. They got extremely rich merely holding on to them for price appreciation and rent collection.

Another problem was that the Japanese yen continued to appreciate even after 1985 because of the Plaza Accord of 1985. Reagan Administration adopted a weak dollar policy—reversing its earlier position—and persuaded Japan, Germany, UK, and France to intervene in the foreign exchange markets to adjust

---

5. "2003 Inventory of Trade Barriers," http://www.mindfully.org/WTO/2003/USTR-Trade-Barriers1apr03.htm

their currencies upward against dollar as twin deficits deepened and some American industries were at the brink of extinction. In the 1980s, the Japanese yen appreciated from JPY260/$1 to JPY120/$1. Such a massive appreciation of the JPY dampened Japanese exports and corporate profits. Japan began to shift its production facilities to countries with cheaper labor cost and stopped the production of some labor intensive industrial products altogether. The so-called hollowing of the Japanese industrial sector started. The unemployment rate which used to be around 2% shot up to 5% in 2002 and 5.4% in 2003. These are the kind of rates that EU countries would die for, but not for Japan.

As the yen appreciated, the products of other Asian countries cut into the market shares and profits of Japanese export industries, particularly in electronics, steel and shipbuilding. At the same time, the Japanese taxes and spending on social security and welfare programs increased considerably over the 1980s and 1990s, compared with Taiwan, South Korea, Hong Kong and Singapore. The Japanese population is aging fast because the Japanese live longer and birth rates are very low. To its credit, Japan has provided universal healthcare coverage at a reasonable cost. As a percent of the GDP, the Japanese healthcare cost is about half the U.S.

With the collapse of the property market in 1990, the lending volumes of Japanese banks contracted significantly because of severe balance sheet problems. *The Economist* had an interesting article entitled "Dead firms walking."[6] It referred to the fact that there are many bankrupt firms which remain afloat because banks do not demand them to pay back loans because dead firms and wobbly banks are "clung to each other in mutual defiance of reality. Troubled borrowers needed the banks to overlook their problems and keep open the flow of money; the banks, too short of capital to admit that their loans had soured, obliged. Over time, this led to the emergence of so-called 'zombies'—companies that are competitively dead, but, sustained by their banks, continue to walk the Earth and give healthier firms nightmares. And zombies are most prevalent in the service sectors of the economy, especially construction, property and wholesale and retail distribution." *The Economist* goes on to say, "It is hard to think of a single non-manufacturing sector in which Japan excels. High domestic transport costs hinder distribution, travel and tourism. A lack of competition in energy and

---

6. "Dead firms walking: Japan's unproductive service industries are holding back its improving economy from achieving even better performance," *The Economist*, September 23rd, 2003.

telecoms keeps business costs high. Professional services, such as law and accountancy, remain hidebound."

When the property market declined roughly 50% from the peak, many banks were in fact bankrupt since most of their loans were secured by inflated property values. The stock market lost about 80% of its value, and there has been a deflation. The Japanese government reduced the interest rate to zero and incurred a massive amount of public debt to prime the pump. Yet, such policies did little to revive the Japanese economy, instead ran up a huge public debt exceeding 150% of GDP. The Keynesian policy did little to revive the Japanese economy which was suffering from supply-side problems.

Sign of Revival

Many Asian countries had to make some painful reforms after the 1997 Asian financial crisis partly because the IMF forced such reforms on them, but Japan did not need IMF assistance and it did not have to take bitter pills. The Japanese people are a model of pliability in appearance but they have an unusually stubborn steak when it comes to making any reform. This is the same stubborn streak that made them believe that killing 20 million Asians in the most barbaric ways, starting as early as 1919 in Korea—for demanding independence—and 1931 in China when Japan started the invasion of China. To Japanese nationalists who is politically strong enough to change textbooks today and swing elections, such atrocities either did not take place or was for the good of Asians. After ten years of economic stagnation, however, Japan's financial regulators forced the biggest banks to clean up their balance sheets. This is at long last happening although it has taken over a decade to do so. Some marginal borrowers, in the meantime, had time to regain solvency. Some reforms have taken place in telecom and the information-technology sector. The Japanese retail sector is also beginning to change since zoning restrictions were relaxed in the 1990s allowing a few global retailers, such as America's Wal-Mart, Britain's Tesco and France's Carrefour, to enter the Japanese market. At least one large Japanese retailer "began to cut off inefficient wholesalers and streamline its logistical system. In some cases, it has done this by taking shipments directly from manufacturers, just as Wal-Mart does."[7]

Prime Minister Koizumi made an effort to streamline the service sector. He succeeded in passing a law to reform Japan's mighty postal system, which is also a huge financial service center (banking and insurance). It cost him his job. Japan has a long way to go but every little reform is being resisted. As a result, addi-

---

7.   ibid

tional reforms will be painfully slow even as Japanese monopolies such as NTT and J-Power (the country's biggest electricity wholesaler) are now being broken up. It should have been done in the 1970s but this is Japan. The U.S. government has engaged the Japanese government on trade and regulatory reforms annually since 2001. A strong Japanese economy and freer access to the Japanese market are good for the world including for the Japanese people although not to Japanese monopolies. The talks are partially responsible for the postal system reform and bringing down unreasonably high mobile phone calling rates and Japan's agreement in principle to remove the fixed costs that NTT charges to its competitors. The interconnection charge is unusually high in Japan. Custom processing fees at Japanese airports for express delivery services have also come down.

The U.S. has also asked Japan to take a whole host of other reforms such as applying more rigorously the antitrust laws and allowing foreign banks to engage in trust and banking businesses on an equal footing with domestic banks. Prime Minister Koizumi seems to believe in the free market. He said to the Diet on October 12, 2004, "there can be no rebirth and development for Japan without structural reforms." The Japanese economy is a tangled mess of concessions to special interest groups and monopolies to public and semi-public corporations. Every trade and occupational group has special agenda. Corruption is another problem. It usually involves giving contracts for rather useless public works to cronies and those to whom politicians owe favors.

The Japanese economy is finally showing a sign of revival. Its stock market has been rebounding since 2003, and even property markets have been recovering somewhat. The banks have been cleaning up their balance sheets. The economic boom in China has been feeding the Japanese industries. The Japanese economy will grow at a decent rate assuming that the Chinese economy remains robust.

Lessons Learned

Important lessons learned from the Japanese experience are as follows:

1. Pro-business policies, high savings rate, low interest rates, good labor-management relation and a sound social environment have driven its economy to the second largest economy in the world after World War II.

2. The post-1990 Japanese economic slump does not necessarily discredit its early economic policies. However, such policies did not serve the Japanese well when its economy matured and created the supply-side bottleneck. Its

protectionism, resistance to reforms, over regulations (e.g. land use policy), monopolies (e.g., utilities) can hold down the economy and the living standards. Over valuation of currency because of undue emphasis on exports also brings down the living standard of a country.

3. Japan's stubborn attempt to rationalize its aggression and atrocities and then try to whitewash them by revising textbooks have not sat well with its neighbors. Japan needs to face the truth about its past as Germany did. This will not only eliminate unnecessary frictions with its neighbors but also set the conscience of the Japanese free.

Chapter 12

Singapore: A Small Country with Big Ideas

Focus

The economic growth of Singapore compares favorably to any economy in the world and its standard of living is ranked the highest in the world. It has achieved this through a free market economy. Singapore is also known for its unique style of law and order (swift and harsh punishment against criminals). Its Central Provident Fund (CPF) is a form of privatized social security system and has done much good to the people. Why has Singapore done so well? The answer is partly Lee Kuan Yew.

Lee's Maneuver Against the Communists

Singapore was a small fishing village until Englishman Sir Thomas Stamford Raffles recognized its potential as a large port and developed it into an international port. It is strategically located at the Straits of Malacca where all the ships pass between the Indian Ocean to East Asia. The increasing prosperity of the city during the British colonial time attracted immigrants from China, Malaysia, Indonesia, India and Europe. After WWII, Singapore wanted to gain independence from the UK. The process took many years partly because of armed Communist insurgency. Lee Kuan Yew returned to Singapore in August 1950 from UK and became a trade union lawyer before turning into politics. Lee graduated from Cambridge University law school with first-class honors. His role as a successful trade union lawyer gave many opportunities to meet Communist leaders. He did not have much respect for lawyering or the due process of law. He even admitted that he won a legal case although his client was guilty. He turned to politics instead. Lee Kuan Yew created the People's Action Party (PAP) by forging an alliance with the Communists, who were unable to form their own political party because the British were all out to eradicate Communist insurgents before granting independence to Singapore. In the 1950s, some viewed Lee as a clandestine Communist, a tool of the Communists or a fool. The first ever General Election was held in the same year. Fool or not, the PAP was successful in election because the Communists were popular among some people and Lee was seen as a moderate.

Upon grabbing power in 1959, Lee and his colleagues cut ties with the Communists.[1] Contrary to some speculation of his being a Communist, "Lee Kuan Yew and his colleagues dismounted from the Communist tiger, so to speak, where they wanted to get off—not where the tiger wanted to take them."[2] A power struggle began immediately after the election victory. Lee decided to emasculate the Communist cells by using British power while the British still retained power over defense and foreign relations. The strategy was successful and the British rounded up most Communists. Was Lee a Machiavellian? There is no doubt about it. The PAP, dominated by the Lee's faction then, continued to hunt down Communists relentlessly. The notion that a country needs two party system, like the U.S. to be prosperous and maintain freedom, has been proven wrong once again in Singapore as in Japan.

Singapore's Economic and Social Policies

The PAP was good for the Singaporeans. GNI per capita in current U.S. dollars increased from $450 in 1962 (the earliest years that the World Bank has data on GNI using Atlas Method) to $27,490 in 2005. The annual growth rate was 10.0%. It is a virtual tie with Japan's 10.2% but slightly lower than South Korea's 12.3% during the same period. During the same period, the rate was 7.8% for China and 6.4% for the U.S. Singapore has achieved this growth rate without protectionism. That is what makes Singapore different from Japan or South Korea. The key to the economic boom in this small island without any natural resources (not even enough water) has been its economic policies and free trade including free investment and ownership of corporations. Every country's economic growth rates slow down as the economy matures although the rate of slow down is different from country to country. During the last 5–10 years, the Chinese economy picked up the steam and the Indian economy is just warming up. The South Korean economy rebounded strongly after the Asian Financial

---

1. Lim Kay Tong, "Lee Kuan Yew: 1923—Politician" (1998).
2. See R S Milne and Diane K Mauzy, Singapore: The Legacy of Lee Kuan Yew (1990) p. 4. They wrote two respected books on Lee and other books on the political and economic history of Singapore and Malaysia.

Crisis. Singapore's growth rate cooled during the past 5 years while Japan economy turned cold since 1990.

Some economists believe that GNI-PPP in international dollar is more meaningful than GDP. One problem is that the time series on PPP started in 1980. GDP-PPP is much higher than straight GDP in countries where the cost of living is low. In 2005, China's GDP-PPP was almost four times larger than GDP and it was almost five times larger in India. On the other hand, in Japan and Western Europe, GDP-PPP was lower than GDP. The benchmark is the U.S. Between 1980 and 2005, Singapore's n GDP-PPP grew at the rate of 7.4% compared with 5.1% of the U.S. See Table 11 for the growth rates of other countries, higher than all comparators except China and South Korea.

Table 11:

GNI-PPP Per Capita and Annual Growth Rate
Selected Countries

(In current International $) *

	1980	*1990*	*2000*	*2005*	*198 0–0 5*
China	$410	$1,310	$3,770	$6,600	11.76%
France	$9,810	$17,970	$25,530	$30,540	4.65%
Germany	$9,690	$18,110	$25,950	$29,210	4.51%
India	$640	$1,370	$2,400	$3,460	6.98%
Japan	$9,070	$19,080	$26,300	$31,410	5.09%
Korea, Rep.	$2,420	$7,510	$15,140	$21,850	9.20%
Singapore	$5,020	$12,230	$23,700	$29,780	7.38%
UK	$8,530	$16,360	$24,840	$32,690	5.52%
U.S.	$12,220	$23,130	$34,690	$41,950	5.06%

*   Source: WBDI except % calculated by the author.

Singapore has always been a center of commerce because it has remained a free port even after the withdrawal of the British. In the early 1970s, it became a center for oil exploration in the region. This brought in a large number of expatriate populations and made it possible for Singapore to evolve into a center of petrochemical industries. Today the economy is well diversified and most of its exports consist of high-technology products. According to UN trade data, the exports of such products with high R&D intensity (such as aerospace, computers, pharmaceuticals, scientific instruments, and electrical machinery) as percentage of all manufactured exports in 2003 comprised 58% in Singapore compared with 31% for the U.S., 26% for the UK and 24% for Japan.

Singapore has been almost entirely rebuilt, too much so according to some people. Its highways and city streets are spotlessly clean and beautifully landscaped. The Changi airport is one of the busiest in the world and much more beautiful than the Frankfurt International Airport, the largest in Europe. Its port is not only the world's largest container port and the busiest in terms of shipping tonnage handled but also a leading center of shipbuilding, ship-repair, offshore support, salvage work and port-related services. Singapore is today at the leading edge of information technology, knowledge industry and innovation. It has excellent transportation, communications and financial institutions.

Lee's right hand man and Finance Minister, Dr. Goh Keng Swee, was firmly in control of monetary and fiscal policy. He kept inflation low and the economy free while providing financial incentives to attract foreign multi-national corporations (MNC) to Singapore. The government also invested in the development of an industrial estate at Jurong. The Economic Development Board (EDB) was set up to help local and foreign corporations establish factories in Singapore. Today, Jurong is a town with many high-tech industries. Singapore also went on to promote human resources and technology development by setting up the Skills Development Fund and R&D assistance funds.

The first economic recession after independence came in 1985. This was partly due to the weakness in the petroleum sector following the second oil crisis in 1980. Because of the rapidly falling oil price, the demand and price for Singapore's petroleum-related exports plummeted. There was also a sharp drop in demand for electronics goods in the U.S. Singapore's unemployment rate rose to 6%. The recession was also Singapore's own making to the extent that the government let wages rise in excess of gains in productivity and the National Wages Council guidelines. Consequently, Singapore adopted policies to restrain excessive wage increases and cut employer contributions to the Central Provident Fund (CPF). It combines social security, medical insurance and private savings accounts. While cutting CPF contributions, the government imposed a tax on expenditure to make up for the loss in government revenues. This was preferred by the people over higher tax rates, which might have driven foreign companies out of Singapore. Growth resumed and reached double-digit figures in the late 1980s.[3]

Singapore had a population of 4.19 million in 2003. The majority of the population is Chinese but there is a sizable number of the Malays (14%), Indians (7.6%) and non-resident foreign population. Singapore's quality-of-life is ranked

---

3.   ibid p. 70.

the highest in the world.[4] The foreign population includes corporate executives, traders and professionals from all over the world as well as domestic helpers from the Philippines, Indonesia, etc. on work permits, never on permanent visas. The non-resident population has increased from 1% of the population in 1970 to 18.3% in 2005. Temporary workers provide cheap labor for the growing economy without creating the kind of lawlessness or citizenship issues that the U.S. is facing. Once I was traveling with several business colleagues from Jakarta to Manila. One of us was a lady from mainland China. The travel inevitably required an overnight stay in Singapore, which is an airline hub in that part of the world. The Singapore Airline counter asked the lady asked whether she was pregnant. She said yes. The airline staff barred her from boarding the plane—a Singapore rule. Singapore needs manpower but does not want any foreign babies. The rules are simple. The contract workers must return to their home countries first upon completing the contract. They can be re-admitted if their contracts are extended by employers. Contract workers are not allowed to bring family members, whether an infant or the old, with them. The employers as well as contract are criminally liable if the rules are not followed strictly. This is true in Hong Kong, Japan and South Korea also. Citizenship is never promised and none is given.

The number of tourists who visited Singapore in 2005 was 8.94 million compared with 4.37 million for the entire country of Japan. Visitors to Singapore find their television programs rather tame in sexual and political content although there are numerous cable stations operating in Singapore. Like in the UK, the government has a monopoly over news. News channels, however, are not free to say anything they want without solid facts. In the U.S., the press has the final say on anyone and any matter and there is very little that anyone can do about this.

In Singapore, the government has an unrestricted right to reply to broadcasts it deems erroneous, biased or otherwise misleading. The government demands an equal and free time to present its side of story. Ultimately, the people decide whose stories are more credible. If the international broadcaster denies an unfettered reply, it can be held to be interfering in domestic affairs and its broadcasting permits can be revoked or at least fined as much as $10,000. "If you don't recognize the government right of reply," Information Minister Yeo asserted, "you

---

4.   The quality-of-life index is developed and maintained by the Economic Intelligence Unit.

won't make money in Singapore."[5] In Singapore, pornography is not considered a matter of freedom of speech.

Singapore found a capitalist way to solve social problems. The CPF has contributed enormously to retirement security, healthcare and housing ownership of Singaporeans. It is an advanced version of George W. Bush's plan for Social Security Reform. It works efficaciously. Singaporeans can even borrow money for housing purchase and mortgage payments. The CPF should be studied by other countries. It is a fund over which the participant has a say in where to invest the money, such as to buy life annuity from a participating insurance company, make a fixed deposit with a participating bank or keep it in a Retirement Account with the CPF Board which pays a minimum of 2.5% interest per annum. Savings in the Special and Medisave Accounts provide for hospitalization and certain outpatient services and the purchase of medical insurance for catastrophic medical costs. The funds in these accounts earn 1.5 percentage points above the prevailing rate on the Ordinary Account interest rate—4% currently. A participant can withdraw CPF savings when one turns 55, after setting aside CPF Minimum Sum S$90,000 for old age retirement. (The exchange rate recently has been around S$1.6/US$1.) One's CPF Minimum Sum makes monthly pay from age 62.

The Housing Development Board (HDB) develops estates and towns, builds condominiums, sells them to individuals and rents some units. About 90% of these units are owned by those living in them. The quality and size of the housing units vary greatly. This is a socialized housing program run on a capitalist principle. There is no forced racial integration or subsidies. Buyers can even choose the ethnic composition of the neighborhoods they prefer (mixed, Chinese only, Malay only or Indian only, etc.). Most Singaporeans have nothing but praises for HDB. Practically everyone owns a house, which gives stability to Singapore society. How government-developed houses can be liked in this manner would be a puzzle for most Americans, but the public housing authorities in Hong Kong and South Korea although they compete head on with private builders are doing well also. The spectacular failure of the U.S. public housing was due to the high crime rates, drugs and no ownership stake in housing.

Contribution rates to the CPF vary by age, but basically it is 33% of earnings (12% by employer and 20% by employees). The rate drops after age 50 to 11.5% for those in the age bracket of 55–60. Since it combines retirement, health insur-

---

5.   **See** Arnold Zeitlin, "New restrictions on broadcasters assailed at conference" May 23, 2001.

ance for all ages, individual investment account and housing mortgage at a reasonable rate, Singaporeans consider it a good deal. By comparison, an average American household pays about 38% of their income for private medical insurance and social security taxes (excluding the portion paid by employers). Americans do not own, or cannot borrow against, their social security savings. The U.S. social security is a government fund but the Singapore CPF is an individual savings account managed by the government. There is no comparison. FICA contribution does not even earn any interest to speak of, compared with CPF. The FICA fund is not owned by contributors. It is just a rip off, pure and simple.

In 1990, Lee Kuan Yew stepped down from the position of Prime Minister. Under Prime Minister, Goh Chok Tong, he served as Senior Minister. Goh has also done well. Singapore was affected by the Asian Financial Crisis, although Singapore was financially sound. Singapore's external balance was and is still strong and the monetary authority took steps to keep reserves safe. Its banks had the highest credit ratings in Asia and its current account balance was exceptionally strong.[6] The attack on the Singapore dollar had no basis and was largely fanned by short-term currency speculators such as George Soros. Although this brief recession during the second half of 1998 was not of its own making, the government was concerned that its economy had lost its competitiveness. It once again undertook the kind of reforms that it undertook in 1980: control labor cost increases exceeding productivity gains, a reduction of contributions to CPF and a reduction of personal and corporate taxes. It also strengthened the development of workforce to promote information technology (IT) and the Knowledge-Based Economy (KBE).[7]

The Singapore Business Federation was created for this purpose. All firms, both local and foreign, were required to join it and pay a levy so that it could promote the KBE better. It promotes the recruiting and retaining of talent in the electronics, chemical, engineering, and life sciences including biotech. The government of this tiny island set aside US$1 billion for venture capital to be deployed during 2000–2003. On a population-adjusted basis, it is like the U.S. government spending $68 billion in three years for venture capital alone. In addition, the government set up three substantial biotech funds, amounting to S$1 billion (about US$619 million). Advanced technology is also Singapore's answer to China's cheap labor costs. Singapore has a per capita income of some 30 times that of China.

---

6.   14.48% of GDP in 2000, 18.97% in 2001, 21.38% in 2002 and 30.86% in 2003.
7.   See Ibid p. 71.

Each time it encountered an economic recession, Singapore undertook sup-ply-side reforms. In 1999, it was cited as the world's most competitive economy and the world's second freest economy (after Hong Kong).[8] The government is known in business circles to be clean and corruption free. The government pro-motes meritocracy, a high quality labor force, pro-business policies and political stability. Local labor laws allow relatively free hiring and firing practices. There is no minimum wage law. There are no taxes on capital gains, sales or development. Government revenue excluding grants was still reasonable at 26% of GDP com-pared with 38% of the UK and 45% of France. "Foreign firms are taxed on the same basis as local companies. Also, there is no withholding tax on the remittance of profits. There is however, a property tax of 12% ... Industrial disputes are usu-ally settled through mediation by the government. When this fails, the matter is decided by the Industrial Arbitration Court, whose rulings are binding."[9] In spite of this, workers are paid extremely well by any standard. This is an example of supply-side policy functioning.

Lee Kuan Yew currently holds the specially created post of Minister Mentor Prime Minister in the current government led by Lee Hsien Loong, his son. He was carefully groomed for the job by first serving as a military officer and then moving on to a government position as a cabinet minister. It gives a taste of a dynasty although he got the position through parliamentary process. No doubt, his father helped him. He is doing a good job. At this stage of Singapore's devel-opment, it is the institutions and established policy direction that guide the coun-try, not personality.

National Unity

Singapore, which is a multi-racial country, has managed inter-racial relationship well. A further unifying element is that the national defense of Singapore requires every Singaporean male sound in body and mind to serve for two or more years. South Korea has a similar system. It is surprising that Singapore not in war or a threat of war is implementing such measures. It is all about preparedness, disci-pline, national unity and skill training. In 1984, Singapore introduced the con-cept of Total Defense, not only to defend the country from military attack but also to work together in civil defense, economic defense, social defense and psy-chological defense. This is a national movement of a sort. It brings Singaporeans together in a common purpose, and unites this multi-ethnic society. Westerners

8.   "Singapore", last updated in July 2002.
9.   ibid

today demand unlimited individual freedom but Asian governments demand, and most Asians accept, that individual freedom can be and should be curtailed for social harmony and national unity such as accepting a military draft system.

The Singapore military is one of the most modernized in Asia and the government spends approximately 28% of its operating expenditures or 5% of GDP on national defense. In percentage, this is almost twice more than what the U.S. spends on national defense now. The career military force is only 20,000 strong, but it has 55,000 men on active National Service and another 225,000 placed on a 10 years stand-by after finishing their National Service. It has 300,000 men in arms or in reserve while the U.S. with 70 times the size of Singapore population has less than 1.1 million in active duty and reserve. In percentage, the U.S. has one-third of 1% of the population in active service and reserve but Singapore has about 7% of its population in active duty and reserve. These reservists may spend up to 40 days of active service every work year. Singapore is a close ally of the U.S. Singapore has consistently supported a strong U.S. military presence in the Asia-Pacific region. Since 1990, Singapore has allowed the U.S. to have access to Singapore airbases and the U.S. Navy logistics unit to be based in the Singapore port.

Lee sees the U.S. as a stabilizing force in Asia. He was concerned with the evacuation of U.S. military bases from the Philippines (on the request of the Philippine government) because this could create a military vacuum that could tempt China or India to reach out to that part of the world. China in a way did by claiming the Spratly island chain, supposedly oil rich, as its territory. Singapore is a member of the Five Power Defense Arrangement together with the UK, Australia, New Zealand, and Malaysia—the Commonwealth allies.

Crime, Punishment and Social Order

One can either hate or love Singapore's policies on criminals. Michael P. Fay, who attended a Singapore American school, pelted several expensive cars with eggs and spray painting. The punishment was caning. Bill Clinton called the punishment extreme and pleaded with the Singapore government to grant Fay clemency, but to no avail. After Fay's punishment was served on May 5, 1994, the U.S. trade representative threatened that he would try to prevent the WTO first ministerial meeting from taking place in Singapore. The U.S. media, including the *New York Times*, joined in to condemn Singapore. A huge majority of the public in Singapore, however, backed their government, and said that a foreigner living in their country should not be above the law. A significant number of

Americans felt that Singaporeans had a right to use corporal punishment if it so chose.

Another incident, well publicized, was a couple of naïve Australians who tried to make easy money by trafficking small quantities of illicit drugs, but they were caught and sentenced to death in Singapore. It is an unusual and cruel punishment by Western standards, but such a policy keeps thousands from getting addicted. The threat of harsh punishment is the only thing that works against criminals. Few Western countries can do it but some Asian countries have done it. As a result such policy, Singapore is one of the safest countries in the world (see Figure 7, based on data compiled by Miss Yeo Soek Lee of Department of Statistics, Singapore). Only violent crimes (murder, rape, robbery and aggravated assaults) are included, because the aggregate of crimes includes petty crimes which some countries do not report. Singapore compares favorably to individual Japanese cities. The low crime rate vindicates Singapore's low tolerance to crime and the practice of harsh punishment.

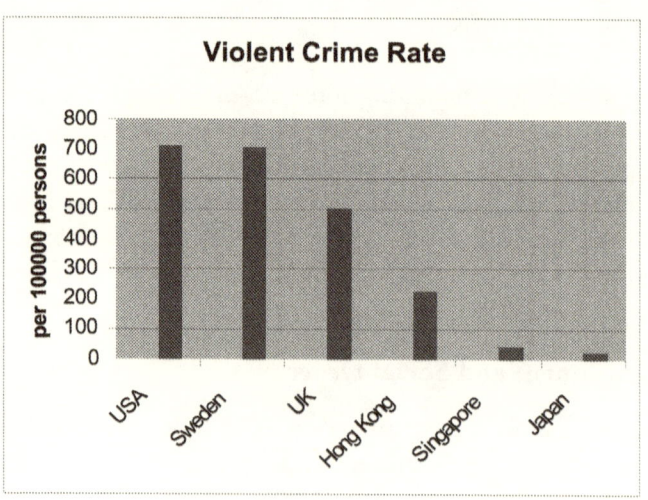

Figure7

There is a saying that justice delayed is justice denied. There is an interesting comparative albeit proxy data collated by the World Bank on this. It takes 69 days to enforce a contract in Singapore compared with 288 days in the UK, 250 days in the U.S., 380 days in the Philippines and 425 days in India. Justice is dispensed swiftly in Singapore as well as in Japan (60) and South Korea (75 days). A swift adjudication does not necessarily indicate unfair justice. Years of televised trial against O. J. Simpson only proves how money and famous lawyers get away with murder rather than dispense justice.

Lee is a stern Asian father figure. During the fight against Communism, he did away with the right of habeas corpus or an open trial against known criminals or political agitators on the grounds that "witnesses were too cowed to come forward to testify against them". These are the words of a former lawyer who graduated from Cambridge University law school with first-class honors. Lee argued that Asians "want higher standards of living in an orderly society. They want to have as much individual choice in lifestyle, political liberties and freedoms as is compatible with the interests of the community." Singaporeans agreed with it and supported Lee all the way. Each Singaporean citizen is free to worship their gods without worrying about a silly ACLU and the separation of the church and state. Businesses do not have to worry about outrageous litigation costs and awards, crippling strikes or environmental terrorism. The city's air, water and land are clean. The notion of appropriate freedom as Lee sees it may be objectionable to many ACLU sympathizers, but no one is completely free to do whatever he or she wants to do—even in Amsterdam. There are few countries in the world which can offer better systems for economic development, social order, religious freedom and a social safety net at an affordable price than Singapore.

Lessons

Singapore provides a powerful lesson to the world. It has created a high growth economy, full employment, high wages, a high standard education, a low crime rate and a strong social safety net by:

1. practicing the free-market and free-trade economy;

2. keeping wage increases in line with productivity increases;

3. creating a social safety net based on individual savings and investment accounts;

4. being tough on criminals;

5. maintaining interracial harmony and national unity;

6. maintaining a low tax burden;

7. providing government incentives to develop new and advanced technology;

8. maintaining an excellent standard of education;

9. creating a government housing program based on ownership rather than rental public housing; and

10. keeping a clean, efficient and small government (only 6% of its workforce is directly engaged in the public sector); and making civil servants pro-growth by linking their salary increases to the overall economic growth rate.[10] (This is a reason why they think of how to promote economic growth rather than imposing onerous regulations).

The development history of Singapore shows that leadership matters particularly during the formative stage of national development. Lee is the author of the Singapore policies and ideology. Lee did not fall for the American version for the American system of political correctness or justice which protects the criminals rather than the people. He practiced supply-side economics: small government and low taxes. He did not hesitate to provide incentives for technology and human resource development and wage guidelines. Singaporeans like the fact that their government does not play politics or mince words. If the government reduced corporate taxes, they knew that this was to keep jobs in Singapore, not to favor big corporation at the expense of the working people. Once national policies and ideology are well established, who runs the government becomes a secondary matter.

---

10. Rajendra Sisodia, *Harvard Business Review,* 1992.

Chapter 13

South Korea: Rags to Riches

Focus

South Korea was the next country to take off in Asia. Its history of economic growth after 1960 is as compelling as that of Japan and Singapore. In spite of having no natural resources to speak of (more so than Japan), no locational assets like Singapore and no technological or human resources because the Japanese occupied practically all managerial, professional and technical positions in Korea for over 30 years before1945, South Korea has achieved remarkable progress. The division of the country and the war that followed devastated the country, physically and economically. The Korean War is still not finished, technically speaking, and national defense costs a lot of expenditures. A threat of another war, now with a nuclear weapon, hangs over the peninsula. How has South Korea overcome all these obstacles and has emerged as an industrial power to contend with? This is the focus of the chapter.

An Unfortunate Victim of the Cold War

South Korea was a hard luck case. It was the first country to fall to Japanese colonialism. Instead of being liberated after the surrender of Japan, the Allies decided to divide Korea. It was a victim of horse trading between Franklin Roosevelt and Joseph Stalin. The U.S. has also paid dearly for Roosevelt's unwise and naïve decision to make Stalin happy at the expense of other countries. The U.S. paid dearly for his mistake. Korea turned into the first battlefield during the Cold War in which the U.S. incurred 136,937 casualties (25,801 deaths). South Korea suffered 257,000 military casualties and 860,000 civilian casualties. Over a half million houses were incinerated or blasted by bombs, and four million refugees abandoned their homes in North Korea to come to South Korea with nothing but what they could carry on their backs. North Korean and Chinese casualties were even larger.

South Korean youth and intellectuals believe that Franklin Roosevelt was entirely responsible for the division of Korea. He did so when he went to the Yalta Secret Meeting (February 4–15, 1945) surrounded by left-wing liberal Harry Hopkins and many State Department officials. Recently KGB agent Iskhak Akhmerov revealed that Harry Hopkins was "the most important of all Soviet wartime agents in the United States" in the 1960s.[1] Even the convicted Communist agent in the State Department, Alger Hiss, was part of the Washington delegation. But the major responsibility for the failed policy of dividing Korea into two belongs to Roosevelt. He was so ill from strokes he suffered in the summer that he did not even read the State Department brief suggesting that the U.S. take a dominant position in Korea. Instead, he created the joint trusteeship between the U.S. and the former USSR for no good reason at all. That was equivalent to dividing France in half and giving one part to the USSR because France was occupied by Germany and Roosevelt needed to reward Russia.

Harry Truman aggravated the situation by abandoning Nationalist China to Mao and pulling out American troops prematurely from South Korea thus inviting the invasion of South Korea from North Korea. Truman also had a knee-jerk reaction and fired Douglas MacArthur for wanting to win the Korean War by bombing Manchuria, where the Chinese troops were crossing into Korea. The Korea peninsula had fixed borders well before most European countries had them. Koreans speak the same language and are of the same ethnic origin, unlike populations in most Western countries. The younger generation of South Koreans sees the U.S. as a self-centered racist country.

The war left South Korean cities badly destroyed. Poverty was widespread, unemployment rates were sky high, and corruption in government was rampant. American economists called South Korean a basket case in the 1950s. South Korea's per capita annual income was less than $100 per person when the war ended, and its future looked dismal. South Korea did not have natural resources. About 80% of the countryside is too hilly to plant crops, The country did not produce enough food to feed its people.

Dr. Syngman Rhee, the old patriot and president since 1948, was clueless on the economy (PhD in political science from Harvard). He had no idea how much a pound of rice or sugar cost because he was surrounded by cronies and "yes" men who always delivered good news. Young university graduates had no jobs. On April 19, 1960, angry students toppled the Rhee regime. South Korea experi-

---

1.   See Dan Flynn, "What Your Textbooks Won't Tell You About the Cold War"; http://www.academia.org/campus_reports/2000/november_2000_4.html

enced a brief period of American style parliamentary democracy headed by another U.S. educated political scientist Chang Myon, but the experience was not a good one for most Koreans, who were not accustomed to political chaos on top of economic crisis. There was also the constant fear that political chaos in South Korea would invite another invasion from north.

Park Chung Hee

On May 16, 1961, Major General Park Chung Hee, whom most Koreans had not heard of before, staged a military coup. The rationale for this coup was that corrupt politicians were endangering national security. Park was not the most senior military officer and was a graduate of the Japanese Military Academy, which was despised by the population. Another serious flaw in his past was that he was, at one time, a member of the South Korean Communist Party although he later became an effective Communist hunter. After the liberation of Korea from Japan, many Korean intellectuals joined the Communist Party because the USSR was the only country that supported Korean independence movement against Japan. The U.S. made a secret agreement with Japan not to interfere in Japanese expansionism provided that Japan does not try to take over the U.S. colony, the Philippines. The UK had a similar agreement with Japan vis-à-vis Hong Kong.

His rise as the leader of the coup stems from a support of a whole class of young colonels he taught at the Korean Military Academy years ago. They saw in him a man who could change the culture of corruption which permeated the top echelon of the military and the government. Koreans at that time were extremely distressed with the future of the country and angry with its political leaders. Park was a short man with a farmer's face (gaunt and dark) but he was tough and disciplined teacher at the Military Academy, He used to lead young cadets on all day marches. In one such drill, a cadet died from heatstroke. Park was expelled from the Academy because of this incident, but the cadets developed a grudging respect for Park not only because he was a tough taskmaster but also because he was patriotic and knew his military arts. Later, as a general in charge of a combat division, he also gained the respect of young officers because he lived an austere lifestyle rather than skimming off the military budget to support his lifestyle, which was common among generals at that time. This was at a time when a general's salary was a sack of rice.

After the coup, Park's first action was to declare martial law and arrest and execute some notorious gangsters who were used by the former regime. They switched ballot boxes and intimidated voters. Lesser gangsters were rounded up and sent to the Cheju Island to build a highway. Just after the revolution, the military police made sure that no one jaywalked, which was a norm rather than an exception at that time. The people immediately realized that this was not business as usual. Park demanded punctuality and he got it. He then began to clean up corruption in the bureaucracy. That was a process, took a long time and could not be accomplished completely. Corruption has many faces. In South Korea, the salaries of civil servants were so low that a really honest person would starve. Corruption has many faces. In poor countries, the salaries of civil servants are so low that a really honest person would starve. Park admitted that there was widespread corruption in his administration and he raised the salaries of civil servants at a much higher rate than the inflation rate. At the same time, he fired high ranking civil servants living much beyond their means. There was no trial or due process of law. Prima facie evidence was good enough for him. He would say to his top aides or ministers suspected of corruption, "Why do you not retire. I understand you are a wealthy man." The culture of South Korea began to change.

Park, now an undisputed strongman, took the highly unpopular move of trying to normalize diplomatic relations with Japan which the people and the National Assembly objected to very bitterly. Nationwide demonstrations were staged against normalization unless Japan apologized for its past wrong-doings first, which Japan did not do. Massive demonstrations raged in university campuses and city streets and went on for months. Any democratic leader would have given up on the idea of normalization, but Park declared martial law to control the demonstrators. He believed that the South Korean economy cannot be revived without trade with, and investments from, Japan. Eventually, he rammed through the normalization legislation. Enlightened dictatorship has a role to play in developing economies where the people are bottled in irrational hatred or self-defeating behaviors. In the short term, $800 million in economic aid was at stake. The normalization eventually helped both countries, particularly South Korea. Park's first Five Year Economic Development Plan (1962–1966) was successfully implemented. The GDP grew at a double-digit rate (in U.S. dollars).

Park, a student of Japanese history, followed the patterns of Japanese economic development. South Korea manufactured and exported labor-intensive goods first (such as textile, garments, toys and wigs). This was also the recommendation of Walter Rostow, the economic and security adviser to President John F. Kennedy and Lyndon Johnson, and the author of widely read book: *The Stages of Economic Growth*. What South Korea had in abundance at that time was a cheap but trainable labor force just like China was in the 1970s. The Confucian tradition emphasized education above money or other worldly possessions. Some business men who started the textile industry and other small businesses succeeded and became *chaebol* (rich and family-owned conglomerates). They were not created by Park as some accused Park of doing so.[2] In fact, right after his coup, Park arrested several *chaebol* leaders for collusion with the former government but he realized that the country needed them if the government's ambitious plans to modernize the economy were to succeed. Capitalism certainly required capitalists.

Later, Park supported those *chaebols* that implemented his ambitious economic development projects. These *chaebols* included Chung Ju-yong (the founder of the Hyundai group), Kim Woo-chung (the founder of the Daewoo Group), Lee Byung-chull (the founder of the Samsung Group) and others who were small businessmen at that time but business savvy and willing to collaborate with government plans. Kim Woo-chung once said that "Daewoo is not my company. It is a government company." This was true because if the government cut off credit lines, the group would collapse "overnight". All *chaebols* became big by following the government's five-year economic development plan. The plan was prepared by the Economic Planning Board and had specific priority investment lists, which were necessary at different stages of economic development. This was a guided capitalism but worked well for South Korea at the time when the private sector was in its infancy. The government would arrange bank loans to the companies willing and capable to undertake such ventures. None of these companies were owned by Park's relatives or cronies although some of his followers misused their office. He personally listened to the difficulties that businessmen faced in exporting and dealing with government bureaucracy. He took care of such problems and all the bureaucrats knew that the businessmen had the ears of the President.

The government undertook some industrial development projects directly. In 1969, it created the Pohang Iron and Steel Company (POSCO). Many foreign countries and businesses were skeptical of Park's decision to invest in a million ton steel plant when there was a global overcapacity. Park, however, went ahead. The construction of the first steel plant began in 1969, and steel rolled out merely three years after ground breaking. This company was privatized later but at the time, observers could not have imagined that POSCO would produce over 30 million tons of crude steel in 2004. It was the 2nd largest steel company in the world in 2007 with plants in South Korea, China, the U.S. (USS-POSCO),

---

2. See *The Origins and Development of Chaebol, South Korea"* Library of Congress, June 1990.

Mexico, etc. He has an ambitious project plan in India. It is one of rare foreign companies in which Warren Buffet invested heavily.

Why this public enterprise succeeded, while other steel companies owned by governments in other countries failed, provides a valuable lesson. The key to the success of a company is accountability. Most public enterprises do not have an "owner" in its true sense. Most politicians exploit such enterprises for their personal gains, but Park made the POSCO accountable to him as much as any business owners would. He went even further and prevented labor organizations from making excessive wage demands. However, it did not take long for most POSCO workers to enjoy the fruits of their patience. They received high wages, generous fringe benefits and stock options. Over the long run, POSCO workers have gotten far more out of their expanding company than they would have if they had joined a strong union at the outset and starved the company to the bare bones.

In 1973, Park launched the construction of the 428 km Seoul-Busan expressway through rugged mountains and rivers entirely for which Korea is famous for. All large and medium-size South Korean companies participated in the construction since the World Bank was not interested in funding such an "unnecessary" project. Korean construction companies lacked experience in executing that size of construction, but they exceeded everyone's expectation in speed and cost savings. As a result of this experience, South Korean construction companies later built ports, roads, dams, hospitals and houses in the Middle East and South East Asia in record time and low cost. The expressway project was like a battle ground just as the POSCO project was. The construction offices were open 24/7 practically all year round. The construction was completed in a mere two and a half years. The Hyundai Construction Company, the mother company of the Hyundai Group, completed the longest segment of the expressway over most difficult terrains. Chairman Chung Ju Yong used to be on the job site by 6 o'clock in the morning, kicking his engineers' shin for maximum pains for any delay or mistake. The Company went on to become one of the largest construction companies in the world and received large contracts during the Middle East construction boom and during the first oil "shoku". This brought in dollars when South Korea needed them badly to import oil.

Hyundai went on to diversify from construction to car manufacturing, shipbuilding, electronics, etc. From the point of view of the government, Hyundai was a chess piece in a drive to steer the Korean economy to heavy and chemical industries, which Park saw as the only way for South Korea to leap forward. The Korean conglomerates were not many but they competed fiercely in domestic and international markets, underbidding each other. When the Hyundai Group (heavy industries and construction) got $1 billion dollar contract to build industrial port of Jubail. There was a hue and cry from established Western companies that Hyundai was not qualified for the highly technical work and the company would go bankrupt because its contracted price was ridiculously low. This held up the award of construction for many months but Hyundai proved them wrong by completing project ahead of schedule. It did so by assembling the underwater structures at Hyundai's Ulsan shipyard and towing them all the way to Saudi Arabia rather than assembling them underwater on site. This is something that engineering graduates could not imagine but Chung was an elementary school graduate who succeeded in business by using his wits and common sense. He was partly lucky at that time because there were no big storm to knock off a fleet of ships carrying the giants structures.

Not all strongmen are good for the country but Park was. He had many enemies but none accused him of stuffing his pockets with money during his 18 years in power. He left very little other than a small condominium unit to his daughter when he was assassinated in 1979. By this time, his wife was already assassinated by a Communist agent.

Park's little-known accomplishment in the West is that he launched a nationwide program for rural development, known as *Saemaul Undong*. This movement is well known in Southeast Asia and other less developed countries of the world. In most developing countries, relatively opulent cities and an impoverished countryside were and still are a big social problem. China is facing such a problem at the moment. In 1971 in South Korea, an average farm household earned 61 percent of the average urban household income. He grew up in a farm like most Koreans of his age. His heart was there as much as in industrialization.

It started as an an experiment rather than a blueprint plan. In planning jargon, it was a process. In 1971, the government delivered 335 bags of cement and reinforcement steel bars to each of its 34,665 villages to keep farmers busy during winter. This was a government gift, and Park asked farmers to keep busy even during off-season and improve their villages including their houses according to their own plans and designs. Each village came up with different ways of using the materials. Some built a common laundry areas, common compost areas, small bridges, other minor infrastructure improvements (roads, irrigation and drainage structures), meeting halls, etc. Some villages did not make use of the materials and the government gift went to waste. The following year, the government ignored those villages which did not make efficient use of the building materials but provided more aid for those villages which did. This is just the opposite of what governments and international organizations usually do: give to those who have failed. Villages got the message. The villagers learned that consensus on how to use such materials was important. This called for meetings to decide priorities and leadership if they were to improve village infrastructure and other community projects. Thus competition started among the villages and every village tried to succeed.

Later, the government provided loans to farmers to improve their homes. Thatched roofs were replaced with tile or tin roofs. Kitchens and toilets were improved. The loans were also used to create income-boosting s. One of the more common projects was to build vinyl greenhouses, which enabled growing fruits and vegetables during the winter. Instead of drinking rice wine and playing card games all winter, the farmers were now busy making money. When government money is used to put idle labor to work, it is money well spent rather than subsidizing the people to stay lazy or unemployed. The loans to the farmers for income-boosting projects were at a concessionary bank rate, but export industries received low interest loans also. At that time, all bank loans were kept much lower than the "curb market" or black market interest rates.

The program was so successful in initial years that four years into *Saemaul Undong*, the average farm household income exceeded that of urban households. This did not last very long. On a longer term, the rural and urban income gap was reduced considerably but not closed completely. Despite the success of the *Saemaul Undong* for 20 years or so, the program was phased out as a result of financial scandals and politicization of the program during the next administration. A corrupt leader—his immediate family member in this case—could always find a way to corrupt a worthy program for political and personal purposes. During an election season, the government forgave all the loans in spite of the fact that most framers were capable of paying back the loans. What started as a successful self-help program turned into a government handout program.

Park's strategy of entering into heavy and chemical industries turned out to be much tougher than Park anticipated and took South Korea to the brink of financial disaster. This was partly because of external economic conditions and partly because of over ambitiousness. Losses in some such ventures were heavy. A small current account surplus in 1977 turned into a huge deficit in 1978, which kept on growing in 1979 to 8% of GDP. It was amid such gloom and doom that Park was assassinated in 1979. The year 1980 was also a bad year in economic terms. The global economy as a whole suffered from another oil shock. South Korea imports 100% of oil from abroad. A recession hit the U.S. as well as South Korea. There were serious doubts as to whether the ambitious ventures that Park launched were the right strategy because the current account deficit kept increasing. South Korea cannot print U.S. dollars. Therefore, when its creditworthiness is in doubt and the country incurs sustained current account deficits, there is no money to import goods and services.

The per capita GNI of South Korea under Park, however, increased from $110 in 1962 to $1,620 in 1979. The per capita GNI growth rate during the 17 year period was 17.1% per annum in US$ dollar. It had a higher per capita income growth rate than China in the post-Mao era. Exports of goods and services almost reached $20 billion from $126 million in 1960. Park's legacy is, however, highly controversial today. He won earlier elections fair and square but, in his later election, he defeated Kim Dae-jung by a slim margin. Park decided to make a constitutional revision so make sure that Leftist and "pro-North Korean" Kim did not win the next election. The constitutional revision favored the incumbent. He was reelected in 1978 under the new constitution but the legitimacy of the new constitution was widely questioned. Only a year later Park was tragically assassinated during a dinner party by his trusted intelligence chief because of political infighting between his intelligence chief and his Secret Service chief. Most South Koreans are grateful to Park's accomplishment but many South Koreans, particularly from his opposition stronghold (southwestern provinces), do not share the view.

Park's Successors and Democracy

The two successors to Park, Chun Doo Hwan (1980–1988) and Roh Tae-Woo (1988–1993), were also military generals and from the same province. Chun grabbed power by a military coup although he stood for an election two years later. He suppressed an opposition uprising in the opposition stronghold of Guwanju by gunning down several hundred demonstrators. But the Korean economy did well under Chun. He followed Park's policies and took tentative steps toward liberalizing international trade and permitting labor unions. Roh Tae-Woo was Chun's right hand man and was the commander of a parachute division which suppressed the Guwanju uprising by guns. Yet he was elected to president in 1988 by the overwhelming support from his stronghold, southeastern provinces. Roh further advanced labor movements and democracy.

The GNI per capita grew at the rate of 12% between 1979 and 1997, which is remarkable by any standard. Between 1970 and 2005, the GNI per capita grew at the rate of 12.3%. Roh allowed labor unions to grow by leaps and bounds. As a result, labor disputes escalated enormously. South Korean labor unions behaved more like German labor unions than Japanese labor unions.

The first opposition leader Kim Yong Sam, ideologically center right, was the first civilian president (1993–98) since 1961. He accelerated globalization and democracy movement. He had the misfortune of having to deal with Clinton's appeasement policy toward Kim IL Sung and later his son Kim Jong IL, known as Framework Agreement. President Kim Yong Sam of South Korea committed to pay for the construction of two nuclear power plants in North Korea. By then, South Korea had several nuclear power plants based on the U.S. technology. This technology unlike the Soviet nuclear power plants—such as the ones being built in Iran now—makes it very difficult to extract plutonium for making bombs.

Another lifelong opposition leader Kim Dae-jung, with a left-leaning ideology, followed Kim Yong Sam. He was elected with only 40 % of the popular votes. It was the first time South Koreans chose a center-left president. Kim took office amid the deepening Asian Financial Crisis and it preoccupied his presidency in the first 2 to 3 years. It bankrupted Kia Motors in 1997 and spread to the Halla Group, the Daewoo Group and other corporations and banks. It appeared that 35 years of economic progress was unraveling within a year. The Asian Financial Crisis originated from Russian defaults and the Thailand financial crisis, but South Korea put itself in a vulnerable position because the current account balance turned negative in 1990 and the deficit kept on increasing to $23 billion in 1996. These were large amounts given the size of the South Korean GDP. Asian countries were unaccustomed to currency crises that have afflicted many Latin American countries. By this time, South Korea had little alternative but to accept IMF loans because country had squandered all the foreign exchange reserve in defending an unrealistic exchange rate.

South Korea, therefore, swallowed the bitter pills that IMF prescribed, and carried out economic and fiscal reforms that fell corporations and banks. Some of them were saved by mergers and foreign acquisitions. Hyundai Motors acquired Kia Motors and General Motors bought the Daewoo Motors. Some large banks merged with other banks with stronger balance sheets and other were acquired by foreign banks. South Korea recovered from the financial crisis relatively quickly compared with some other Asian countries and resumed growth in 1999. There is a saying "What does not kill you will make you stronger". This was also the case with South Korea. The financial crisis was painful and some companies never recovered from it but the IMF imposed reforms sent an important message that the government would not bail out large corporations from their mismanagement.

Under Kim Dae-jung, labor unions and their members gained more power and money. Still, the number of labor disputes went up sharply. Labor demands had no direct relation to productivity gains. "Foreign investors have said that Korea's inflexible labor market is one of the main obstacles to investing in Korea, more so than the North Korean nuclear issues."[3] In spite of such gains, labor leaders complained, "The government says the economy is successful. But only a few benefit from the economy. There is nothing in it for us."[4] Korean labor groups alleged that South Korea had the greatest inequity between the rich and the poor and the gap was widening. These are all blatant lies. According to the the Gini index published occasionally by World Bank, South Korea had more even distribution of incomes than India, Malaysia, the UK or the U.S.[5]

The successful presidential candidacy of center-left Roh Moo-hyun (a human-rights lawyer) handpicked by Kim Dae-jung in 2002 surprised many Koreans. His candidacy was helped by those who missed out on the previous economic boom, and which was closely aligned with the U.S. lost the election as a result of this. The new center-left government has been pursuing an appeasement policy toward North Korea to the disappointment of the Bush Administration. This acquittal gave the leftist and young voters the ammunition that they needed to say that Americans are arrogant and racists. The conservative Grand National Party (GNP) closely aligned with the U.S. lost the election as a result of this. The new center-left government is not cooperating fully with the U.S. on the North Korean nuclear issue.

In 2002, South Korean tax burden, including social security taxes, as a percentage of GDP, caught up with the U.S. but were higher than that of Ireland or Japan. South Korea has national health care, and its burden on the economy has been also rising rapidly. These center-left governments have been pouring money into North Korea for humanitarian and economic assistance. This controversial policy was initiated by Kim Dae-jung and was called the Sunshine Policy. Under the policy, South Korea has been providing a generous amount of food, fertilizer and cash to the North (billions of dollars in private and government cash transfers). The objective was to open North Korea as Nixon opened China. It did but at a low level and without any appreciable relaxation in tension. The policy may have even helped expedite the North Korea's nuclear weapons program. Meanwhile, North Koreans are still starving. For "security" reason, the bags of rice and

---

3.   Florence Lowe-Lee, "Improving Labor Market Flexibility, A Key to Economic Success", Korean Economic Institute 5.8 (2003).

4.   See "South Korean Cultural Ecology"

5.   Gini coefficient for South Korea was 31.6 in 1993 compared with 37.8 for India in 1997, 48.5 for Malaysia in 1995, 37.1 for UK in 1991, and 40.8 for the U.S. in 1997. The higher the index, the larger is the disparity among income groups.

fertilizers were carried by North Korean ships and have no marking indicating that it came from the South.

Roh more or less followed Kim's Sunshine policy under a different name. South Korea is now a reluctant partner in enforcing the UN sanction against North Korea. North Korea has threatened that the South would pay "a high price" if it collaborated with the U.S.-led sanction against the North. Previously, it has threatened to turn the South into a sea of fire. This is possible even without the use of nuclear bombs because some 20 million South Koreans live within the range of the North's long-range artillery. South Koreans are afraid that the mad dog Kim Jong Il is capable of starting another war. The on-again-off-again six-party negotiations seem to have gained momentum after the UN sanction froze North Korean bank accounts in Macao. Kim obviously needs the money badly and is also weighing the relative benefits of selling its weapons to rogue states or terrorists vs. wheedling as much money as possible from the U.S., South Korea and Japan. A pitfall in dealing with Kim is that the U.S. will not be able to monitor his nuclear program unless IAEA inspectors gain an unrestricted access to all parts of North Korea.

Between 2000 and 2005, the South Korea's per capita GNI in U.S. dollar grew at the rate of 10% per annum—using the World Bank's Atlas method of adjusting foreign exchange rates. Such a high rate of growth was partly because of the strength of Korean Won after the Asian Financial Crisis and partly because of the rapid growth of the Korean economy. Some of its corporations are now world class companies such as Samsung Electronics (now larger than Sony Corporation), POSCO (a steel industry leader), Hyundai-Kia Motors (9th largest producer in the world in 2005–2006 with an ambitious expansion plan) and the shipbuilding industry which is ranked #1 in the world with Japan closely behind it and China emerging as # 3 out of nowhere. The investments in heavy industries that Park started to make have been gaining strength year over year after a shaky start. The economic boom in China is also fueling the South Korean economy. Labor unions are still militant and the work ethic has been deteriorating. However globalization is putting a lids over the demands of militant labor unions.

There were times when South Koreans feared to open its market but no longer. Even the center-left ruling party has become a free trader. This reflects the shift in the public opinion. According to a survey in May 2002—sponsored jointly by *The Korea Times* and research institutions—South Koreans supported redistribution over growth by a margin of 73% against 27% but in December

2004 they chose growth over redistribution by 52% against 48%.[6] This is a swing of 25% in 2 ½ years on such a fundamental issue.

Since 2004, South Korea has been all out making free trade agreements (FTA) with different countries. Chile in 2004 was the first but it was followed by Singapore in 2005, the nine member Association of Southeast Asian Nations (ASEAN) in June 2007. South Korea inked the Korean-U.S. trade agreement (KORUS) with U.S. Trade Representative Susan Schwab in July 2007. Immediately thereafter, China showed interest in FTA with South Korea. "The European Union, Canada, Australia, New Zealand and the Gulf Cooperation Council are next on Seoul's FTA target list." according to Stratfor's article, "Free Trade as a Key to South Korean Aspirations" 7/5/2007. South Korea now wants to become another Singapore rather than another Japan. This is a right move at this stage of South Korea's economic development. Japan has hung on to protectionism too long. It is still making little progress with FTA partly because of the stubborn protectionist sentiment within.

---

6.   "52% of the People Choose Growth Over Redistribution," *The Korea Times*; January 27, 2005.

Chapter 14

Malaysia: Islam and Secularism

Focus

Malaysia is a multi-racial country with a delicate balance of Malay Muslims and non-Muslim populations, mostly the Chinese. The Malays and other indigenous groups, mostly Muslims, comprise 58% of the population; the Chinese 24%; and Indians, mostly Hindus, 8%; and other races, 10%. The relationship between the Malay Muslims and the Chinese has been volatile. What makes the situation worse was the income disparity between the two groups. There are lessons in how they have resolved the problems and achieve remarkable respectable economic progress.

Ethnic Conflict and the New Economic Policy

Malaysia was a British colony as Singapore was. They together were known as Malaya at the time. Malaysia today consists of Peninsular or West Malaysia and East Malaysia (the northern part of Borneo Island). The two parts of Malaysia are separated by 400 miles of South China Sea. With a population of 23.5 million people (2003) in an area of 328,550 sq km, it is sparsely populated by Asian standards. Malaya became valuable to Britain when large deposits of tin were found on the peninsula. It later became the leading producer of tin, latex rubber and more lately palm oil. To mine tin and tap rubber trees, the British brought in a large number of indentured laborers from China and India. In the process, the British created a complex multiracial country, which did not mix well. At times, it was thick with racial tension. Each ethnic group has maintained its own language, religion and culture.

Over time, the Chinese became almost as large as the Malay population in in Peninsular Malaysia. More significantly, they have come to control the commerce and industry. If there is any doubt whether one race is superior in making money over other races, one needs to go no further than the Chinese communities in Southeast Asia (Malaysia, Thailand, Indonesia and the Philippines). They are minorities in these countries but they have become far more affluent than native populations. From the point of view of the Malays in Malaysia, the Chinese, formerly indentured laborers and their descendants, were taking over their country. The underlying tension erupted into a racial riot in May 1969 when the Chinese-dominated Democratic Action Party (DAP) scored well in the Parliamentary election in Peninsular Malaysia and had a boisterous celebration. The Malays reacted violently. An official account indicates that 196 were killed and 439 injured. Most of the killed were Chinese. The police, predominantly Malays, are said to have arrived at the scene of riots and intervened on behalf of the Malays. What followed the riot was a national debate on the root cause of the riot and the government concluded that the deeper cause of the riots was the economic imbalance between the Malays and the Chinese.

This led to the formulation of the New Economic Policy (NEP) in 1972–73. It provided a plan and a target for giving Bumiputra (indigenous people) a higher share of the economy. The NEP decided that Bumiputra (consisting mostly of the Malay and some other indigenous groups) should have at least 30 percent ownership of the economy within one generation. Dr. Mahathir Mohammad, who at the time of the 1969 incident was a young and radical member of the ruling United Malays National Organization (UMNO) ed up providing intellectual rationale for the NEP. During his banishment from UMNO for his defiance against UMNO bosses, Mahathir wrote a controversial book, *Malay Dilemma*. Its main argument is that Malays could not compete with the Chinese on an equal basis because of genetic and cultural reasons. Mahathir practiced medicine before turning into a politician. This is the first known book written by a person to insist that his race is <u>genetically</u> inferior. Mahathir then went on to argue in his book that Malays needed special protection and privileges to even the playing field. Perhaps this argument is similar to the argument for Affirmative Action although African Americans believe that it is not the gene but the history of slavery.

Mahathir's book was banned in Malaysia, but the NEP was his vindication. He eventually became the Prime Minister of Malaysia and served in that capacity for 22 years. As a prime minister, he was not as radical as most people feared that he might become. The NEP was, however, controversial among Chinese Malaysians. But an important detail that saved the NEP was that its objectives were to be achieved through economic growth, not by the redistribution of existing wealth or business ownership that was in the hands of the Chinese. That distinguishes the NEP from Marxism or the Rhodesian policy of appropriating plantations owned by the whites and distributing them to the native population.

Furthermore, the NEP embraced a credible economic development strategy. Among other things, the Malaysian economic policy was to shift from import substitution to export promotion.

Various new incentives were introduced to attract export industries such as electronics industry and other multi-national corporations (MNCs). [1] The strategy was successful in attracting many Japanese MNCs in search of cheap labor and business-friendly countries rather than American firms which Malaysia targeted initially. Export processing industries grew rapidly in the 1970s.

Malays and Islam

I was briefed at some length about the racial tension and government policies when I took a consulting assignment to Malaysia. I ended up learning a lot about the Islam as well as ethnic tension. My first assignment was in the east coast of Peninsular Malaysia as a public finance specialist. During my field trip to an agricultural development project area, I came to a government sponsored land development scheme, owned cooperatively by workers (known as settlers) and managed by a government agency, the Federal Land Development Authority (FELDA). Each settler owned 10 acres and worked collectively under the management of FELDA. This agency was the largest land owner or manager of agricultural land in Malaysia. Each FELDA scheme had a village surrounded by 5,000 acres oil palm trees. Outside the plantation area is usually jungle. In one of such a scheme, I met a very beautiful Japanese girl in her twenties.

She worked for a Japanese Peace Corps-like agency and had been working and living in the village alone (without any Japanese colleague) for several months. Her house was a typical farmer's house, a wood frame on stilts. It was hard for me to imagine such a young woman living alone safely among villagers surrounded by jungle and palm trees. But I realized later that she was much safer there than in any place else in the world. The Malays are devout Sunni Muslims, closer to fundamentalist Christians than any other group that I can think of. Muslims believed that Jesus was a prophet—therefore to be respected—but that Prophet Muhammad was the last prophet. Malay Muslims lived, by and large, a clean life. They usually do not take alcoholic beverage and they obey the Islamic laws

---

1.   See Jomo K. S., Chen Yun Chung, Brian C. Folk, Irfan Ul-Haque, Pasuk Phongpai-chit, Batara Simatupang and Mayuri Tateishi, Southeast Asia's Misunderstood Miracle: Industrial Policy and Economic Development in Thailand, Malaysia and Indonesia (1997) p.98.

(sharia) as well as secular laws. There was no case of a Muslim trying to kill infidels just because they are infidels.

Malaysia is harsh against drug traffickers as Singapore is. This was not a country for pot-smoking hippies during the '60s and '70s. I developed a healthy respect for the Malays Muslims who fasted from sunrise to sundown and abstained from smoking and sex during the whole month of Ramadan. The religious police patrolled the streets during Ramadan to make sure that Muslims observed fasting in public places. Islam requires its followers to be obedient and submit to the will of God. The enforcement of Islamic law is, however, a state matter in Malaysia and is applied to Muslims only because Malaysia is nor an Islamic state. An incident within a month of my arrival in Malaysia, however, taught me what it means to be a Muslim in Malaysia. A Malay widow was romantically involved with a representative of the UN High Commission for Refugees in the town of Trengganu, a conservative north eastern state in Peninsular Malaysia. His job was to take care of Vietnamese refugees arriving in Malaysia by the hundreds on boats.

One day he was given notice to leave Malaysia within two days because of his relationship with a Muslim widow. No proof of sex was necessary because close proximity (*kalwat*) was a sufficient ground for the action. Under such law, a woman or girl who comes in close physical proximity with a man must marry the man. Otherwise the woman is jailed although not beheaded like in Saudi Arabia under the Wahabbi religious law. The UN staff, a non-Muslim, could have married the woman but he could not do so without first converting to Muslim. It is customary under such a circumstances that the infidel is simply ordered to leave the country in order for the woman not to be jailed.

I could not believe that this was happening on the planet earth in 1976. I was also curious as to how such a demanding religion came to have 1.5 billion followers all over the world although there are differences in the ways Muslims practice their religion depending on the country. One important reason is that once a king or a ruler converted to Islam, all his subjects were forced to adopt the Islam. The Arabic word Islam means the submission or surrender of one's will to Allah. This brings out a fundamental difference between the Koran and the Bible. According to the Bible, God gave the man the commandments to follow but also gave a "free will" at the same time. God would account for the sins of a man on the day of judgment. This is not so in the Islam. The Muslims, by and large, do not have the choice and do not have freedom to convert to other religions.

After three years, my new job took me to Kuala Lumpur (usually called KL) as the Chief Technical Advisor of a UNDP project. The new job was to advise the

Ministry of Land and Regional Development. An interesting person I met in the job was Tan Sri Dato Seri Radin Soenarno, the Secretary General of the Ministry. Tan Sri is the highest title that the Government of Malaysia confers to a person, and Dato Seri is the highest title that a sultan of the state of Perak, where he once served as Chief Secretary, confers to a person. A sultan is the titular head of a state but also has real powers such as executing religious laws and order any person including a federal civil servant to leave the state. Sultans take turn to serve as the King of Malaysia. Radin (his proper name) is the most interesting Muslim intellectual I met in Malaysia. He is a historian by training and a devout Muslim. His B.A. thesis entitled "Malay Nationalism" is a required reading for Malaysian civil servants although he wrote it as a Bachelor of Science thesis. He later received his graduate degree in development economics from the University of Pittsburgh.

There are many well-educated Malays like him in Malaysia, but he is somewhat different from most of them. He was able to distance himself from the current politics and government policies and see the situation from the point of view of a historian. Radin's views were often unorthodox. While he was the chief economic adviser to the Prime Minister Mahathir, he did not agree with Mahathir's *Malay Dilemma*. I expected an intellectual like him to be less pious, but I was wrong. He prays, does not drink and observes fasting. All good Muslims are supposed to be fundamentalist Muslims and he was. But this is not to be confused with militant Muslims.

UN advisors including myself joined an advisory committee where all the national policy papers submitted for inter-departmental comments and eventually to the cabinet were reviewed for the department's comments. This was a very unusual practice. Radin was fond of discussing almost any national or international topics. Neither he nor any other Muslim tried to "sell" or rationalize their faith to me. I found this also true in Indonesia. He had a tolerant view of other religions and cultures and sent me a Christmas card although I was not a church-going Christian at that time. He later moved up to become the Director General of the Economic Planning Unit (EPU). Most Malaysians resent the arrogance of the white people. When I visited Radin in the late 1980s at EPU on a mission representing ADB, I wore a white shirt, a tie and a jacket—somewhat unnatural in a tropical country—although I used to wear a bush jacket or batik shirt when I worked in Malaysia. He told me jokingly, "We think the people who dress like come to Malaysia to rip us off." EPU was the final authority in approving development projects and borrowing money for project financing. Naturally, many bankers and representatives of engineering firms went there for information and negotiations.

Mahathir is a Malay intellectual who despises and rejects the Western culture. On June 20, 2003, he said that Europeans including "those who migrated and set up new nations in America, Australia and New Zealand" wanted to impose a global culture that includes unlimited freedoms and "the practice of free sex, including sodomy, as a right…. Marriage between male and male, female and female are officially recognized by Them. What we regard as incest is not regarded as serious by them. The culture and the values which they will force us to accept will be hedonism, unlimited quest for pleasure, the satisfaction of base desires, particularly sexual desires."[2] Many Malay Muslims are tempted by Western sins but they do not respect the Western values and cultures. The West is "unclean" and evil. They do not want the infidels to "pollute" their faith.

Radin had a mixed feeling about democracy for developing countries. When he returned from an official visit to Taiwan, I asked him what he had learned. He said that a Taiwanese official said that the only way to rule the unruly Chinese was with an iron grip. This would be also true in Singapore. Its government uses iron hands with velvet gloves. China uses a rope to plant fears to the disobedient. Malaysian civil servants, who are mostly the Malays, are well educated compared with their rural counterparts. They are well paid and are not corrupt. The government is seen as the protector of the Malays against the more money-smart Chinese. Radin, however, did not believe in the genetic inferiority of the Malay, which is the premise of Dr. Mohamed Mahathir's *Malay Dilemma*.

The thrust of the NEP was for the government to invest in trust for the Bumiputra in land development, agro-businesses and industries, sometimes in joint ventures with Chinese Malaysian owned companies. The government also used petroleum revenues, from the offshore oilfields developed in the mid-1970s, for this purpose. The government also made investments in heavy and chemical industries, patterned after the South Korean strategy of developing automobile, steel and petrochemical. Malaysia had a mixed success. Even to its supporter, the progress was too slow and financial losses were too heavy. This was particularly true of its venture into steel production. That venture failed economically and financially. [3] This was particularly painful for Malaysia during the Asian Financial Crisis (1998–2001) when Malaysia's GDP declined. During the financial crisis, the NEP was accused of causing the depreciation of the Malaysian currency. Mahathir moaned one day, "All the economic progress for Malays brought about

---

2.   See The Age.com

by the NEP and other efforts stalled."[4] The economy has, however, recovered since then. For the entire 1990s, the economy grew by 7.5% per year, very impressive considering the situation affecting Malaysia as well as much of Asia.

An economic strategy that worked well in the mid-1980s was to depreciate the Ringgit, deregulate and privatize the economy and increase investment incentives. The small and medium scale manufacturing sector expanded rapidly. In 1990, the Malaysian Government declared that the NEP objectives had been achieved although the government has continued to pursue elements of these objectives under a different name. There is no longer a quantitative target for "restructuring the economy". In spite of the redistribution policies of the NEP, the Malaysian economy performed well because the restructuring objective was achieved from growth rather than redistribution of existing assets across ethnic communities. The continued development of natural resources, export-based agriculture (palm oil and rubber), electronics, textiles and other industries served the country well.[5] The Malaysian economic growth rate of 9.11% in US$ from 1960 to 2003 stands up well against most countries. The cost of living in Malaysia is low. Therefore, the GNI per capita in PPP of $9,512 in 2003 was almost two and half times that of the GNI per capita. It is one of better countries to live in for expatriates. Kuala Lumper is now a modern city with the two tallest twin towers in the world.

Lessons Learned

Malay Muslims and the Chinese have come to live together in relative peace and have achieved impressive economic growth. The key to this success has been economic growth. The people of different cultures and races have different abilities to succeed in the commerce and industry. The restructuring or redistribution policy that Malaysia has adopted is not as efficient as an unadulterated market economy. But in spite of it, the Malaysian economy has performed well because

---

3.   Heavy industries were expected to be long-term investments, but even by such a standard their performances have been disappointing. A number of these projects suffered heavy financial losses. The government had to shield the industries from international competition and subsidize capital. Perwaja Steel has been the worst and was riddled with corruption and considered unsalvageable. See GH Kok, "Mahathir's legacy: A trail of mistakes to avoid," malaysiakini.com reader; Dec 5, 2003

4.   March 17, 2000

5.   For fuller discussion, see John H. Drabble, *An Economic History of Malaysia, c.1800–1990: The Transition to Modern Economic Growth.* (2000).

of its abundant natural resources, correct macro-economic policies and economic reforms. Malaysia decided to keep the nation together rather than achieve a higher economic growth rate by using a winner-take-all policy. Rapid economic growth is a necessary condition for such a policy to succeed because no nation can have genuine peace if redistribution means taking wealth from one group to give it to another.

Chapter 15

Philippines: Democracy and Mediocrity

Focus

Just after World War II, the Philippines had a higher per capita income than Japan. Even in the 1960s, its per capita income was well ahead other Asian countries. It has now slipped behind Thailand. The people are keenly aware that their country has been falling behind their Asian neighbors. In 1994, the World Bank estimated that 41% of the population was poor.[1] Most do not have access to safe piped water and proper sanitation. A large proportion of the population lives in squatter settlements and slums. The per capita GDP-PPP in constant international dollar declined between 1980 and 2003 while that of other Asian countries more than doubled. This means that, when the cost of living and inflation are factored in, the Filipinos have become worse off during the past 23 years.

A high incidence of crime, kidnapping, Muslim terrorists and corruption at high places frustrate the population as much as the poverty. What should a country like do to get out of poverty and deteriorating living conditions?

Background

The Philippines had over 81 million people in 2003, and this over-populated island nation is still growing rapidly. Its population consists primarily of the Malay stock with a mixture of Chinese and Spanish descents. Spain colonized the country in the 16th century. The Philippines became part of the prize that the U.S. took from Spain in 1898 at the end of the Spanish-American War. The Spaniards brought the Catholic Church and today the Filipinos are overwhelm-

---

1. This is the percentage of the population living below the national poverty line. Those below the line do not have a sufficient income to take enough calories or enjoy other basic necessities such as shelter and medical care.

160

ingly Catholic. Islam was introduced to the southern islands of the Philippines around 1500 by traders from the Indonesian islands.

The Philippines was once an idyllic tropical country where the living conditions were good and the people were happier. Today the crime rate is extremely high and the unemployment rate has been climbing from 5% in 1980 to 10% in 2000. Good paying jobs are even scarcer. In large cities, a high proportion of workers is drivers, security guards and domestic workers. Security guards are necessary because there are too many criminals. Drivers are necessary because hiring a driver is relatively inexpensive but finding parking spaces and driving through congested city streets are incredibly difficult.

On July 15, 2004, the headline story of the daily newspaper, the *Philippine Star*, was "Gov't: Troop pullout begins." This was in reference to the decision of the Government of the Philippines to pull out a small Philippine humanitarian mission out of Iraq ahead of schedule to save the life of a truck driver who had been captured by terrorists and was being threatened with beheading unless the Philippines withdrew the 51-man contingent. In fact, the Philippines pulled out the contingent to save the life of the driver. Giving in to terrorist demands is very common in the Philippines. Interestingly, the July 15 issue of the *Star* had another telling front page story entitled "We'd rather die in Iraq than starve at home." The newspaper article said "Clutching a bag of used clothes, Edgardo Lumapas scampers under a makeshift tent outside a Manila recruitment agency promising jobs in Iraq despite a government ban after the kidnapping of a Filipino truck driver. [For him it was] a chance to earn up to $600 a month as forklift operator in Iraq." He was quoted as saying "We'd rather die in Iraq than die of hunger here in the Philippines." Without millions of Filipino overseas workers such as Lumapas who is willing to do the work that the Arabs, Japanese and Hong Kong Chinese are unwilling to do themselves, the Philippine economy would be in an even worse shape.

The ADB estimated he overseas contract workers (OCW) transmitted about $7.6 billion in 2003 alone, equivalent to 7.5 percent of the Philippines' GDP. There has been a steady exodus of Filipinos as maids, entertainers, nurses and engineers to make living overseas. This has been going on since the first oil shock in the 1970s, but the trend has accelerated in recent years. Even a medical school graduate who topped the medical board examination migrated to the U.S. as a nurse because he was making very little as a physician in the Philippines. This raised the ire of Filipino politicians. He is supposedly sending $500 a month to his family in the Philippines. There is no social safety net in the Philippines other than family. Even with such overseas workers' remittance, external debts have been climbing. The central government debt has been climbing. In 2003, it was 78% of the Philippine GDP compared with 19% in India. Debt services for these loans as percentage of GNI increased from 5% in 1970 to 12% in 2003. More borrowing whether from the World Bank, IMF or private banks has done little to boost the economy of the Philippines.

Causes of Failure

What is holding back the progress of he Philippine economy and social conditions? These are the main reasons:

1. the breakdown of law and order, particularly the inability to contain Islamic separatists and plain terrorists, and the failure to reduce kidnapping and other economic crimes;

2. the culture of corruption handed down from the days of former dictator Ferdinand Marcos and his cronies to the current bureaucrats, judges, military leaders and the general citizenry;

3. frequent labor strikes which make the Philippines an unreliable place for multi-nationals to invest in;

4. the Catholic Church which has not played a constructive role for the Philippines;

5. crony capitalism and the landed "aristocracy" created by land grants of the Spanish king;

6. gross mismanagement of the country after Aquino's power power revolution; and

7. the Philippine version of democracy copied from the U.S. system of democracy.

The seven points above require explanations. The percentage of managers surveyed who consider corruption as a major constraint was 35%.[2] This is the second highest in Asia after Indonesia, another country whose economy is lagging well behind other Asian countries. The corruption of the Philippine government officials including revenue collection officers is not just for survival but to live

---

2. See "Investment Climate Surveys", the World Bank, 2004.

large. The bribes paid to Indonesian government officials are shared by all persons in the department by fixed percentages. Too bad there is no equity in the distribution of bribes in the Philippines!

One cause of the lawlessness is the inability of the Philippine government to subdue Muslim rebels. Past administrations have tried to appease Islamic terrorists and separatists in the South but amnesties and treaties did not have lasting impacts. The government has been too quick to offer compromises. Total victory is one thing that the government has not tried. A state of lawlessness and terrorism has discouraged tourism and investments in the Philippines. Some economic crimes such as carjacking are reportedly committed by underpaid soldiers and policemen.

The Catholic Church has played a dubious role in the Philippines. Its practice of forgiving sins by confessing them to ordained priests ritualizes repentance and takes away individual responsibility. The rich and powerful Catholics in the Philippine keep mistresses and make money dishonestly without ever intending to stop the habits. They just hope that they will confess all their sins before they die. Another practice of the Catholic Church, established by Popes rather than the Bible, is to forbid any form of birth control. A high population growth rate per se is not a bad thing for growing economies but it is in a stagnant economy. The power of compounding is such that the population of the Philippines grew from 27 million in 1960 to 71 million in 2000. The country has not been able to provide jobs for the growing number of the population and poverty is widespread.

President Cory Aquino and her advisers, consisting most of human right lawyers, squandered the opportunity created by the People Power Revolution. When Marcos was deposed, the Filipinos thought that their troubles were over but they were far from over. The Aquino Administration did not seize the moment and fix the broken systems. Aquino's maiden name is Corazon Cojuangco, a rich and powerful Chinese-Filipino mixed blood clan from Talac province. She was sent to the U.S. after her grade school in the Philippines and returned to the Philippines radical surgery, not the human rights lawyers whose whole focus was to go after Marcos' money and legacy. The Philippine version of democracy and the due process of law did little for the Philippine economy and its fight against criminals, terrorists and corruption. The new government was indebted to the masses and the military that supported the Revolution. They took a populist politics: blame everything to Marcos

The Aquino Administration spent much of its energy and political capital on going after Marcos' ill-gotten wealth. It was rumored to be worth around $3 billion. She did not see any money returned during her administration. A vastly reduced amount was recovered two administrations later. Another obsession with Marcos corruption led to the mothballing of a $2.2 billion nuclear power plant which was practically complete and ready to generate 640 MW which the country needed badly. Aquino's expensive lawyers went after Westinghouse, which built the nuclear power plant, on the ground that it was "unsafe" and that Westinghouse bribed Marcos.

The lawyers could not prove any of these charges. Although Westinghouse paid a Saudi Arabian agency a commission to facilitate approval and it is a fair guess that a good part of the money went to Marcos, Westinghouse did not commit any crime. Mothballing the power plant only dealt a devastating blow to the floundering Philippine economy. The electricity shortage became ridiculously frequent and severe, and brownouts and voltage fluctuations went on throughout her administration. No industrial plant could operate properly under such a condition. Factories had to buy private generators. The next administration under General Fidel Ramos had to spend far more money to build inefficient power plants by Enron and others while the good one was and still is rusting away.

Economic growth and trickle down are necessary to reduce the level of poverty and corruption in poor countries. How can politicians, judges, military generals and civil servants live when their salaries do not even cover the basic requirements of life such as enough calorie intakes for their families. The government cannot afford to pay them more because the economy is weak and government revenue collection agencies are hopelessly corrupt. Bribery money is openly negotiated and passed at tax offices. It is a vicious cycle. The country is poor because of corruption but corruption cannot be reduced because the country is poor. There are other factors that hold back the Philippine economy as mentioned earlier in this chapter, e.g., crony capitalism and the landed "aristocracy". Because of these factors, the income distribution is skewed and wealth does not trickle down. Trickle down requires moral capitalism and competent law enforcement. But the Philippines does not have them, particularly the latter.

The failures of the Philippines are partly due to adopting the aspects of the American legal and political systems that are not appropriate for the Philippines. The Philippines is the only developing country in the world which has an equivalent of the U.S. Constitution's Fifth Amendment, i.e., not to incriminate oneself. It is a wrong thing to have for the Philippines which is infested with terrorists, separatists, racketeers, tax evaders and corrupt cops as well as common criminals. The Filipinos are quick to catch on to political correctness strict privacy law over bank accounts (more so than the U.S.) and aversion to nuclear power plants.

Corporate and individual bank accounts cannot be opened for routine tax evasion or criminal investigations unless the court authorizes it on very rare occasions. This happened only once in recent years during the investigation of Joseph Estrada's graft and corruption charges. Absolute financial privacy makes it almost impossible to prosecute economic criminals.

Even the privileged hates their government. Once I was invited to a Rotary Club lunch where Aquino's Secretary of Interior in charge of local governments and the police spoke. At the end of his spirited presentation on how the Aquino administration will make difference, a Rotarian stood up and said that the worst thing that the Filipino did was to fight for and get independence from the U.S. Everyone clapped. On another occasion, I was invited to speak at the National Conference of Philippine Planners which discussed, among other issues, the proposed constitution. Cory's proposed constitution prohibited the forced removal of squatters, even from railway and public road rights-of-way. The chairwoman of the 40-member committee drafting for the new constitution was in the meeting. I questioned her about whether this provision might not increase squatters. She did not think so. But the squatter policy did encourage further illegal occupation of land, which was bad enough even without a constitutional sanction. After the constitution was adopted, large areas owned by the government as future building sites, railway rights of ways and private properties were grabbed by thugs acting as professional squatter developers. They "developed" such land, put up shacks and collected rent from the real squatters. Squatters resisted any attempt by landowners to reclaim their land.

Law enforcement was so lax during the Aquino administration that dynamite fishing destroyed some of the most beautiful coral reefs in Southeast Asia. Illegal logging by her trusted cabinet secretaries, in cahoots with the military commanders, denuded mountainsides in some of the most scenic areas of the Philippines. This caused frequent flooding and killed fish life too. The Philippines needed a strong leader like Lee Kuan Yew or Park Chung Hee but Aquino had nothing in common with them.

The country had an educated population and ample access to development loans from international financial institutions. The problem has not been money, but rather its productive use. That cannot happen without extensive economic reforms. In 1991, the Philippines asked the Americans to move out of the Subic Bay Naval Base and the Clark Air Base because of national pride fanned by Leftists and anti-American elements. They blamed the bases for rampant prostitution although prostitution was widespread all over the country. Their base removal deprived the Philippines from the reliable flow of base rental money from the

U.S. and made the Philippines vulnerable to external threat such as the Chinese claim for the Spratly islands off the Philippine coast.

Aquino's successor Fidel Ramos was elected president in 1992 and served one 6-year term until 1998. He was a far better president than Aquino. He carried out some important reforms. He reduced tariffs, privatized state-owned industries, cut government expenditures, and tried to prosecute tax evaders. In addition, he provided incentives for foreign capitalists to invest into the Philippines, like Malaysia and Singapore did two decades earlier. He was only moderately successful in this because of internal and external problems. His administration still faced an unreliable supply of electricity, poor transportation and inadequate communications infrastructure. Although the security situation improved somewhat, this did not last after he left office. The New Constitution restricted a president to only one six-year term. This constitutional provision was to prevent another Marcos but it prevented Ramos to deepen the reforms he started and carry on with infrastructure development.

Under him, the GDP in US$ expanded at the rate of 10.4% per annum. In spite of this relatively robust GDP growth, the unemployment rate stayed high, falling only marginally from 9% in 1991 to 8% in 1995. However, there was some optimism that the Philippine economy was on the right track. Some believed that the vicious cycle of poverty would be broken, but this speculation was premature. Ramos' successor, Joseph Estrada, was a former film action star. Estrada promised to eradicate poverty and eliminate graft and corruption. On the wide screen, Estrada was always a "good guy" who fought for common people. Estrada had gained the reputation of being a compassionate person to the poor when he had served as a mayor earlier.

He turned out to be a crook and a gambling addict. He was corrupt and took huge kickbacks and kept them in secret bank accounts. He gambled all night, and kept several mistresses in palatial homes. The disappointed public ousted Estrada in January 2001 through yet another people power revolution. His vice president, Gloria Macapagal-Arroyo, an economist by training and a classmate of Bill Clinton, was sworn in as President in January 2001. Under her, modest economic growth and stability have returned, but she has been unable to make sweeping reforms which she said that the Philippines needed. She cannot do much other than hanging on to her precarious office of presidency because the ouster of Estrada which put her into the office of president was supported by the military and the Supreme Court. As an economist, she is far more aware than Aquino was on what the Philippines needs but she does not have the political capital to make necessary reforms.

Lessons

Democracy is not an answer for a country that requires massive reforms and where the masses are gullible and illiterate on economics. National security and law and order are necessary for economic and social development. Due process of law, particularly a version of the Fifth Amendment to the U.S. constitution that the Philippines adopted from the U.S. legal system, are luxuries for a country with massive corruption and crime problems. Corruption in various forms and in places including in revenue collection agencies has destroyed both social equity and government finance. A revolution can be a solution for a country such as this but not when the revolutionaries cannot take advantage of it to reform the country. Reforms require a strong leader with a vision and the support of the military power but the Philippines had no such leader.

Chapter 16

China: An Emerging Superpower

Focus

Since Deng Xiaoping opened the country in 1978 and steered it to capitalism, China has turned into the biggest economic phenomena in the last half century. The boom in China is having huge impacts all over the world. While the impacts have been largely positive, they have ominous implications also.

Losing China to Mao

The fall of China to the hands of Mao Zedong was a tragic event. It cost the country 30 years of misery and an estimated 40 million death. The State Department blamed the fall of China on Chiang's corrupt Army. MacArthur had a somewhat different take on what tilted China to Mao: "In China, Generalissimo Chiang Kai-shek was gradually pushing the Communists back, being largely aided and supplied by the United States ... Instead of pushing on to the victory, an armistice was arranged ... [by the State Department] and General [George C.] Marshall was sent to amalgamate the two components"[1] MacArthur remarked that age, and perhaps the war, had worn Marshall "down into a shadow of his former self." After months of fruitless negotiations, an indecisive Marshall withdrew. However, in this interval of seven months of negotiations, the Nationalists had received no munitions or supplies from the U.S., while the Soviets had reinforced Mao's Army. MacArthur spent most of his military career in Asia and he knew Asia better than anyone in State Department or the Department of Defense, which were dominated by military brass from the European theater of World War II. These Washington high ranking officials saw nothing valuable in Asia except Japan. Marshall's successor Dean Acheson did not once visit Asia

---

1. Douglas MacArthur, *Reminiscences* (New York, Toronto and London: McGraw-Hill Book Company, 1964) 320

even when the first blazing hot war during the Cold War was being fought in Korea.

Corruption was indeed everywhere in China after WWII. The national economy was in ruin and there was a hyperinflation in China, which resulted when the Chinese Nationalists relied on the printing press to finance the war. It was not difficult for Mao to discredit the Nationalists. "The monetary expansion was so severe that during World War II, Nationalist printing presses were unable to keep up, and Chinese currency printed in England had to be flown in over the Himalayas."[2] Between 1935 and 1949, prices rose more than a thousand fold. Yet, after the war, Washington had little interest in extending financial help to bail China out of hyperinflation. The Marshall Plan was the thing to do for Europe but not for Asia. Was racism a factor? No doubt about it. Was the U.S. wrong not to assist its WWII ally, China? The U.S. is not obliged to treat every WWII ally equally but the U.S. made winning the Cold War much harder than necessary when Nationalist China fell to Communists. The history of the Cold War would have been entirely different if the Nationalist China was saved.

MacArthur was not alone in seeing the situation differently than State Department. A young Congressman and a veteran of the Pacific War, John F. Kennedy, remarked that American aid would not be forthcoming unless a coalition government was formed was delivering a crippling blow to the Nationalist Government. He went on to say, "So concerned were our diplomats and their advisors with the imperfections of the diplomatic system in China after 20 years of war and the tales of corruption in high places that they lost sight of our tremendous stake in a non-Communist China."

After World War II, generals who had fought in the Pacific theater did not get any important positions in Washington. The Defense and State Departments were dominated by Europe-first generals who could not care less about the fall of the entire Asia, except Japan perhaps and its former colony the Philippines. The State Department spread the word that the Nationalists were beyond salvation and Mao's takeover of Taiwan was inevitable. To their disappointment, it was Taiwan that had evolved as a viable and prosperous democracy while Mao was killing millions and driving China to poverty. State Department liberals cheered Mao's "egalitarianism"—rather than calling it what it was. The Western presses and intellectuals had nothing but admiration for Mao since Mao was pursuing

---

2.   Jay Habegger; the Foundation for Economic Education, Inc., "Origins of the Chinese Hyperinflation," *The Freeman* 38.9 (September 1988).

equality for all the Chinese. The loss of millions of Chinese lives did not concern them.

Most tourists who rushed to China in the 1970s and the early 1980s found that China was two decades behind other Asian middle-income countries and that much cultural heritage was destroyed during the Cultural Revolution. One could easily imagine the Red Guards running through the streets waving *Mao Thought*, burning and destroying everything old, including books and artifacts associated with the past. A tourist would have also visited a show-case commune or two where Chinese Communist Party (CCP) officers had books and data in their hands showing how well their communes were doing. Many journalists and writers from the West visited such places before the country was open to ordinary tourists and went home and praised Mao's great achievements. Mao was a great military strategist but was no better than Stalin when it came to economic development.

He launched the Great Leap Forward (1958–60) according to the Soviet economic development model. He wanted to increase steel production greatly. Farmers were even encouraged to make iron out of their shovels and hoes. The result was disastrous. In just two years, the GDP of China plunged by 32% (in 1995 constant US$). China's per capita GDP in 1960 was $94 (in 1995 constant US$), barely above survival levels, but it sank to $65 in 1962. Mao shut the country to outsiders. One estimate indicates that his foolish policy and the resulting famines killed an estimated 40 million Chinese. This is twice the number of people killed by Stalin.[3]

Mao had to relinquish his position as head of state, although he retained his position as the Chairman of CCP. His influence over the government and the party was gone. Under Liu Shao-chi, the new chief of state, the economy of China recovered smartly, and the people praised him. The loss of adulation from the people was painful to Mao to the point that he wanted to destroy Liu and Communist leaders loyal to Liu. By this time, Mao had developed paranoia, reportedly because of advanced syphilis. He supported his wife Chiang Ching's diabolic to purge all the "revisionists". The Cultural Revolution raged on and destroyed the country until October 1968 when Liu Shao-chi was finally expelled from the party. Mao once again had the country in his grip but the Revolution killed, purged and jailed millions of party leaders, generals, writers, economists and intellectuals. Even Mao's old comrade-in-arms, Deng Xiaoping, was not

---

3.   Mathew White, "30 Worst Atrocities of the 20th Century," *Historical Atlas of the Twentieth Century*.

spared. Deng's son became permanently disabled after being thrown out of a window by the Red Guards. Deng was Liu's right-hand man.

The year 1976 was an auspicious year because the mad Mao, his old and loyal comrades Zhou Enlai (Premier) and Zhu De (chairman of the National People's Congress) all died. The Gang of Four headed by Mao's widow ruled the country for a couple years, but in 1978, Deng Xiaoping emerged as the leader and went about steering the country away from *Mao Thought*.[4] Deng urged the people to examine ideology critically and think about the economic consequences and responsibility rather than class struggle.[5] This would not surprise a 4th grader in the West, but this was a great counter-revolutionary thought in China.

Deng opened the country step by step. The first was Shenzen city in Guangdong Province. It was designated as a Special Economic Zone (SEZ). Guangdong is situate across the Pearl River from Hong Kong and was already "contaminated" by Hong Kong capitalism. It was an unqualified success and convinced CCP to expand the experiment to other coastal areas of China, on a larger scale. Shanghai, Tianjin and Dalian emerged as special cities. This new policy had an immediate impact on the Chinese economy. What the government did was to build infrastructure, invite foreign companies to invest in these special zones, relax Communist-era regulations and let the Chinese keep the money they earned. The Overseas Chinese invested first and others followed later brining in capital and technology to take advantage of the dirt cheap labor and the huge potential Chinese market. The government was willing to keep the wages low and keep exports booming.

The march to capitalism was not smooth. Deng found it necessary to come out of retirement briefly and make the Southern Speech of 1992 in Guangdong to put down the leftists. The Chinese capitalism is still not a typical capitalism but it is red hot. Its GDP in constant 2000 US$ grew at the rate of 8.6% between 1975–1985, 9.9% between 1985–1995 and 11.2% between 1995–2003. In per capita GNI-PPP, the growth was even more spectacular. It grew from $410 in 1980 to $4,980 in 2003. See Table 11 for comparison with other countries. The per capita GNI of China in current US$ was $840 in 2000 but jumped to $1,740 in 2005 after an upward revision.

Much has been said about the economy of China taking over the U.S. If the GDP growth rates of the two countries in 2005 (3.5% for the U.S. and 9.9% for

---

4. For detail, see Rongxing Guo, A Multiregional Overview (New York: St. Martin's Press, 1999) 41.
5. ibid

China) are extrapolated to the distant future, the GDP of China would surpass that of the U.S. in the year 2034. But the chances of China's GDP growing at the rate of 9.9% per year or better to such a distant future is practically nil. The economic growth rate of every emerging country has slowed down as its economy matured. Even if these assumptions were correct, the per capita GDP of China would be less than one-fourth of the U.S. in 2034—using once again the population and economic growth rates of 2005. China could conceivably surpass the U.S. in terms of GDP-PPP soon. China's GDP-PPP was about five times larger than GDP because of low living costs in China. If the growth rates of China and U.S. between 1995 and 2003 are extrapolated, the GDP-PPP of China will exceed that of the U.S. in 2015. China is the second largest economy in the world in terms of GDP-PPP already, which is a more meaningful figure than GDP in measuring the wealth or the living standard of a country.

Such explosive growth of the Chinese economy has had a profound impact on the economies of the world. Between 2001 and 2003, China has accounted for one-third of global economic growth (in PPP), twice as much as that of America. "While America's industrial output has shrunk over the past three years, China's has increased by almost 50%.... Last year it consumed 40% of the world's output of cement.... one-third of the growth in global oil consumption, 90% of the growth in world steel demand, and more than the whole of the increase in copper demand."[6] In addition, China consumed 37% of cotton, 30% of coal, 21% of aluminum and 21% of wheat between 2004 and 2005. The commodity boom that the world has seen in recent years has been largely due to China. The Middle East, Australia, Brazil and other resource rich countries have cashed in on the China Boom. A downside of such a boom is the high price of crude oil, copper, etc.

The economies of the entire world has been in boom with minimal inflation because of inexpensive imports from China and exports of raw materials and technology to China. The U.S., however, has been suffering huge trade deficits against China decade after decade and they are still growing. China has now replaced Japan as the largest holder of the U.S. dollar. The Japanese bought real estate and golf courses with their dollar surpluses at a wrong time and lost money, but China wants to buy Unocal and other key industries with its huge dollar reserve. Congress was not wrong to send the signal that such acquisitions were not acceptable. China does not even allow 51% foreign ownership of any Chinese company.

---

6.   "The Great Fall of China?" *The Economist*, May 13, 2004.

Aspects of Chinese Capitalism

This red hot "market" economy does not have democracy, commercial laws that do not change constantly, private land ownership and an independent judiciary. The main objective of the Chinese Communist Party (CCP) is to promote economic growth and keep the Chinese well fed. Political and religious freedom or even income equity are not CCP's idea of good governance. Written laws do not mean much because CCP can change them at will. The government is ubiquitous. Therein lies the vulnerability of China as well.

The development of Shanghai and its suburb Pudong exemplifies the modus operandi of the CCP—both good and bad. Pudong is a new suburban city across the Huang Pu River from "old" Shanghai. Those who watched Tom Cruise's *Mission: Impossible III* saw some of Pudong's skyscrapers. It has been called the largest construction site in the world. One-fifth of the cranes in the world is supposed to be in Pudong. I was involved in reviewing the Pudong development plan, prepared by local planners, with several Hong Kong-based British and other international consultants. I believed the plan unnecessarily costly and would create more problems in future. Chinese authorities wanted to adopt some physical features of New York, Paris and London. This made Pudong a hodge podge duplication of these great cities. The very decision to expand Shanghai across the Huangpu River rather than expand to west was a costly decision because it required building many bridges and tunnels. The city will become automobile and highway dependent like all Western cities, which in due course would create traffic congestion and pollution and waste energy and human time for commuting.

Building a separate Pudong International Airport at the extreme east end of Pudong was a mistake when there was an underutilized Hongqiao International Airport nearby that was expandable when the traffic increases. To increase the usage of the Pudong International Airport, magnetic levitation train (Maglev) was built in 2004 but only from Pudong's Longyang Lu Station of Metro Line 2. It is a fast train but it cost Shanghai Province $1.07 billion. "Since the beginning of operation, the Maglev has only carried 4,000 riders on an average day, which is less than one-sixth of its capacity."[7] It is a huge waste of money but money seems to be the last thing that Chinese planners worry about. There is more of it where it came from, any number of state-owned banks.

The Huangpu is a wide river mouth that empties into the Yellow Sea. Its width is 1,300 feet compared with 870 ft for the London Bridge. During the first

---

7.   "Pudong's Blueprint: to Double 2000 GDP in 2005", PD Online Staff Zhu Lizhen

stage infrastructure development alone (1990–1995), two bridges, five tunnels, two highways, four 10,000-ton berths as well as telecommunications systems and other utilities were constructed. Between 1996 and 2000, a deep sea port for Waigaoqiao, the Metro Line Two and more highways were built.

We could not make the Chinese government change the physical plan in any way at all because the government had already decided to implement the plan as is. That begged the question why invite planners and economist from outside the country to review it. What the government wanted was a seal of approval from international experts. Money seems to be the least of its worry. Well, what is extra several billion dollars to China for creating a showcase? Perhaps, not much. We ended up spending most of our time on advising on service sector reforms which of course were very important for the growth and function of a city. Between 1990 and 2003, Shanghai succeeded in inducing McDonnell-Douglas, Volkswagen and some "7,488, resulting in a total investment of US$ 28.5billion, of which $14.8 billion was contracted directly from overseas capital."[8]

Between 1991 and 2003, 1,297 skyscrapers and other tall buildings were built. More have been built since then and even more are under planning.[9] A question is their utilization or the vacancy rate. Pudong has been able to attract a large number of factories, research facilities and office users from all over the world, but Pudong had an office vacancy rate of 65 per cent in 1999 (*Shanghai Star*, 28 May 1999). The residential units were also overbuilt.

Dangers of Implosion

The world hopes that the China can sustain its economic growth on a long term basis; will do so without using unfair trade practices (such as the piracy of intellectual properties), dumping excessive pollutants to the atmosphere and water or putting poisonous substances in foods and pet foods; and will provide more freedom to its people. In the global world, China's economic, humanitarian and environmental problems are those of the world as well. Pollutants affect not only Siberia, Korea and Japan but the rest of the world as well. There are several danger signals that the future of China may be far more rocky than in the past.

Danger Signal #1: Real Estate Bubble

The government authorities appear unconcerned about the real estate glut in spite of Pudong's 65 per cent vacancy rate (1999) and they are confident that

---

8.   ibid.
9.   ibid

vacant spaces vacant space will be filled soon. A private developer in a market economy would go bankrupt with such a high vacancy rate but most of such buildings are built by public entities and financed by government banks. As long as the government can pay for vacant buildings, no one seems to be complaining or concerned.

Speculative buying is rampant in the residential market. Don Lee's article which I read in *The Standard of Hong Kong* but published in many major newspapers says: "Once one of the hottest property markets in the world, Shanghai has seen sales of homes virtually halt in some areas of Shanghai, prompting developers to slash prices and real estate brokerages to shutter thousands of offices. For the first time, homeowners here are learning what it means to have an upside-down mortgage—when the value of a home falls below the amount of debt on the property. Recent home buyers are suing to get their money back. Banks are fretting about a wave of default loans." This is beginning to happen elsewhere also. George Friedman's excellent "Geopolitical Intelligence Report"[10] says, "In China money is not considered a limited resource. The combination of the yuan peg and subsidized loans allow firms to expand broadly without regard for profitability. The residential construction sector is perhaps the best example.... China's need for housing is astronomical, and as expected, some one-sixth of all loans granted go to efforts to build more housing. But the structures being built are not structures Chinese citizens need. As such, China has a housing shortage, but 700,000 empty apartments."

There are many new millionaires in China, but many investors in China can also buy houses with a financial statement not authenticated by either a bank or genuine employer. Real estate companies did not mind this practice because property prices continued to rise. If a buyer defaults on payment, the real estate company repossesses the property and sells it to next buyer at a higher price. But this cannot go on forever. As it did in Japan, a property market bubble could lead to China's first implosion. If it does, it will be ugly not only for China but also for the world.

The average annual wages in Pudong was yuan or RMB25,620 (US $3,500 more or less). To buy a standard two bedroom apartment in Pudong, a wage earner has to pay 100% of his or her wage for thirty years. There is a mismatch of price and income. Yet, out of pride, the government built modern hi-rise condominiums costing an equivalent of $100 per sq ft. This comes on top of leased

---

10.   May 31, 2005

land, not a fee simple land. Building empty skyscrapers add to GDP too until the bubble bursts and the economy shrinks.

Danger Signal #2: Stock Market Bubble

With China's sustained economic boom, one would think that investing in the Chinese stock market might be the smartest thing to do. The Shanghai Stock Exchange Composite Index lost half its value from June 1999 to June 2005. Then from January 2006 to mid-May 2007, the index shot up from 1200 to 4000. That is s a 233% climb in 17 months. As I am writing this paragraph, the price to earnings ratio (PER) is 43 compared with 11 for South Korea and Brazil, and 19 for Japan. This is the kind of PER during the heydays of the Japanese economy. Although the Chinese stock markets are closed to retail investors outside of China (except B shares, mostly overpriced junk stocks reserved for foreigners), a major correction in Shanghai and Shenzen stock exchanges can ruin the security of many Chinese retirees who put their life savings in the stock market. It could also impact the real economy of China and. therefore, the rest of the world economies. The government has tried to cool the market but has not succeeded yet.

Both Shanghai and Shenzen exchanges are full of state owned enterprises whose financial statements cannot be trusted fully.

Danger Signal #3: Ever-changing Laws and Foggy Information

Direct investments in ventures in China are also wrought with hazards. The Taiwanese Association of Investment Victims in China provides a long list of telling episodes on such cases.[11] For example, when joint ventures begin to make money, the government can change the rule favoring local players, demand new technology transfer or face cut-throat pricing from Chinese imitators. The privately owned enterprises (POE) have increased considerably from nothing to more than 10 million small to medium-sized enterprises (SMEs) in 1999 but the government has controlling interests in all important companies in petroleum, oil exploration, automobile and steel manufacturing, insurance, mining, telecommunication including cellular phone, banking, computers, chemicals, appliances, consumer electronics and shipping. Furthermore, a POE in China does not enjoy

---

11. See Ming Shi, "The Risk of Gambling with the Communist Party is Too High—Written on the eve of the IPO of the four largest state-owned Chinese banks in Hong Kong," *The Epoch Times*, May 6, 2005

the protection of commercial laws. No matter who owns an enterprise, the CCP is the lawmaker, judge and jury.

Accurate information is hard to come although there has been progress in this area. Chinese officials still report the results that they are expected to achieve. Access to officers handling statistics requires special permission and is not given as a rule. When I went to Dalian to appraise a water supply loan of about $150 million, I wanted to talk to a statistics officer to get the real number of persons in the city including "floating population" (a Chinese version of illegal migrants from rural areas to cities in search of jobs). Even such mundane data as population is difficult to obtain in China because the practice of birth control and the numbers of the "floating" population are politically sensitive matters. The actual population growth rate is higher than official number. One child per family is still the government policy in urban areas but in rural areas the actual practice is two children per family because of many exceptions granted to rural households. Even in urban areas, not everyone obeys the law although the penalty for violating the law is a loss of five years of salary or dismissal if parents work for the government. Therefore, underreporting of births is common. In any event, the government is now revising the one child per family policy. As a result, the population of China will increase considerably faster than before.

Danger Signal #4: Corruption

Corruption in China is massive. The Chinese citizens cannot own foreign currency, but some government officers have been caught with a huge sum of U.S. dollars. On one of business trips to Shanghai, I was supposed to have met a middle level government officer for a rehabilitation study of the old Shanghai downtown. But he did not show up at the airport and his deputy showed up instead. I asked him what happened to his boss. His colleague said that his face was on television. I asked, "Why?" He was reluctant to speak but he finally told me the story. Two million US$ showed up in the water tank of his toilet. According to the *Global Corruption Report 2003*, the level of China's corruption in 1997 was one of the worst in the world. In the scoring system where a high number means more corruption, China occupied 41st place out of 52 countries surveyed (the higher the number more the corruption). The Chinese government is taking measures to punish corrupt officials, particularly if they are on the wrong side of the political faction. n October 2001, Shenyang's mayor was sentenced to death. In the same year, Chinese authorities investigated 36,000 cases of corruption and jailed 20,000 officials.[12] In 2007, poisonous substances were found in pet foods and imitation Colgate toothpastes imported from China. Some Chinese food inspectors have been prosecuted.

Danger Signal #5: Trade War

China is also under intense pressure to stop the rampant piracy of intellectual property rights of other countries and to let the yuan float. The exchange rates are the mechanism through which the price of goods and services across international boundaries are determined. When they are manipulated, the entire trading system is distorted. An upward revaluation of yuan is not necessarily a good thing for American consumers but the fair thing to do to American companies and workers. Any time, such matters are discussed, extreme free traders warn against the dangers of a trade war and point to the history of the Great Depression. Such a concern is overblown in this day and age. The U.S. Is not abandoning free trade but tariffs and trade sanctions have a place in this world.

China plays a rough game when it comes to its trade disputes with other countries. Here is how China fought for its right to export garlic to South Korea. "The row started when South Korea raised its import duty on Chinese garlic to 315 percent from 30 percent between November 1999 and May 2000 as agreed previously. China's garlic exports to South Korea were valued [only] at $9 million [small for the size of either country's economy]. But China retaliated by banning imports of South Korean mobile telephones and polyethylene estimated at more than $510 million last year."[13] South Korea capitulated and the dispute was over quickly. This is the kind of "language" that China speaks and understands. The U.S. should learn from the Chinese art of trade war: not tit for tat but using an overwhelming force such as imposing general tariffs on all goods if possible under a WTO sanction.

A delegation of high ranking U.S. officials including Treasury Secretary Hank Paulson and Chairman Ben Bernanke went to Beijing and lectured on the danger to China of building up such a huge foreign currency reserve. That show had no effect. China is, however, aware that Congress may slap tariffs on Chinese goods. The U.S. has a "garlic" card in Chuck Schumer, the Democratic Senator from New York State, who is itching to do so. The Chinese could retaliate by selling their U.S. Treasury instruments. That will be an interesting match to watch.

---

12. *Global Corruption Report 2003* (Internet version: Transparency International, 2003) 132.

13. Excerpts from "China South Korea Sign Garlic Accord," *People's Daily*, August 01, 2000.

Danger Signal #6: Banks

A huge number of state-owned enterprises are losing money and non-performing loans (NPL) are piling up fast. Independent banks and firms such as UBS, Ernst & Young, the McKinsey Global Institute and Price Waterhouse Coopers have estimated bad debts of Chinese banks to be "upwards of 50 percent of China's gross domestic product."[14] It means NPL of $1 trillion equivalent. The government does not accept such a number and has been cleaning up bank balance sheets. In addition, it has been recapitalizing its banks by issuing tens of billion dollars bank IPOs, such as the China Construction Bank ($8 billion), the Bank of China ($11.2 billion), the Industrial and Commercial Bank of China ($22 billion), etc. These banks are owned mostly by the government. As the foreign-ownership shares of Chinese banks increase, the banks are likely to adopt Western banking practices and contain if not reduce NPL. Citing Beijing National Accounting Institute President Chen Xiaoyue, *Business Week* said, "Two-third of China's 13,000 listed companies don't earn back their true cost of capital."[15] The truth might be even uglier.

Danger Signal #7: Labor Unrest and Regional Income Disparity

The Chinese government has been keeping a tight lid over a growing amount of civic and labor unrest. In 1993, there were 10,000 industrial actions across the nation and the number has been rising. Almost all of them are considered illegal because labor law permits strikes only against private businesses, which accounted for less than 5 percent of the nation's enterprises. Some strike leaders have been arrested but officials had to back off when the strike was too large to confront.[16]

Discontent over regional disparity between the affluent coastal urban areas and the interior areas is rising. The farmers are mad at the local government for taking their land at will and for leasing it to developers for a huge profit although a new law may prevent this in future. Farmers are also angry about price controls, which in fact subsidize the urban workers and keep the farmers poor. Additionally, the movement of rural workers to urban areas has been restricted although

---

14. See George Friedman, *Stratfor*, "Geopolitical Diary: Cosmetic Change in China's Economy"; *Stratfor* is a leading security consulting intelligence report firm, which offers intelligence and strategic forecasting services on world events.

15. See Alistair R. Anderson, Jin-Hai Li, Richard T. Harrison and Paul J.A. Robson, "The Increasing Role of Small Business in the Chinese Economy," Journal of Small Business Management 41.3 (2003), Questia, 14 Feb. 2005.

16. "The Great Fall of China?" *The Economist*; May 13, 2004.

the government has relaxed this regulation. All such policies, particularly regional disparity, have the potential of rocking the country.

Friedman says, "China's rulers have always struggled to keep the outward-oriented coastal regions in sync with the more insular interior. Whenever one of the two regions becomes too disparate relative to the other, China suffers a catastrophe that re-establishes the balance."[17] China has to redirect industrialization to the interior areas now. This will be costly and require delicate financial engineering such as withdrawing easy money from coastal cities and raising interest rates while providing financial incentives and government direct investments to the interior regions. The government fired the Shanghai mayor, who was the member of the all-powerful Political Bureau on corruption charge although his more grievous crime was not toeing the government line to slow down investment in Shanghai. However, the government cannot afford to kill the goose that lays the golden eggs. The coastal urban centers will have to continue to produce and export more to finance the development of the interior regions.

Danger Signal #8: Democracy Movement

A real danger to the CCP is the demand for democracy. Everyone wants more freedom of speech and religion. Sooner or later, the government will have to respond to these demands. For now, the government has revealed no intention to do so. It continues to impose censorship of the Internet and the media. In 1994 Rupert Murdock's STAR (Satellite Television for Asian Region) was forced to remove *BBC World* from the network because the Chinese government was unhappy with the BBC's coverage of China and threatened to block STAR TV in the mainland if the BBC was not dropped. STAR bowed to this demand. The latest to bow to the Chinese government are Google and other Internet companies. They have agreed to block all search words that the Chinese government considers unacceptable such as democracy.

History teaches us that, above a certain level of economic prosperity, political freedom becomes increasingly valuable and likely because of the inescapable need for educated men and women who eventually become too many to be oppressed. The great challenge for the West as well as the Chinese is to see China make a peaceful transition to democracy. Democracy is also the key for the Taiwan issue because if there is more political and religious freedom in China, Taiwan may join China.

---

17. "China: Banking on Shifting Growth to the Interior" Stratfor Summary; April 28, 2006.

It would be wrong to leave this section with an impression that China is doomed. The Chinese economy faces many uncertainties and a rocky period is ahead. However, this will not cripple China. The government is resourceful and clever. It will find a way out. Over the next 10–20 years, China is destined to become an economy that would rival Western Europe or the U.S.

Military Threat

China and the U.S. are potential military enemies because of Taiwan, the Middle East oil and Asian hegemony. Neither China nor the U.S. wants a war against the other, East and China's thirst for oil, and Asian hegemony. One should not dismiss such a conflict even between two economies mutually dependent. Neither China nor the U.S. want a war against each other, but China is preparing for the worst just in case. "The Pentagon reported [in March 2006] that China is moving forward rapidly with an offensive capability in the Pacific. The capability would not, according to the report, rely on the construction of a massive fleet to counter U.S. naval power, but rather on development and deployment of anti-ship missiles and maritime strike aircraft, some obtained from Russia."[18] In January, 2007, China blasted its own orbiting weather satellite, which the U.S. government took as a warning that China can take down its spy and other satellites important to the U.S. military. Chinese rockets also shined laser beams to U.S. satellites. There is little doubt that China is preparing for a possible space war.

Earlier, China forced down American eavesdropping flights along China's coast, which Washington insisted took place at least 12 miles off the Chinese territory. Beijing has threatened to invade Taiwan if it declares independence. Mao's China actually took over Tibet in a 19th century style attack and invaded India. China claims that Tibet was part of China. If such distant history is justification for taking over Tibet, Tibet may have the right to say that a large part of China belongs to it. Tibet occupied Chinese capital Xian before Tibet became a pacifist country. China claims that Genghis Khan was Chinese and an ancient Korean Kingdom Koguryo, which stretched from Pyongyang (North Korean capital today) to a large part of Manchuria, was a Chinese kingdom just because part of it was located in what is now China.

In Central Asia, the Shanghai Co-operation Organization (SCO) comprising four Central Asian countries, China and Russia is "increasingly challenging America's military presence in the region."[19] China and Russia are doing a mini-

---

18. For detail see George Friedman, *Stratfor*; "U.S. Perceptions of a Chinese Threat", *Geopolitical Intelligence Report*; 05.31.2006

mum to stop North Korea and Iran from developing nuclear programs. They do not support the American strategy for the Middle East or any harsh sanction against Iran, let alone any military action. China is also claiming the ownership of energy fields off the coasts of Vietnam, the Philippines, Malaysia, Japan, and Brunei although China pledged not to use military means to settle disputes. On June 4, 2005, former Secretary of Defense Donald Rumsfeld remarked at the regional security conference in Singapore, "China is … building up its military without being threatened by any other country." China was placing hundreds of missiles in the range of Taiwan and "was also sharply increasing its military spending and buying large amounts of sophisticated weapons."[20]

China and the U.S. have different political agendas on North Korea. The U.S. hoped that China would exert enough pressure on North Korea to make it abandon the nuclear programs. China might be able to do so if it wants to because the North Korean regime will crumble without Chinese trade and assistance for food and energy but China does not want that to happen. China is happy with a anti-American North Korea providing a buffer between China and South Korea with U.S. Military presence in it. A unified Korea under South Korea is the last thing that China wants. In the fast changing world, North Korean loyalty to China cannot be taken for granted. Its loyalty is on sale to the highest bidder whether it is to China or a consortium of the U.S., South Korea and Japan as long as the security of the Kim's regime is assured. Kim needs money to feed his vast army and loyalists.

The U.S. is an inconvenient superpower to China because among other things the U.S. Navy dominates the Pacific and Indian Oceans and still remains the protector of Taiwan. The U.S. is obliged to defend Taiwan if China attacks under the Taiwan Relations Act. Whether the U.S. will do so or not is another matter. China can lob missiles but does not yet have the capability to land a large number of troops on Taiwan. Increasing military cooperation between the U.S. and Japan is also a concern to China. Unfortunately, over the years, the U.S. has made one concession after another to China. Taiwan has been forced out of the U.N. and most international agencies. Taiwan in fact does not exist as far as international agencies are concerned. The U.S. cannot even invite the president of Taiwan to visit the U.S. without angering China.

19.   "Aphorism and suspicion", *The Economist*; November 19th, 2005; 23.
20.   Matt Kelley, Associated Press Writer; June 4, 2005.

Lessons

The Chinese economy is another proof that any form of capitalism is infinitely better than communism. China has shown that a market economy can thrive under an autocracy as long as it is pro-business. China has become something of a fascist economy (resembling pre-WWII Germany or Japan) with strong nationalism, the control of foreign exchange market and no-democracy. But democracy becomes more valuable to modern men when the people have full stomachs. It remains to be seen how long the CCP can remain in power without granting political and religious freedom to the people.

Chapter 17

India: Better Late than Never

Focus

With the population of over 1.1 billion, the population of India is second only to that of China (2007). Even as late as 1990, India appeared incapable of lifting itself out of poverty and economic stagnation. What kept the Indian economy so depressed for such a long period. Lately, Indian GNI is growing almost as fast as that of China. What woke it up in the mid-1990s?

Experiments with Socialism

A fatal mistake that Indian leaders made after independence (1947) was to embrace a socialist or "mixed economy". The first Prime Minister of India, Jawaharlal Nehru (1947–64) as well as Indian intelligentsia and politicians deeply distrusted capitalism because the British did some of the most shameful things in Asia in the name of capitalism. Its "tea" trade was financed by opium exported to China. John Stuart Mill, a founder of capitalism and free trade, was a senior officer of the East India Company and defended the Company until its demise. This was capitalism, without moral content, engaged in criminal activities. It is not surprising that Nehru took a particular liking to Harold Laski (a leading British Labor Party intellectual) who thought that a country could achieve social justice and prosperity through a "mixed economy."

This led to the state ownership of large parts of the Indian economy. India invested what little capital it had and foreign aid it received from the British and the old USSR in heavy industry. This was in line with the Soviet model of economic development. The overall investment in physical infrastructure and in industries was woefully inadequate. Yet the government would not let the private sector invest in primary industries. The government on the other hand ignored its role in developing basic infrastructure such as transportation, power supply and distribution, communications and irrigation facilities. Its control over the price of agricultural products held back the agricultural sector. The food shortage was so severe that India had to ration food in spite of massive food aid from the U.S. through PL 480. All the control and state planning and ownership of industries served the formidable Indian bureaucracy well because it gave the Indian Administrative Service (IAS) elites ways to grant exceptions and make money. The private sector could not invest and expand its production capacity without a government permit.

I went to Calcutta, India, on a two-year assignment for the Ford Foundation in 1965. The living condition in the city was more miserable than any large city in the world. Municipal water was scarce and even when available, it was unsafe. On the first night at Calcutta's best hotel, I woke up with violent stomach pains. The hotel called a doctor in the middle of night. I thought it was some kind of poison but the doctor thought that it was a stomach bug—nothing earthshaking. Most restaurants and tea stalls do not boil water long enough to kill bacteria. It was no wonder that the infant mortality rate was 146 per 1,000 live births compared with 26 in the U.S. in 1960. Life expectancy at birth was only 47 in 1965.

The caste system dictated every aspect of Indian life. The Ford Foundation general service unit in Calcutta, which supported the Calcutta project, preselected a driver for my family. I found that he would not handle any luggage or even my briefcase. I promptly fired the man, who probably had a family and had waited for my arrival for a long time. Later I found out that he belonged to a high-caste Hindu community, and was not allowed to touch anything made of leather such as my briefcase. I felt sorry for my impetuous decision after finding this out, but by that time I had already hired a Muslim driver. It was too late to reverse my decision. A neighbor of mine died in hospital after a car accident because he refused to eat foods prepared by a lower caste hospital worker. its "holy"cow, dietary restrictions and the caste system pervaded every aspect of daily life including the division of domestic works among the people of different castes. Things appeared to have remained unchanged for a thousand years.

I was later assigned to the Asansol-Durgapur area, some 170 km west of Calcutta on Grand Trunk Road. The road is the subcontinent's first, largest and oldest highway built centuries before the British came to India. It linked what is now Bangladesh to Calcutta, Delhi, Lahore (Pakistan) and then went over the Khyber Pass finally ending in Kabul, Afghanistan. The Damodar River which flows through this region had a recently-built dam which supplied water for industrialization, hydroelectric power and flood control. Asansol and Durgapur both had a steel plant. Durgapur also had an Alloy Steel plant and the Mining and Allied Machinery plant built with British and Soviet foreign assistance. This region was to become a symbol of a post-colonial success story.

A problem was that in spite of such massive investments in the region, there were few downstream or ancillary industries developing in the area. This was predictable because the private sector was weak and heavily regulated. The Durgapur Steel Plant, built with modern British technology, had 30,000 employees, far too many for a steel plant producing only 1 million tons of pig iron, ingots and railway wheels per year. By comparison, British Steel in 1994 had about 40,000 employees but produced about 12 million tons of steel and diversified steel products.

The Durgapur Steel Plant was more of an employment agency for those with political or union connections than an enterprise. The bloated number of union workers drained more than money out of the steel plant. The unions become so militant that even the general manager of the steel plant was unable to enter the plant in fear of being beaten by his workers. Labor strikes were frequent. The production cost of steel was so high that it was cheaper to buy steel from Japan than produce it in Durgapur. India's steel could not be exported and the steel industry survived on protectionism. Japan had neither iron ore nor coal but produced steel more cheaply and was selling it all over the world. The labor cost was many times cheaper in India. It had all the raw materials (coal and iron ore) locally including cheap electricity from the hydroelectric power plant nearby. The location was perfect for a steel plant. It did not make sense that the cost of producing steel in India was higher than in Japan but for the political patronage and out-of-control labor unions.

A group of Ford Foundation advisers, of which I was a junior member, took a tour of key industries in East India. The steel plant that we visited during the trip included the Tata Iron and Steel Company (TISCO). It was an old plant owned by a private enterprise that started operation with the first wave of Indian industrialization in 1912. We found out that its production cost was much lower than the Durgapur plant, even though its plant was old. The general manager of the plant told us that the company wanted to expand production but that the government did not give the company a permit. The government was trying to build more government-owned steel plants like the Durgapur Steel Plant rather than leave steel production to the private sector. Steel Plant and the town of Durgapur. In 2003, the plant finally began to make money but all these years, Indian taxpayers subsidized a massive amount of money.

In spite of massive losses, the Durgapur Steel Plant did not fold up as a private company would have. Similar situations affected most public enterprises in India. With a new wave of reforms 30 years later, in the 1990s, some changes have been made in the Durgapur Steel Plant and the town of Durgapur. In 2003, the plant finally began to make money but all these years, Indian taxpayers subsidized a massive amount of money.

The story of the Durgapur Steel Plant was not an isolated incident. Similar failures were widespread throughout India. It extended to other manufacturing sectors and also to the service sector. All major banks and insurance companies were nationalized in 1969 and these accounted for over 90% of the financial sector's assets in the early nineties. At the end of the 1980s, about 45% of the economy's capital stock was in the hands of the public sector. The most brilliant college graduates went to the public service. They knew what they were doing. Money, power and prestige awaited them. They maintained an iron grip over the country's policies, the economy, production, investment, foreign exchange operations, price control, foreign trade, licensing and subsidies. Even more junior Indian Administrative Services (IAS)officers at district and subdistrict levels were in control of not only the routine government operations but also the judiciary and the police.

The central government was under the socialist Congress Party. This was the party of Jawaharlal Nehru. Later, his daughter Indira Gandhi inherited the party. In spite of the disastrous economy of India under the Congress Party, Indira Gandhi was reelected in 1971 under the slogan of "Abolish Poverty." Such slogans, when used by politicians, mean that they will create more entitlement programs. Such promises are effective even in industrialized countries but in countries where the population is mostly poor and economy-illiterate, they tend to work every time. In 1975, such a slogan elected Mrs. Gandhi once again but she was found guilty of violating election laws. Her socialist government was also losing popularity because it could not reduce, let alone abolish, poverty. Riots broke out and spread to everywhere. To avoid losing her power, Gandhi declared a state of emergency in 1975. She then ordered the arrests of the main opposition leaders. In her opinion, this was for the good of India but she made the mistake of believing in it. She allowed free elections to take place in 1977. The Indian people voted her out of office. But the name Nehru and Gandhi still had a magical power in India. She returned to power in 1980 only to be assassinated by her own Sikh guards four years later.

Post-Socialist India

Indira Gandhi's son Rajiv Gandhi became Prime Minister after the assassination. Prior to that, he was a professional pilot for Indian Airlines. He began the process of turning India away from the socialist economy in 1984 and reducing the power of the bureaucracy, led by the IAS. The economic performance of India began to improve. In 1988, GDP in current US$ went up by 10%. Rajiv Gandhi lost office in 1989 because of financial scandals. During his comeback attempt in the 1991 election, he was also assassinated. The curse of the Gandhi!

His political ally, Narasimha Rao, was elected the prime minister and continued the process of reform. Reagan's supply-side economics was a new topic in India and even old socialists finally admitted that the tired old socialism was not working. P Chidambaram, a former socialist and junior minister under Rajiv Gandhi, was appointed Commerce Minister and received credit for doing away with several red tape regulations and boosting Indian exports. Chidambaram symbolizes the kind of transformation that the Indian intelligentsia went through from being a hard-core leftist to a Reaganomist. They turned pro-business and anti-big-government. After seeing the demise of the USSR and the meteoric rise of China, the market economy no doubt appeared worthwhile to try to Indian intellectuals. Reaganomics and Thatcherism had already found its passage to India some years ago although no politician dared to embrace them. Manmohan Singh, the Finance Minister then (the Prime Minister now), dared the process of reducing the powers of "permit raj", the IAS-dominated Indian bureaucracy which, for a right price, can give exceptions to regulations and issue licenses to do business and production in India. This was not an entirely new idea. In fact, Rajiv Gandhi started it.

Singh then introduced a package of broad reforms in 1991: (a) privatization; (b) tax reforms; (c) a market driven exchange rate system resulting in a sharp devaluation of rupee; (d) deregulation to allow the inflow of foreign capital; and (e) a greater autonomy to the Reserve Bank on monetary policy. Along with such reforms, India reduced its import substitution policy and liberalized trade.[1] India now laid the foundation for capitalism. The proof of the pudding is in the eating. The Indian economy took off in 1992. The conservative Bharatiya Janata Party (BJP) was voted in in 1998 and deepened economic reforms. The growth rate accelerated further. GDP in current US$ grew by 9% in 2003 and 7% in 2004. The BJP lost power in 2004 but the Congress Party that replaced it was no longer the same socialist party that it once was. The growth rate in 2005 was 7%, second only to China. External indebtedness was reduced; foreign exchange reserve rose from $5.8 billion to $130 billion in mid-2005; and international trade boomed.

Money has a way of finding a safe haven and seeking a greater return. When the control over money was relaxed and an environment friendly for investment

---

1.   Mihir Rakshit," India's Economic Reforms: Some Macroeconomics of India's Reforms Experience" downloaded on 6/23/04.

and profit was created, the money accumulated in India and money from abroad poured into India. Although a vast area of India has not changed much, there are several urban-industrial growth centers that are changing fast and spreading growth to the entire country. Bangalore is turning into a Silicon Valley. When an American calls customer service with a computer problem, someone in Bangalore answers the phone with the unmistakable Indian accent. That is not all. Indian engineers are writing the latest software for American firms and are designing "gas turbines, aircraft engines, medical gear ... for GE and other clients." This is what Americans call outsourcing. It cannot be stopped unless Americans are willing to pay more and drive American companies out of business. Today, Tata Steel's Jamshedpur plant produces four million tons of steel and has an ambitious expansion plan.

Business Week (August 22, 2005) says, "At the Indian Institute of Technology (IIT) campus in Kharagpur, near Calcutta, a small team of engineers is beavering away on what they hope will prove a killer competitor to the BlackBerry.... at IIT Madras, students and professors have spun off a startup that's working on a no-frills network computer aimed at the Asian corporate and government markets that will sell for just $100." Nokia is building a campus in Madras to produce cell phones. South Korea's Pohang Iron & Steel Company plans a $12 billion steel complex in Orissa State by 2016, where good grade iron ore is abundant. Tata Steel said that India should reserve natural resources for national companies. In fact, there was a concern that India would run out of iron ore sooner than later. Tata Steel had an ambitious expansion plan. According to *Forbes*, information technology companies such as Wipro, Infosys and Zee Telefilms are among 200 of the most most successful companies outside the United States with the annual sales of under $1 billion. What the Left did not know then was that the proportion of poverty would drop to 27.5% in 2004–05 (Planning Commission of India). Trickle down worked even in India, which had many structural impediments. Developing countries should not be overly concerned that the incidence of poverty does not drop rapidly in the early stages of economic development. They should continue to intensify reforms and educate the masses. Then, the incidence of poverty will decline, especially if the country does not expand entitlement programs. Remember that the former Communist countries, which tried to eliminate poverty by redistribution of incomes, made everyone poor.

Such an argument is heard in the U.S. and Europe also. The proportion of poverty dropped to 29% in 2000, perhaps to the disappointment of the left. In any event, India as well as other developing countries should not be overly concerned that the incidence of poverty does not drop rapidly in the early stages of

economic growth and intensify reforms, educating the masses and making supply-side reforms. With economic growth, the incidence of poverty will decline.

India has a long way to go for reforming its economy. It is still practically
impossible for Indian firms to declare bankruptcy or fire workers without paying
high penalties. Rent control is practiced all over the country, which discourages
developers to invest in rental housing. India still has too much red tape and corruption is rampant. India needs to spend trillions in infrastructure development.
India's financial institutions are by and large closed to foreign banks and investors. As a result, they do not have enough money to lend. Another reform necessary is to privatize the vast number of state-owned enterprises which are still
making losses every year.

India has bottlenecks in almost every infrastructure category. It includes transportation, power supply, water supply and telecommunications. In 2000, the per
capita consumption of electricity in India was 358 kwh compared with 827 kwh
of China and 2628 of Malaysia. India definitely needs more investment in
human resource development. The literacy rate of the adult population was 61%
compared with 91% for China. The life expectancy of an Indian born in 2004
was 63 compared with over 71 in China. See Table 10 for other social indicators
(the availability of hospital beds, personal computers and Internet) of India compared with China, Malaysia, South Korea and the U.S. The labor unions still
hang on to government corporations like leeches. The old ways do not change
easily, and democracy does not allow a quick shift in policies.

Table 10

Social Indicators
India and Selected Other Countries [*]

| | 2000 | | 2004 | | | |
	Electric power Consumption kwh per capita	Personal Computers per 1,000 pop	Life expectancy at birth total (years)	Literacy Rate Adult pop %	Hospital Beds Per 1000 Persons	Internet Users Per 1000 Persons
China	827	16	71	91	2.5	73
India	358	4.5	63	61	..	32
Korea, Rep.	4968	405	77	..	6.1	657
Malaysia	2628	95	73	89	..	397
The U.S.	12399	572	77	..	3.6	630

[*]   Source: WBDI

One consolation to reform-minded Indians is that the Congress Party's economic ideology has moved to the right of its traditional position as the Labour Party of the U.K. did after Thatcher. The reformist Dr. Manmohan Singh became prime minister in 2004 and appointed P Chidambaram as Finance Minister. Singh is the first Sikh Indian prime minister. Their appointments were designed to reassure the business community that a pro-growth policy would continue. But the Congress Party did not gain an outright majority in the election and had to embrace the Communist Party to form the government.

Conclusions

National Economic Policies

The Great Depression and the stagflation have taught us several important lessons. First, a good monetary policy is necessary for capitalism to work smoothly and contain inflation. Second, supply-side reforms are necessary for all over-taxed and over-regulated economies today which include the West European and U.S. economies. Finally, the Great Depression has taught that high tariffs and trade barriers are mutually destructive. Today, the alternative to the free market economy is welfare socialism. Facts are conclusive that the euro-welfare economies have been losing grounds to both the U.S. and UK economies which went through supply-side reforms around 1980. The euro-economies have created large numbers of unemployed and welfare-dependent populations. They have now stopped raising taxes and adopted some aspects of supply-side reforms. As a result, we are now witnessing a modest revival of the euro-economies.

Although the U.S. economy is still #1 and enjoys almost full employment, it is now a nation of indulgent consumers and governments rather than a nation of producers. Its tax burden has been creeping up in spite of several tax cuts that have been made. In addition, the extraordinarily high cost of healthcare is acting like an additional 5% tax on household incomes compared with other leading industrial countries. Due to the high twin deficits, the U.S. has been piling up an unprecedented amount of external debts. The U.S. has been issuing multi-billion dollar checks to the rest of the world every week to finance the twin deficits. This condition cannot last forever. The U.S. has to reduce current account deficits to prevent the slide of the dollar. The depreciation of the dollar depreciates everything that Americans own and will eventually invite inflation. The U.S. must reduce twin deficits preferably by improving its competitiveness rather than continue to depreciate its currency or raising interest rates. The U.S. government has much to learn from Asian economies on this. The U.S. economy has to become more business friendly; increase incentives for cutting-edge technologies; and force China to abandon its unfair trade practices (including the piracy of intellectual properties, massive subsidies to its enterprises, currency manipulation and the excessive pollution of the environment). The U.S. would do well to explore and tap its available oil and gas reserves as well as develop and make use of viable alternative-energies such as nuclear, coal and solar. The world may or may not have reached the peak oil production but environmental politics and geopolitical turmoils have effectively created a peak production.

Socio-Economic Policies

Poverty can only be reduced by robust economic growth and trickle down. Better education and less welfare for able bodied persons are also important. The Asian economies are the proof of this truism. Trickle down has worked everywhere in spite of the denial of the Left. Developing countries should not be overly concerned that the incidence of poverty does not drop rapidly in the early stages of economic development. They should continue to intensify reforms and educate the masses. Then, the incidence of poverty will decline.

More borrowing from the World Bank, IMF, other international financial institutions and aid programs will contribute little to economic growth without fundamental economic reforms. Most African countries and the Philippines in Asia among others are good example of such a failed approaches.

by more generous entitlement programs. Communist countries have tried that only to find out that such an approach made everyone poor.

Swift and severe punishment against drug dealers and criminals has helped not only Asian countries socially but also economically. The U.S. has been reducing its crime rates by locking up more criminals and drug addicts. As a result, the number of the prison population has been increasing enormously. Too many criminals are still on the loose in inner cities streets of the U.S. terrorizing and killing innocent people. Whenever, efforts are made to lock up more criminals, black activists cry "racism". The ultimate victims are largely African Americans in inner cities. The race industries blame the high crime rates to poverty. Crime rates and the incidence of poverty are poorly correlated in industrialized countries. Asian countries owe a great deal of their prosperity to low crime rates and high social order.

Corporate and while collar crimes are rampant also. This includes not only doctoring up corporate balance sheets in the U.S. but also institutionalized monopoly and crony capitalism in developing countries.

The annual cost of crime and drug and alcohol abuse runs close to $2 trillion in the U.S. This is about the estimated Federal Government tax revenues for 2007. The short life expectancy and high infant mortality rates in the U.S. are partly due to crack-babies, the use of alcohol during pregnancy and HIV-infected mothers.

Max Weber's Protestant values have left the West but they continue to thrive in Asia. Asians in the U.S. have also elevated their incomes above the level of the whites by working harder and studying longer years, not by crying racism. The Left of the world either does not know this or denies these obvious truths. Blaming racism and the history of slavery for the failures of African Americans are counterproductive.

A stable **oil** price and the security of the oil supply are important to maintain a high living standard. But the energy policies of the the West have been hijacked by environmental extremists. The protection of **the environment** is important for health reason but the fear of global warming is not only irrational but also extremely costly. The build-up of CO_2 will increase the temperature of the Earth if everything else remains the same but everything else does not remain the same. The temperature of the sun, the activities of the oceans, volcanoes, vegetation, aerosol and other particles in the atmosphere change the temperature of the earth constantly. The science behind global warming at the present is no better than the time when *The Blind Men* were trying to figure out the shape of *the Elephant* by touching different parts of the animal. Trying to save every variation of a species such as fairy shrimp in seasonal rainwater puddles makes as much sense as banning DDT based on a writing of a sentimentalist. That ban revived malaria and killed millions of children and grown-ups around the world.

Immigration can be a win-win proposition for all countries, but the U.S. has turned immigration into a racket that encourages lawlessness. Illegal immigrants in the U.S. meet the labor requirements of low wage jobs but they increase fiscal burdens on local and state governments and increase the risk to national security and public health, and destroy law and order. They depress the wages of low-income American workers because many of the illegal immigrants do not pay taxes and workers comp insurance and take away jobs that low-income Americans can fill. The solution is simple but it goes against electoral politics. Work permits are the answer, not citizenship programs. Even the legal immigration criteria should be revised to invite able and talented workers rather than chain migration. The U.S. can learn much from Asia and even from Western Europe.

Values and Social Policies

Moral values and social order are the foundations of a civilization and prosperity. The decline of values in the West casts dark clouds over its future. Traditional values are under intense attack in the West from atheists and the courts (the

Supreme Court in the U.S.) sympathetic to them. The laws used to be based on religious values or the societal views of what is right and what is wrong, whether in the East or the West. This is still true in the East but not in the West. In the West, laws are increasingly created by several lawyers in high courts. Through "reinterpretations" of constitutions, they overturn the laws created by elected representatives of the people.

The ultimate avatar of the Western liberals today is inalienable rights to unlimited freedom, hedonism and privacy. Such values and the culture of looking after #1 have led to the increasing number of broken families, troubled youths, drug addiction and mutual destruction. Children are not raised properly. Secular progressives believe that the essence of Christianity is the forgiveness of sins and charity to the poor. The forgiveness of sins comes from repentance, not from continued commitment to sins. Dr. Benjamin Spock sold 50 million copies of *Baby and Child Care* (1946), whose primary message was permissiveness. Later, he came to realize that he was wrong and said, "I think that the children and adults in families that adhere to a specific religion (as I do) or a firm set of moral standards (as I do) are fortunate." The Eastern philosophy, particularly Confucianism, is equally demanding of following a strict set of rules and children paying respects to their parents.

War and peace continues to be as critical issue today as during the time of WWII and the Cold War. But now the Iraq War is threatening to become another Vietnam. In both wars, the U.S. used the rules of engagement meant for fighting regular armies during WWII. Such rules are entirely inappropriate in fighting guerrillas and terrorists. There are no politically correct ways to win such wars. What good are more boots on the ground, cluster bombs, advanced fighter planes and tanks in the hands of those who cannot tolerate any collateral damage or another Mi Lai massacre? An alternative to the brutal use of weapons is a long war that will kill more people and may end in a Vietnam-like retreat. That hasty retreat from Vietnam resulted in the death of millions of Cambodians, Vietnamese and Laotians. There are some early signs that the new tactic of General David Patrias may work. Coalition troops protect civilians 24/7 rather than come and go. Some al Qaeda safe houses, fingered by local populations, are bombed from the air, thus sparing the ground troops from possible accusations of killing civilians. If a war is not critical enough to take the "gloves off", it is better to keep American troops at home. The war against the Islamic terrorists also requires an ideological attack on their perverted belief system. Those Muslims who want to enter Heaven by blowing themselves up in city streets need to be persuaded that such an act of suicide will not be rewarded with 72 virgins. The West won the Cold War by exposing the lies of Communists, not by remaining silent.

The Economies and Social Values of Asian Counties

China has achieved miraculous economic growth without democracy. In coming years, however, China will face increasing cries for democracy, religious freedom, individual property ownership and less government control over matters such as family size. This is the natural tendency of the educated population once the basic needs of human survival (food, shelter and clothing) have been met. The autocratic government of China has also created some explosive situations in the course of developing the country such as regional income disparity, property market bubble, the banks burdened with very high non-performing loans and labor unrest. A trade war with the the U.S. cannot be ruled out because the Chinese government has all but ignored the U.S. demand regarding the protection of its IP, currency float, etc. China has already threatened to retaliate any U.S. move to raise tariffs by dumping its immense dollar reserves. The possibility of military confrontation with the U.S. has also increased because the Chinese military is large and technologically sophisticated. China does not even want to concede the Pacific or space to the U.S.

India's take off is almost as big a story as that of China. But it has a large illiterate people and has a long way to go to deepen reforms and build up infrastructure. But it is a democracy and its prosperity does not pose the same kind of military threat that China's does.

When the rest of Asian economies was booming, the **Japanese** economy dived into more than a decade of recession-stagnation in 1989. Why? The immediate cause of it was the bursting of the real estate bubble. This shrank the assets of Japanese banks so much that they could no longer lend much. Another reason for the stagnation was protectionism. It made Japan a very expensive place to live and kept its service industries extremely inefficient. In cost of living adjusted per capita income (GNI-PPP), the standard of living in Japan fell below that of Hong Kong. Singapore may catch up with Japan soon. Japan is still very wealthy country but it is not not respected in East Asia, particularly in China and the two Koreas. Japan could play a larger role in Asia and the world given its economic power, but it is still regarded as a "little Japanese". Instead of admitting its past wrong doings and moving on as Germany did, Japan has been revising its history textbooks and honoring war criminals. Its Imperial Army killed 20 million Asians—some of them in the most inhumane ways as the Nazis did (e.g., chemical experiments on human beings, the brutal massacre and genocide of women and children, grabbing young girls from villages and turning them into "comfort women" for the Japanese soldiers on the war front). The West has been rather uninterested in the whole subject, but to the Chinese and Koreans, Japan was no better than what Nazi Germany was to the Jews. The Japanese government and the people have not apologized as a nation.

South Korean economy has risen from a basket case to the 12th largest economy in the world. It has been far more nimble than Japan in cleaning up its banks and conglomerates after the Asian Financial Crisis and has been on a spree of concluding free trade agreements lately. It is, however, still mired in an unfinished war with the North. A new generation of Koreans sees Korea as the victim of American naivete or racist policies during the Roosevelt and Truman administrations. The U.S. has paid dearly for its mistaken post-war policy agreed with Stalin in the Yalta Secret Meeting. However, the U.S. has remained a faithful ally and defender of South Korea since the Korean War. To the disappointment of the U.S., however, South Korea has been a reluctant partner in containing North Korea. It has been providing billions of dollars in aid to North Korea even after its Sunshine Policy failed and North Korea admitted to having an active nuclear arms program. The on-again-and-off-again six nation talks are on again after the U.S. returned North Korea's frozen bank assets in Macao. The U.S.'s main concern is that North Korea does not sell its missile and nuclear weapons to Iran or Al Qaeda. Now that the U.S. and North Korea are in direct talks and North Korea declared that it has shut down its Yong Byon nuclear facility, China is concerned. China does not want a rapid rapprochement between North Korea and the U.S. China is happy to have North Korea as a buffer state which is loyal to China. This is a victory of a sort for the U.S. diplomacy but no treaty with North Korea will make any difference unless there is a nuclear verification program covering the entire country.

Singapore offers a model of a free economy and a social security system based on individual savings. The ruling party (PAP) has maintained an overwhelming parliamentary majority ever since Independence by offering economic prosperity, corruption-free government, social security and law-and-order. It should be a model for other countries. The success of Singapore is a compelling story and defies conventional wisdom. The U.S. (as well as other countries) should send Congressmen to Singapore to study how the privatized social security and a harsh criminal justice system have done wonders to Singapore.

Malaysia offers a model of how Muslims and non-Muslims have lived together in relative peace and worked out co-prosperity of different ethnic groups with different business abilities. The goal of growth and redistribution has been achieved with a relatively moderate cost to the economy.

The Philippines provides a lesson that a democracy with no political stability, no consensus on how to build a nation and no will to maintain law-and order cannot attain prosperity. Toppling greedy and corrupt leaders such as Marcos and Estrada did little to the Philippines. Politicians pandering to the public and corrupt judges and military generals have prevented the government from making real reforms.

Index

978-0-595-43364-3
0-595-43364-2